. Benghazi

Cairo

951
BYA
1.2

1922
EGYPT (U.A.R.)
26.6

1960
CHAD
2.7

Khartoum

ort Lamy

1956
SUDAN
12.6

FRENCH SOMALILAND
0.07

1960
CENTRAL
AFRICAN
REPUBLIC
1.2

Addis Ababa

ETHIOPIA
20.0

1960
SOMALI REPUBLIC
2.0

aigui

1962
RWANDA
2.7

1962
UGANDA
7.0

Mogadiscio

1960
EPUBLIC OF THE CONGO
14.5

Entebbe

Kigali

KENYA
7.3

Leopoldville

Usumbura

1962
BURUNDI
2.2

Ö ZANZIBAR
0.3

Dar es Salaam

1961
TANGANYIKA
9.6

ANGOLA
4.9

NORTHERN
RHODESIA
2.5

NYASALAND
2.9

MOZAMBIQUE
6.6

1960
MALAGASY REPUBLIC
5.6

SOUTHERN
RHODESIA
3.2

Tananarive

HPG

AFRICA

and the

COMMUNIST WORLD

HOOVER INSTITUTION PUBLICATIONS

Contributors

ALEXANDER DALLIN
ALEXANDER ERLICH & CHRISTIAN R. SONNE
ROBERT & ELIZABETH BASS
WILLIAM E. GRIFFITH
RICHARD LOWENTHAL
ZBIGNIEW BRZEZINSKI

AFRICA

and the

COMMUNIST WORLD

Edited by

ZBIGNIEW BRZEZINSKI

Published for the

HOOVER INSTITUTION ON WAR, REVOLUTION, AND PEACE

by

STANFORD UNIVERSITY PRESS

Stanford, California, 1963

The Hoover Institution on War, Revolution, and Peace, founded at Stanford University in 1919 by Herbert Hoover, is a center for advanced study and research on public and international affairs in the twentieth century. The views expressed in its publications are entirely those of the authors and do not necessarily reflect the views of the Hoover Institution. This study was supported by funds received from the John Randolph Haynes and Dora Haynes Foundation, Los Angeles, California.

Stanford University Press
Stanford, California
© 1963 by the Board of Trustees of the
Leland Stanford Junior University

Library of Congress Catalog Card Number: 63-17816
Printed in the United States of America

PREFACE

The purpose of this book is to examine Communist policies toward Africa; it is not a book about Africa as such, nor even about African Communism. It is a collective effort by the contributors to present a contemporary analysis of the programs adopted by the various Communist states to establish their influence among the new African states south of the Sahara, to consolidate their positions there, and to use these positions to further their long-range goals. More specifically, the primary focus is on the new African states that have already become targets of Communist strategy. Occasional reference is made to other African areas, but usually either to introduce a line of reasoning or by way of example. No effort has been made to assess the degree of Communist penetration within Africa as such; that will be the purpose of a subsequent study, which will be sponsored, as this one was, by the Hoover Institution on War, Revolution, and Peace.

In its organization, this volume is designed to cover the major facets of Communist strategy for sub-Saharan Africa, as well as its specific tactical expressions and adjustments. Thus the first chapter sketches out the historical and ideological background of the Communist interest in Africa and then deals in greater depth with recent Soviet activity toward it: ideological developments, political strategy, specific tactics, and changes in expectations. The second chapter examines contemporary Soviet economic thought about Africa, comparing it with earlier Leninist notions, and reviews Soviet trade and economic aid to Africa in that context. The third chapter focuses on the activities of the states of Communist East Europe, especially industrially developed Czechoslovakia and East Germany, and attempts to assess the motives, the scale, and the degree of specialization and coordination in these efforts. The next two chapters describe the activities of two Communist states that in recent years have differed with Moscow on issues of Communist strategy. Thus the fourth chapter explains how Yugoslavia has competed with the efforts of other Communist states to establish itself in Africa while at the same time trying to make Communism in general respectable on that continent, and how the factors that made Yugoslav activity possible may perhaps alter its future character. The fifth chapter examines the role of Communist China: its prescriptions for Africa and their underlying assumptions, its activity in the area, and its competition with the Soviet Union viewed in the larger context of their different global perspectives. The concluding chapter is not a recapitulation but an attempt to highlight certain themes concerning the inherent advantages and disadvantages of the Communist strategy, the problems of coordination within the context of Communist diversity, and the possible implications for Communism of its involvement in the struggle for Africa.

Each contributor is fully responsible for the views and conclusions expressed in his chapter. An effort was made to avoid repetition, but the same issue is occasionally treated by different authors when different perspectives on it can thereby be presented. As editor, of course, I assume over-all responsibility for shaping the basic pattern of the book, and, in cooperation with the several authors, for revising the manuscript. My primary concern, however, was to secure contributors of outstanding scholarship and expertise. As the documentation of the book shows, the contributors are well versed in Communist source material; most of their notes are based on systematic research in primary Communist and other sources. Furthermore, two members of this authors' "collective," Mr. Griffith and I, traveled to Africa in the late summer of 1962 to verify on the spot some of the hypotheses and findings contained in a preliminary draft of the volume.

I wish to thank my associates for their collaboration and for the good humor with which they bore up under my complaints, criticisms, and frequent urgings that they engage in "socialist competition" among one another, thereby accelerating their efforts. A special word of acknowledgment must go to Peter Duignan, Curator of the African Collection of the Hoover Institution. He initiated the project, helped in the various stages of its execution, and criticized the manuscript constructively; not least important, he provided, on behalf of the Hoover Institution, the generous financial support that both encouraged and sustained the authors in their labors.

ZBIGNIEW BRZEZINSKI

Paris
April 1963

CONTENTS

CONTRIBUTORS

ELIZABETH BASS was trained at Smith College and Harvard University, and has been employed as an economist in Washington, D.C., and New York City. She is the co-editor, with Robert Bass, of a documentary survey of the Soviet-Yugoslav controversy, and is currently Assistant Editor of the *Current Digest of the Soviet Press*.

ROBERT BASS received his training at Columbia University and has taught modern history at Columbia, Smith College, and Mount Holyoke. He has written articles and brochures on various aspects of international Communism, and is the co-editor, with Elizabeth Bass, of *The Soviet-Yugoslav Controversy, 1948–58: A Documentary Record* (1959). He is on the faculty of Brooklyn College.

ZBIGNIEW BRZEZINSKI studied at Harvard University and between 1953 and 1960 was a member of Harvard's Russian Research Center and the Center for International Affairs. He has traveled many times to the Soviet Union and other Communist states, and in 1962 he made an extensive tour of Africa. His publications include *The Soviet Bloc—Unity and Conflict* (1960) and *Ideology and Power in Soviet Politics* (1962). He is now Professor of Government and Director of the Research Institute on Communist Affairs at Columbia University.

ALEXANDER DALLIN completed his graduate training at Columbia University in 1950. Between 1951 and 1954 he was Associate Director of the Research Program on the U.S.S.R., in New York City, and was a research fellow at Harvard University in 1956. Since then he has taught at Columbia, where he is now Professor of International Relations and Director of the Russian Institute. He is the author of *German Rule in Russia, 1941–1945* (1957) and *The Soviet Union at the United Nations* (1962).

ALEXANDER ERLICH was trained at the University of Berlin, the Free Polish University of Warsaw, and the New School for Social Research in

New York City. His publications include *The Soviet Industrialization Debate, 1924–1928* (1960) and articles on the economics of Poland and the Soviet Union. He is now Associate Professor of Eocnomics and a staff member of the Russian Institute at Columbia University.

WILLIAM E. GRIFFITH studied at Hamilton College and Harvard University. His publications include *Albania and the Sino-Soviet Rift* (1963) and articles on East European Communism and Sino-Soviet relations. He is currently Director of the International Communism Project of the Center for International Studies, Massachusetts Institute of Technology, and Lecturer in Politics at M.I.T. and the Fletcher School of Law and Diplomacy.

RICHARD LOWENTHAL, educated at Berlin and Heidelberg universities, went to Britain as an exile from Nazi Germany and traveled widely after the war as a foreign correspondent for the London *Observer*. Since 1953 he has specialized in the comparative study of totalitarian movements and particularly in the study of relations between the Communist Parties of different countries. He served as a co-author, with G. F. Hudson and Roderick MacFarquhar, of *The Sino-Soviet Dispute* (1961) and is the author of *Chruschtschew und der Weltkommunismus* (1963). He now holds the chair of International Relations at the Free University of West Berlin.

CHRISTIAN R. SONNE is a graduate of Yale and the Columbia School of International Affairs. He holds a Master of International Affairs Degree and a Certificate from the Russian Institute at Columbia University, and is currently working in the field of international finance for Harriman Ripley & Co. of New York City.

ABBREVIATIONS

A partial alphabetical list of African political parties and of organizations (some of them non-African) important in the trade-union, peace, and Pan-African movements. Abbreviations not mentioned in the text and abbreviations for governments and supranational organizations are not included.

AAPSO	Afro-Asian People's Solidarity Organization
AATUF	All-African Trade Union Federation
ATUC	African Trade Union Confederation
CGT	Confédération Générale du Travail
FLN	Front de Libération Nationale
ICFTU	International Confederation of Free Trade Unions
KANU	Kenya African National Union
MNC	Mouvement National Congolais
MPLA	Movimento Popular de Libertação de Angola
PAI	Parti Africain de l'Indépendance
PDG	Parti Démocratique de Guinée
PSA	Parti Solidaire Africain
RDA	Rassemblement Démocratique Africain
UGTAN	Union Générale des Travailleurs d'Afrique Noire
UNFP	Union Nationale des Forces Populaires
UPC	Union des Populations du Cameroun
WFDY	World Federation of Democratic Youth
WFTU	World Peace Council
WPC	World Federation of Trade Unions
ZNP	Zanzibar Nationalist Party

AFRICA

and the

COMMUNIST WORLD

INTRODUCTION

Zbigniew Brzezinski

The African continent, more than any other in recent history, has been the object of bitter and protracted international rivalry. The Dutch, the Spaniards, the Portuguese, the English, the French, the Germans, the Belgians, and the Italians have all competed and often fought among one another for possession of various sections of that vast continent. Their era in Africa is now ending. But this has not meant that Africa has ceased to be an object of international conflict.

New protagonists have appeared on the scene. The departing colonialists were all from the seafaring Western European states, almost neighbors of Africa. Today, USIS outposts, Peace Corps contingents, and economic aid express the growing interest of the United States in Africa's future. Similarly, Africans are the objects of the political and ideological activity of the East Europeans, the Russians, and the Chinese. The engagement of these Communist states in Africa is part and parcel of their global political and ideological aspirations, which have polarized the major world powers into two competitive blocs. Both the Communist camp and the Western community have an acute interest in the future political and economic shape of Africa, although neither is attempting to turn the clock back by practicing old-fashioned imperialism or colonialism. In this age of national independence and political subtlety, efforts to extend domination and control are no longer blatantly displayed. Alliances, close cooperation, and peaceful coexistence are the new labels for what are often very one-sided political and economic relationships. But in many ways, the competition is more intense than ever, and the aspirations of the protagonists more comprehensive, for the struggle between the two blocs involves not only their power relationships, but the clash between two images of the world: one that reflects the political and ideological experience of the Communist world and one that corresponds to the more amorphous and pluralistic vision of the West.

Africa is thus an important arena of political and ideological conflict, and one side's gain is seen by the other as his loss. Given the new conditions and the present balance of power, neither side can afford, even if it desired to do so, to use traditional methods of open coercion and aggression. This forces the conflict into more complex patterns; and competition in ideas, in effective political penetration, and even in granting aid, thus becomes the outward expression of the underlying struggle.

Viewed in historical perspective, this restrained form of conflict is a major step forward, and in many ways it even benefits the new African states. In part, this self-restraint is due to a recognition that the age of colonialism has passed and that nationalism is the basic force moving the masses. The two World Wars, with their stimulating effect on national consciousness in Africa and their undermining of the colonialist powers, as well as the October Revolution, which made the West more conscious of the need to win the respect of the African and Asian peoples, doubtless contributed to this new outlook. In very large part, it is also due to the strong American tradition of anticolonialism, which has finally made its impact on America's allies.

That the Communist world recognizes the intrinsic importance of Africa, with its human and material resources—not to speak of its strategic position—is clear. That it took the Communist leaders some time to perceive its importance, in spite of the traditional Communist emphasis on the underdeveloped nations so well underlined by Lenin's perceptive 1917 pamphlet on imperialism, is not denied by Communist spokesmen. They admit that until the Twentieth Congress of the CPSU in 1956 they held rigid and "dogmatic" views concerning this important region, with the result that even serious study of the area was neglected, or at least lacked the necessary sophistication.[1] That deficiency is now to be erased, Soviet spokesmen assert. But Communist interest in Africa reflects a concern more basic than their obvious interest in gaining control of more votes in the United Nations or in preparing for eventual territorial expansion.

The future of Africa is central to the prophecy that feeds the Communist sense of dedication and historical confidence. The Communists accept change as an immutable aspect of our reality, and they believe that they understand the direction it will take. Today Africa is in the midst of a profound revolution, spanning in decades processes which elsewhere took centuries to mature, molding nations out of often truly primitive tribes, seeking modernity without yet, in some places, having reached even the stage of backwardness. To the Communists the nature of this revolution is crucially important, and not just in the sense of how it will affect their power relations with the United States. More fundamentally, their concern is with the fate of their entire historical perspective; its legitimacy, already refuted by events in Western Europe, now depends on developments in Asia, Africa, and Latin America.

The leading Soviet expert on "the Communist future," Professor S. Strumilin, undertook in the fall of 1961 a systematic effort to reach some conclusions about the probable state of the world in 1980.[2] He did not deal with Africa directly, but what he had to say was both important and relevant. After commenting that Western economic development and improvement in social conditions may in many ways increase the gap between the West and Africa, thereby contributing to "more acute contradictions" between them, he noted:

> It is known that many underdeveloped countries have already started to use the methods of industrialization whose application has produced such striking successes in the socialist camp. We do not know how many of these countries will fully enter the commonwealth of socialist countries in the next ten to twenty years, but we can expect with certainty that their gravitation toward this camp will increase with every year, rather than diminish. We may recall that the growth in the population of the socialist camp attributable to the addition of new members just since 1945, after the World War, reached not less than 830,000,-000 persons by 1960, and of these not more than 80,000,000 came from the countries liberated from Hitler's yoke, while about 750,000,000 are from the underdeveloped part of the world, repsenting some 36 per cent of its population. It can be expected that in the future this irreversible process of the socialist camp's expansion will proceed according to approximately the same rates and volumes.
>
> But let us assume out of caution that not more than 30 per

cent of the population of neutral countries and not more than 10 per cent of those of the imperialist camp take the socialist road during the next twenty years, and that in the first decade—up to 1970—the percentages are only half of these. In this case, the movements of the world's population during the twenty years will appear approximately as in the table below:

World Population (*millions*)

Groups of Countries	1960		1970		1980	
	Total	%	Total	%	Total	%
Socialist	1,050	35	1,597	45	2,295	54
Imperialist	600	20	631	18	660	16
Other*	1,350	45	1,318	37	1,248	30

Groups of Countries	Percentage Increase	
	In 10 Years	In 20 Years
Socialist	52.1	118.6
Imperialist	25.2	10.0
Other*	−2.4	−7.6

* In this group we include the countries that have either freed themselves from colonial slavery or are struggling for liberation.

Strumilin supplemented these figures by projections of present annual production increases in the West and in the Communist world, and he concluded that there, too, the future favors Communism.

Professor Strumilin was reflecting the Communist penchant for demonstrating that the image of a split world, so long inherent in the Communist outlook, is correct, and that the world, and especially the new nations, have only two choices: "socialism" and "capitalism." Furthermore, he was trying to show that the Communists know what the choice will be, and, in keeping with their concept of the unity of theory and practice, that they can bring it about. In essence, he was asserting that the Communist prophecy is a self-fulfilling one, and that the future of Africa is preordained. A reminder of this Soviet point of view is an appropriate introduction to an examination of Communist policies toward Africa.

1

THE SOVIET UNION:
POLITICAL ACTIVITY

Alexander Dallin

The breathless speed of Africa's emancipation from colonial sub-
jection to proud and multiple sovereignty has been unprecedented in
human history. The Soviet Union, like the United States, has sought
to adjust to the new reality and to take advantage of it for its own
ends. In doing so, it has faced both advantages and handicaps intrinsic in the Soviet outlook and experience. More realistically than
the West—although only after years of stubborn denial—it acknowledged the significance of the "collapse of the colonial system." But
the inferences Moscow drew from this had to be validated in a setting
uniquely complex and unfamiliar to it, a setting in which the relationship of Communist and national revolutions appeared in a peculiarly
deceptive light.

The Ideological Perspective

Marx and Engels had virtually nothing to say about Africa, and
neither did Lenin and Stalin. Lenin's keen sense of priorities left
the Dark Continent, as it were, in the field of peripheral vision. For
him and for his disciples Africa was a part of the "national-colonial"
question, to the analysis of which Communists devoted considerable
attention. The universal answers they evolved were assumed to be
applicable to African societies as well.

Lenin's views on the critical relationship of nationalism and
Communism had taken shape gradually, from the debates with fellow
Marxists around the turn of the century to the bold gestures and

global strategies charted at the Second Comintern Congress in 1920. In China, India, and Turkey, Lenin saw national liberation movements threatening colonial rule. Arguing against critics on the Communist left, he came to defend national self-determination as objectively progressive in the struggle against the imperialist states.

Ever since, the official formula for determining the movement's political strategy, based on an analysis of class forces at work in a given situation, has required the Communist leadership to proceed as follows:

> In the first place, to determine correctly the *main aim* of the working class at the given stage and the *chief class enemy* against whom it is necessary to concentrate at the given stage the class hatred and the shock force of all the working people. . . . Secondly, it is necessary to determine correctly the attitude of the Party to the largest *intermediate* section of the population. . . . Thirdly, when elaborating the strategic line, it is important to determine correctly the *allies* of the working class at the given stage of the movement.[1]

The most controversial part of this scheme was, and continues to be, the position of the intermediate elements—political parties (the Social-Democrats), social classes (the "national bourgeoisie"), and national states (the neutralists). And the vacillations of Communist strategy over the years can be usefully understood in terms of changing attitudes toward precisely these groups. Communist parties, and the Soviet state, have both needed and feared allies; the question raised with regard to their partners, time and again, has been, "Who is using whom?" Nowhere has it been more bothersome than with regard to the "national-liberation movements."

The common enemy—imperialism without, feudalism within—has often provided a basis for temporary collaboration between the national (bourgeois) and the Communist movements. The complementary nature of the colonial and proletarian revolutions was derived from the definition of the national upheaval as the precursor of the second, or "socialist," stage of revolution. Whether the first stage should be considered necessary remained open to some debate; that it was not in itself sufficient was held to be indisputable.

Lenin's analysis of imperialism divided the world into exploiter and exploited nations. With the proletariat (or rather, its self-appointed Communist spokesmen) in power in one country, Soviet conflicts with other states amounted to a geographic projection of the class struggle—which suggested an alliance of oppressed classes as well as peoples, a linkage of Communist and national revolutions, with Russia as the bridge between the two.

Ever since the debates at the Second Comintern Congress, the analytical and prescriptive difficulties posed by this approach have revolved around two principal issues: (1) under what conditions, if any, an alliance with the national bourgeoisie is desirable or permissible; and (2) whether the working class (that is, the Communists) should assume hegemony in the alliance before the "bourgeois" stage of the revolution is completed, or only after political victory of the national liberation movement is achieved.[2] In approaching these questions, Communists have always considered the national bourgeoisie to be dual in nature; in their definition, its role can be either progressive or reactionary, depending upon the socio-political context. In general, it is expected that one stratum of the bourgeoisie will "sell out" to the imperialists while another will tend to associate itself, at least for a time, with "democratic" or "progressive" forces. The changing role of the bourgeoisie (as assessed by the Communists) thus dictates changing tactics toward it. Although the whole concept of the national bourgeoisie has proved ambiguous and thoroughly inadequate, it has survived with remarkable tenacity; it is still officially essential to Soviet political thought.[3]

In 1928, after some signal failures of Communist alliances with colonial nationalism (notably in China), Soviet policy took a turn to the left. The Sixth Comintern Congress warned that the national bourgeoisie, frightened by the revolutionary movement, was betraying it; it called on all comrades to "unmask" nationalist leaders and their stooges. Like the Social-Democrats in the West, the "reformists" in the East (Gandhi, for example) were accused of "social treason." The theses of the Sixth Congress proclaimed what leftists had urged in vain a few years before: interclass alliances must come under the hegemony of the proletariat, even in the early stages of the struggle; and once the national bourgeoisie gains power, Communists must not tolerate class peace, let alone support economic development in the interests of the class enemy.

Long after this line was abandoned, Africa remained for Moscow the orphan continent. During the Stalin era Africa attracted no significant attention except in the Comintern, which did little more than deplore the absence of Communist parties in tropical Africa. Even after World War II, Africa was seen only as part of the general colonial system. The interest in it began to increase, but Soviet articles about it were full of errors and gaps of evidence, relied heavily on non-Communist materials, and were characterized by an abundance of glosses and stereotypes.[4]

In 1949 it was decided to study what stages of development the peoples of Africa had reached—by no means an idle academic exercise for Marxists. Yet the political conclusions were once again prejudged: Moscow argued that the newly independent nations, from India to Egypt, had acquired only a fictitious sovereignty. The imperialist powers were said to be locked in a bitter rivalry among themselves, and the United States was emerging as the chief enemy of the U.S.S.R. In this frank return to a "two-camp" view of the world, Moscow found it impossible to sanction neutrality for the colonial and ex-colonial world. It saw the African nationalists as firmly in the bourgeois camp; even the more "progressive" leaders in Africa were held to be incapable of securing the victory over colonialism, to say nothing of promoting the "higher stage" of the revolution.*

Communist refusal to support "bourgeois" national movements implied heavy reliance on the working class. There was in those years a proclivity among Soviet writers to exaggerate both the size and the activism of African labor. The classic example of this is Professor Ivan Potekhin's paper on "Stalinist Theory of Colonial Revolution and the National Liberation Movement in Tropical and Southern Africa," which appeared in early 1950. Potekhin said that "the solution of the colonial problem . . . is impossible without a proletarian revolution," that the proletariat must "play a leading role" in it, and even that "the era of its hegemony in the revolution has begun." This paper—by no means unique—is significant because

---

* Soviet journals of this period contain what must now seem an embarrassing number of vicious attacks on "bourgeois" leaders: for instance, Dr. Nnamdi Azikiwe was called an "African Gandhi" and the author of a "colonial edition" of American pragmatist philosophy; Dr. Kwame Nkrumah was labeled a representative of the "big bourgeoisie" and his party a "screen covering up the domination of English imperialism" in the Gold Coast.

its formulations refer specifically to Africa south of the Sahara, and because Potekhin has since become the leading Soviet expert on Africa.

Even Potekhin's article revealed some awkwardness, or perhaps some intentional hints that things were not in fact so simple. Since in tropical Africa neither the proletariat nor the bourgeoisie amounted to any sizable force, some conscientious Soviet writers found it difficult to fit their evidence into the crude categories imposed by Party dialecticians or to find acceptable descriptions for conditions that were varied and unusual. Nevertheless, the official line remained unchanged. Even the valuable handbook *Peoples of Africa* provided, amid abundant scholarly and factual material, a political résumé fully in keeping with Stalinist clichés.[5] The Communists failed to foresee either the nature or the rate of political change in Africa.

The shift in Soviet outlook and strategy came with the start of the Khrushchev era. It was between the Twentieth and Twenty-Second Congresses of the CPSU (1956–61) that Moscow came to insist that the balance of power was shifting in favor of "the socialist camp" and that the West could no longer deal with Russia from a position of superior strength—a claim made plausible by a variety of economic, scientific, and political successes. Another argument, from 1955 on, was the much more optimistic assessment of the "collapse of the colonial system," a process that heralded new opportunities for Moscow. These opportunities were perceived both because of the "objective" upsurge of nationalism (as dramatized by the quest for dignity, recognition, and organization demonstrated at the Bandung Conference) and because the Soviet leadership was prepared to tolerate a less doctrinaire approach. Indeed, it was self-defeating for Moscow to persist in its rejection of colonial nationalism. Now a determined effort was made to show that Communism was not antagonistic to nationalism; political independence, previously written off as a sham, was now hailed as a desirable step; indeed, the true cause of national progress, Moscow claimed, was better served by Communism than by the bourgeoisie. Africa was part of the area to which this outlook applied.[6]

Whatever their future disposition, the very emancipation of the colonies was considered a major blow struck at the "imperialist" world. In a review of world-wide revolutionary opportunities, Boris Ponomarev, the CPSU's top official responsible for dealings with Communists abroad, stressed the torrential growth of the national-liberation movement and contrasted its upsurge, militancy, and performance with the record of the countries which had harbored what he called the classical bourgeoisie.

Belief in the inevitable gravitation of the hitherto colonial world toward the Soviet orbit further enhanced the attractiveness of the prospect of gradual and painless revolution, which went hand in hand with the new Soviet line. With an admixture of wishful thinking, the Soviet leadership—perhaps temporarily—convinced itself that the international interests of the new states and of "the socialist camp" coincided even beyond their independence. The "zone of peace" concept, bracketing the two blocs, was but one expression of this view. As an authoritative commentator in Moscow explained in 1961:

> Even though the countries having achieved liberation continue in most instances to remain in the system of world capitalist economy, they no longer constitute the rear and reserve of imperialism, as they had in the past. Now the countries are an important ally of the socialist camp in the struggle for peace and international security, for the full liquidation of colonialism.[7]

There was no cogent Marxist explanation of how such a thing was possible. What mattered was the political implications of this view. The most daring of them was the change in Soviet tactics regarding neutralism: Moscow abandoned the time-honored tenet that in a two-camp world neutrality was fictitious, or even an enemy trick. Instead, it now made itself the champion of the new nations' neutrality—if only by a special interpretation that described the creation of a neutralist bloc as "a tremendous loss for the imperialist system."[8]

The Strategy Emerges

Recent Soviet strategy for Africa incorporates the familiar Bolshevik distinction between maximum and minimum objectives. The maximum objective—control of the African continent, with its manpower and resources—is axiomatic to faith in the world-wide triumph of Communism and yet vague enough to prevent specific elaboration.

It is a goal indefinitely postponed because it is unrealistic at present and not worth the risks required to achieve it. The minimum objective has been to deny Africa to the West, and especially to deprive the United States and its allies of political influence, economic opportunities, and strategic bases in Africa. In the short run, Moscow has seen its best hope in the emergence of African states that would pursue "positive neutrality" and cultivate increasingly close economic, political, and cultural ties with the Soviet bloc.

This rather modest program, although still in force, has of late been supplemented by more militant aims: to prevent the consolidation of Africa into a separate and solidly non-Communist bloc; to give greater emphasis to the necessity of advancing to the "second stage" of the African revolution; and to encourage African states to take foreign policy positions more distinctly identified with those of the U.S.S.R.

At the same time, Moscow has retreated from its undifferentiated identification with the cause of Africa, seeking instead with greater flexibility to bank on those states that cast a sympathetic eye on the Soviet Union as a model for modernization and rapid development, and choosing to concentrate its support selectively on "progressive" states most likely to follow a policy congenial to the U.S.S.R.

Despite some confusion among Soviet authorities and several changes of expectations and plans, the general line since 1955 has been to support African nationalist movements as essentially progressive; to dispel local suspicions of Communist subversion; and to present "the socialist camp" as the champion of anticolonialism, African independence, and peace and progress.

This general strategy is based on three main assumptions. First, it is assumed that cooperation with existing African governments is reasonable because there are no better forces, and particularly no reliable African Communist parties, toward which to turn. Second, time is thought to be on the Communist side. It is expected that the growth of trade-union forces, the extension of "front" organizations, and continuing urbanization and industrialization will strengthen pro-Soviet elements within (or against) African governments; and it is supposed that in time those governments can be moved closer to "left" domestic policies and pro-Soviet foreign policies—which will eventually lead to the establishment of intermediate forms of government and the conversion of their ruling parties into serviceable instruments of Communism. Third, it is assumed that Soviet failure to support and woo the nationalist governments would in effect abandon them to influences and blocs inimical to the U.S.S.R.

Stressing the fluidity of African politics and the possibility of realignments—to the unusual extent of describing the categories themselves as matters of convenience rather than of rigid and "objective" fact—Soviet commentators in 1960–62 classified African states as follows, in descending order of preference:

(1) Ghana, Guinea, and Mali as "progressive" one-party states with socialist elements in the government and economy, and with favorable political sympathies toward the Communist bloc.

(2) Other states that pursue an anti-Western policy or a "positive neutralism" appealing to Moscow, even though their domestic policies or foreign ambitions may be suspect, such as the U.A.R. and Morocco.

(3) States maintaining "correct" and "businesslike" relations with the U.S.S.R., in some cases accepting Soviet aid and specialists while resisting Western blandishments, even if these states ban the Communist Party or perpetuate a "feudal" society, such as Ethiopia, Sudan, Libya, Liberia, and the Somali Republic.

(4) States inclining toward a "capitalist path" and "bourgeois democratic" models, among which are Nigeria, Togo, Tanganyika, and Senegal.

(5) "Reactionary" and "fascist" regimes, such as South Africa, and some of the former French African possessions, such as Congo, the Ivory Coast, and Mauritania.

These categories, of course, omit the remaining colonial areas as well as Algeria and Republic of the Congo—an indication of Soviet embarrassment about dealing with colonial wars. Except for the "reactionary" states, where change can presumably come only with the ouster of the present regimes, Moscow hopes for the gradual propulsion of the various states into more "progressive" categories, and the further transformation of the most progressive into the Soviet likeness.

Moscow's Plan for Africa. The Soviet prescription for an "independent" foreign policy for African states begins with the assertion that the imperialists remain in substantial control of Africa: "In the majority of states that achieved independence as a result of forced constitutional concessions on the part of the colonizers, the imperialists have succeeded to this day in retaining their commanding positions in economic, political, and military affairs."[9] Hence the major thrust is to separate the new African states from the West. To this end, the whole arsenal of anti-imperialist propaganda, joint diplomatic and demonstrative *démarches*, and a measure of Soviet aid have been mobilized.[10]

At least for the present, Moscow demands no alliances and in fact offers none. But besides claiming substantial credit for the success of the national-liberation movements, the Soviet Union also assures the new countries that it will "paralyze" the aggressive intentions of the Western colonizers. By offering "the socialist camp" as a reliable shield for the new nations against the West, Moscow suggests that reliance on the Soviet bloc is essential for Africa's future.

In domestic policy Moscow describes the choice which the new states face as limited to the alternatives of a "capitalist" and a "noncapitalist" path. It has taken great pains to convince Africans that "true progress can be assured only on the road of socialism: this is true of all countries, whatever the level of their economic development, size and population."[11] However, the more sophisticated Communist theorists and policymakers have recognized that "not all the newly liberated countries can make the immediate transition to socialism."[12] Thus the Party Program in 1961 spoke of a "complex multi-stage process" of transition, in which certain intermediate forms of social organization could be acknowledged.

Despite much awkwardness about the class nature of these transitional forms, it has generally been taken for granted that they must be based on the continued "alliance" of the African proletariat, peasantry, and bourgeoisie. Until 1961, an optimistic tone about the alliance prevailed. Eugene Zhukov, the dean of Soviet experts on the "East" (understood to include Africa), wrote in 1960:

> For many countries of Asia and particularly of Africa, backward in their development, with a predominantly rural population, and now engaged in liberating themselves from the yoke of imperial-

ism, the "struggle not against capital but against medieval remnants" will remain the principal task for some time to come. This makes possible the prolonged cooperation of the workers, peasants, and intelligentsia of underdeveloped countries with certain bourgeois circles, that part of the national bourgeoisie which is interested in an independent political and economic development of the country and which is ready to defend its independence against all encroachments of the imperialist powers.[13]

By 1961, however, as high an official as Boris Ponomarev could express considerable skepticism about the efficacy of the class alliance. After achieving independence, "progressive forces," he said, were bound to meet "counter-efforts of reactionary circles leaning on the support of foreign imperialists." Perhaps with Nasser and Kassem in mind, Ponomarev went on to argue that a "dictatorial" policy by the bourgeois elite should be met by a "narrowing of the social base of the struggle"—in other words, by a turn to the left in Communist policy.[14]

What major demands should the working class (or the national coalition) make after winning independence? Moscow's list includes agrarian reform, industrialization, "political democracy" (permission for the Communist Party to function legally), other social and economic reforms. The ouster of foreign "monopolies" and rapid economic development are of course central to the whole argument in favor of a "second revolution." But in many of the new states there is no influential bourgeoisie and very little capital in African hands, and this has led governments to assume responsibility for economic development. Hence there is bound to develop a new kind of "state capitalism"—"a form more progressive than private property."[15]

The conflicting opinions, with different implications for the evolution toward "socialism" in Africa, were apparent, for instance, at a "theoretical discussion" by Communists from 21 countries in September 1961. The published summary warned against "a blanket definition" of state capitalism; some participants even argued that the term did not apply at all to African countries with only a weak bourgeoisie, or none at all:

In such countries power is exercised by a bloc of the democratic and patriotic forces, in which the working masses are the dominant element. But even in these countries the state sector cannot be described as socialist. What is its nature? Marxist literature distinguishes three types of production relations: exploitation in societies with antagonistic classes; comradely cooperation in socialist society; and relations of a transitionary nature. Proceeding from this, forum participants suggested that the latter type applies to African countries in which there is practically no native bourgeoisie. And if this is so, then the state sector in their economies is neither capitalist nor socialist, but transitionary.[16]

The tendency to mint transitional categories to describe African trends and realities also appears in Potekhin's "basic" Africa pamphlet produced in 1960: "It is not at all impossible that this all-national anti-imperialism will *merge* with the struggle for the reconstruction of society along socialist principles."[17]

Thus the notion of a peaceful transition to socialism, originally formulated to apply to advanced, capitalist, parliamentary states, has been extended in the opposite direction to include the backward areas, in a novel variant of the concept of continuous revolution.

The Non-Capitalist Path and National Democracy. What is at stake is the formulation of alternative roads to power. While the search for itineraries to Communism is an old one, the challenge of Africa has contributed to an increased willingness to accept intermediate stages short of outright Communist rule.

An analysis of forces at work in tropical Africa evidently convinced Moscow that neither Communist nor "front" organizations were strong enough to lead effectively. This, in turn, reinforced the decision to maximize the influence of the Soviet state on the national governments of Africa. Wherever possible, such Soviet efforts were to be reinforced by pressure from within the country. Indeed, since 1958 Soviet specialists have outlined a series of steps by which the "progressive" elements in a united front, after its conquest of power, increasingly line up against the imperialists, "come out for the restriction of private capital" within the country, contribute to the "loss by the reactionary big bourgeoisie of its economic and political positions" and in turn pave the way for a new national front under "working class leadership," meaning ultimately the establishment of "a democratic dictatorship of the people."

To legitimize support of national-bourgeois regimes with a maximum of ideological plausibility and propaganda appeal, Soviet theorists devised the concepts of a "non-capitalist path" and "national democracy." Neither was conceived specifically for Africa, but both were to be applied extensively there. While orthodox Marxism had considered the capitalist stage essential to society's dialectical progress, the new theory implied that it was possible for any pre-capitalist society to skip over the capitalist stage.*

In Africa, the optimists among Soviet scholars and politicians insisted, such a "qualitative" leap would be assisted by several factors: (1) the weakness of the national bourgeoisie, both numerically and economically, and the prospect that the working class would grow more rapidly than the bourgeoisie; (2) the importance of the state sector of the economy in setting the course for a non-capitalist development; and (3) the survival of communal landholding in large parts of tropical Africa.[18]

This argument, it is true, placed Moscow in an awkward position vis-à-vis Peking: Soviet insistence on the feasibility of an African short cut to socialism came precisely as Moscow was condemning Chinese efforts to take a short cut to Communism. Soviet Communists vehemently reminded the Chinese that the laws of history could not be repealed and that (in the words of Eugene Zhukov) "it is impossible to jump over a certain historical stage." Soviet ideological gimmickry in the Khrushchev era thus clashed with the Soviet prescriptions for gradual takeover. Soviet arguments against the "stage-jumpers" in Peking were negated by Soviet insistence that the new states could, or should, be "stage-jumpers" themselves. The problem remained unresolved, as did the question whether Moscow believed

---

* This was essentially a political problem of long standing. Lenin in 1917 seized power even though, some critics argued, Russia had "not yet" gone through the entire capitalist stage. Similarly Moscow chose to reformulate the doctrine which evolved the possibility of by-passing capitalism, rather than sacrifice the opportunity for hothouse transformation of the Caucasus and Central Asia, a few years later. In the 1950's the theory was elaborated to the point where the proletariat was no longer considered essential for a proletarian revolution.

it easier to build Communism in a more advanced or in a more backward state—in Nigeria or in Mali, for instance.*

The concept of a "national democracy" was formally introduced and defined in the Statement of Eighty-One Communist Parties, adopted in December 1960:

> In the present situation, favorable domestic and international conditions arise in many countries for the establishment of an independent national democracy, that is, a state which consistently upholds its political and economic independence; which fights against imperialism and its military blocs, against military bases on its territory; a state which fights against the new forms of colonialism and the penetration of imperialist capital; a state which rejects dictatorial and despotic methods of government; a state in which the people are assured broad democratic rights and freedoms (freedom of speech, press, assembly, demonstrations, establishment of political parties and social organizations), the opportunity to work for the enactment of an agrarian reform and other democratic and social changes, and for participation in shaping government policy.

But since a state so defined could not be called "socialist," there was considerable debate over the new concept and its meaning. The prevalent interpretation soon emerged: "Without being socialist, the national-democratic state realizes the demands of the anti-imperialist, anti-feudal, democratic revolution," and fulfillment of these demands "will inevitably create the conditions for the transition of the underdeveloped countries to the non-capitalist path of development."[19]

It remained unclear whether the non-capitalist path began only after a national democracy had started enacting reforms, or whether

---

* Here also is the clue to the amazingly contradictory record of Soviet statements regarding African society—whether the proletariat, the bourgeoisie, or the peasantry is weak or strong, gaining or losing, active or passive. The impotence of the national bourgeoisie and the existence of the village "commune" in Africa were strong arguments for those who maintained that a non-capitalist path was open to all African states, however underdeveloped. Thus, in a peculiar application of what has been called the dialectics of backwardness, unreadiness for capitalism became equated with readiness for socialism. Yet Moscow's attempt to make a virtue of underdevelopment could not conceal the inherent contradiction between Communist perceptions of regularities in the historical progress, and Soviet invitations to passage directly from the dark realm of African necessities to the socialist dreamland of expanding freedoms.

it was a precondition for the very establishment of such a state: it was agreed only that a national democracy *could become* socialist. As early as 1961, however, Soviet commentary had begun to imply that the socialist destiny of national democracies was by no means inevitable, and that reverses would probably occur. From this it could be inferred that Soviet support of national democracies was not to be irreversible; unlike "People's Democracies," national democracies might conceivably be let down by Moscow in a crisis.

Techniques of Political Influence

In pursuing its aims in Africa the Soviet Union has done much that is safe and little that is risky. A variety of techniques has been brought to bear in the effort. Since 1955 there has been a formidable development of African studies in the U.S.S.R. The purposes of this many-faceted endeavor may be summarized as follows: (1) to understand Africa and provide Soviet policy-makers with information, intelligence, and advice; (2) to train cadres of Soviet experts on Africa in the various relevant disciplines; (3) to equip Soviet technicians, journalists, scientists, and others going to Africa with the requisite competence; (4) to impress Africans with the idea that the Soviet Union is the major country most concerned with Africa's past, culture, and accomplishments, and is therefore presumably better able to understand them; (5) to establish contacts with other Africanists abroad; and (6) to apply its conclusions in the academic cold war between scholars in the East and West.[20]

Since 1957 the academic work has been coordinated under government supervision, with the active participation of the Academy of Sciences. Large funds and heavy allocations of manpower have been made on a priority basis to a variety of institutions, the principal one being the Africa Institute established in Moscow in late 1959. Its director, Ivan Potekhin, has been remarkably frank about the political ends of its research and publication program.[21]

The output, which includes brochures, popular handbooks, dictionaries, specialized monographs, and collective studies, has multiplied under a carefully coordinated program of research and publishing. The increase of interest in Africa was symbolized in 1961 by the changing of the names of the two leading Soviet journals of Oriental Studies: *Contemporary East* and *Soviet Orientology* became *Asia and Africa Today* and *Peoples of Asia and Africa.*

One aspect of the research effort worth singling out is the extent to which Moscow engages in academic propaganda among the African elites. It has skillfully launched treatises on a few major themes that are bound to appeal to the sensitivities of African intellectuals—to whom history is a major weapon, much as it was in the Balkans half a century ago. Soviet publications contend, for instance, that Africa was a flourishing civilization before colonialism intervened; this "excuses" the present condition of Africa, blames the colonial powers for Africa's backwardness, and permits Africans to take pride in their pre-colonial past.

Soviet accomplishments in African studies have been substantial but highly uneven. There is still a shortage of specialists and linguists. The quality of work varies considerably; some areas (such as West Africa) are far more familiar to Soviet scholars than others. Potekhin himself is pushing ahead, evidently over the resistance of some Party academicians who feel he is going beyond the limits of reasonable promise. Yet, with its blind spots and distortions, the recent efforts have made the Soviet Union one of the world's leading countries in the study of Africa.

Other Soviet efforts, as in diplomacy and propaganda, have put Moscow more directly in touch with the African states and their representatives abroad. The Soviet Union has been prompt in recognizing the new African states and, wherever allowed, has established legations, embassies, consulates, trade missions, and other official agencies in Africa. It has sent sizable staffs even to small states. Since the end of 1958, the Foreign Ministry in Moscow has had a separate African Department (since subdivided).

One characteristic of the Khrushchev era has been the extensive use of "personal diplomacy," including the dispatch of high officials for negotiations, trade talks, and attendance at national celebrations in Africa. Khrushchev himself has received and accepted several invitations, and between September 1959 and June 1960 a series of press dispatches (including Soviet ones) indicated that he was planning to visit Guinea, Ghana, Liberia, Ethiopia, and the U.A.R.;

since the Congo crisis erupted, however, there has been no talk of his visiting Africa. For its part, the U.S.S.R. has received visiting dignitaries from Africa—notably premiers Abboud of Sudan, Shermarke of Somalia, and Dia of Senegal—with formal banquets in the Kremlin, guided tours across the country, and extensive coverage in the press. Journalists in Accra have even alleged that Khrushchev has engaged in extensive private correspondence with Nkrumah and Touré, to whom he has expounded his views on disarmament, foreign trade, and economic development. In 1961 Moscow awarded a Lenin Prize to Touré, in 1962 to Nkrumah, and in 1963 to Modibo Keita.

An informal but significant effort, which has attracted considerable public notice, is the extensive use of "cultural" contacts, in the broad Soviet sense. Beginning with Ivan Potekhin's sojourn in Ghana in 1957, person-to-person contacts have multiplied. African delegations have been visiting Russia *en masse*, often at Soviet expense, with attendance at Youth Festivals perhaps the most impressive occasions. The award of scholarships to African students for study in the U.S.S.R. has been a major Soviet enterprise, supported by the establishment in 1960 of Moscow's "Friendship University" for African students. These efforts have not brought total success, of course; African students in the U.S.S.R., for instance, always seem to include a group that Soviet officials consider troublemakers and "provocateurs." By 1963 Moscow could no longer deny some ugly instances of discrimination and incompatibility.[22] Still, the total Soviet program for training individual Africans and promoting an image of the U.S.S.R. as a helping elder brother is bound to produce some of the desired effects.

The Soviet propaganda effort has increased rapidly since the late fifties. The Soviet press has given extensive coverage to Africa, and vast quantities of printed matter are distributed in Africa by the U.S.S.R. or local proxies. Soviet broadcast time has considerably increased since April 1958; the original English and French transmissions have been supplemented by broadcasts in Swahili, Amharic, Hausa, Somali, and Portuguese. All the standard techniques are used: special appeals are made to young people, women, and intellectuals, and "pen-pal" clubs and quiz programs are organized. Information centers attached to Soviet embassies dispense news bulletins, movies, and gift books to African libraries. To these overt methods of influence certain covert ones are doubtless added.[23]

Moscow and African Communism. Moscow's most reliable instrument in any target area has usually been the indigenous Communist Party; its existence and eventual installation in power has been a *sine qua non* in Communist thinking. Here tropical Africa has posed another challenge, for it has no regular Communist organizations worthy of the name.[24]

Efforts at establishing such parties had been made, of course. The Rassemblement Démocratique Africain (RDA), established in 1946 as a kind of popular front, came under the articulate and often controlling influence of French Communists; although it did not embrace all the nationalist groupings, it became the first politically effective indigenous organization with branches throughout French Africa. But the Communists themselves were too weak to take over the RDA. In 1950–51, its leadership, under Félix Houphouet-Boigny, broke with the Communists. The RDA as such fell apart but was succeeded by regional political movements, of which the most important are the present ruling parties of Guinea (Parti Démocratique Guinéen) and Mali (Union Soudanaise), and the Union des Populations du Cameroun (UPC), a movement whose temper was militantly radical and crypto-Communist.

Throughout the 1950's the Communists had no overt organizational base in what became the Brazzaville bloc. The same years saw the disaffection of individual Communists in Nigeria and the Gold Coast (most of whom had been attracted to the cause while studying in England). In South Africa, the party, after suffering a severe decline in membership and a heavy turnover among its African contingents, was outlawed in 1950.

Moscow recognized fairly early that African Communism suffered from a lack of native leadership and cadres: virtually every one of the handful of African revolutionaries trained in Moscow had left the movement. Africa, moreover, seemed to be politically volatile and immature beyond the limits of Communist toleration: time and again, some ephemeral "Marxist" group would dub itself a Communist party, only to have its leaders and its total membership (sometimes identical) defect without remorse or second thoughts.

African Communism as an organized movement had thus never stood high in Soviet expectations or esteem.* As a matter of fact, liaison between African and European "headquarters" was at times maintained through channels (such as the French trade unions) deemed more reliable than the Communists themselves.

Until 1961 it was evidently a calculated Soviet policy not to encourage and not to recognize the formation of new Communist parties in tropical Africa. Such a Soviet policy is by no means novel; Lenin applied it to Turkey, Khrushchev to the U.A.R. It would thus be misleading to conclude that the Soviet Union has refrained from encouraging Communist parties in order to appeal more effectively to the "nationalist" parties and governments of Africa. On the contrary, it was in large measure the weakness of indigenous Communism that made it desirable to revert to the "alliance" policy.

Since 1955 Communists in Africa have worked to infiltrate nationalist organizations, to take over trade unions, and to stand behind broadly "progressive" causes. If Ghanaian sources can be believed, Potekhin during his stay in Accra (in the fall of 1957) advised the Communist youth group there (active under the name "The Nucleus") to join existing organizations and work from within them.[25] This has in fact been the policy in recent years: overt or clandestine Communists have tried to stand behind, or near, the thrones. How many real Communists are at work is still anyone's guess.[26] What remained, until 1961, were small parties either operating illegally (like the Senegalese PAI) or fighting the existing governments without Soviet support (like the UPC in Cameroun).[27]

A novel effort was made, in 1961–62, to associate the "progressive" ruling parties of Guinea, Ghana, and Mali with international Communism. The attendance of their representatives at the Twenty-Second Congress of the CPSU, in October 1961, symbolized this trend, though Moscow was careful not to lump them with the Com-

---

*Since Moscow had just made a determination that any country, however backward, was capable of going socialist, it was loath to acknowledge the "objective" causes of Communist failure in the stronghold of anticolonial unrest. The near-absence of a proletariat, the scarcity of urban centers and good communications media, the strength of traditional loyalties, and overwhelming illiteracy had also obtained in other countries, such as Mongolia and Vietnam. Moscow, moreover, rarely acknowledged the "objective" differences between Asia and Africa, such as the widespread absence of agrarian crises and overpopulation in tropical Africa.

munist parties properly speaking, and their speakers were obviously aware of the remaining gap. The subsequent experience, however, seems to have weakened the Soviet belief in the eventual convertibility of these national-revolutionary parties into crypto-Communist ones.

More recently, Moscow has assumed an optimistic tone about the prospects of African Communism.[28] To be sure, the less propagandistic among Soviet accounts reflect an awareness of the difficulties, but none seems to question the axiom that Communism eventually must triumph in Africa, too. To fulfill its historic role, the leading Communist writers insist, the working class in Africa must be organized into its own Marxist-Leninist party.[29]

Where and when parties must be established has been a matter of some dispute. Moscow itself has remained silent on the subject; some spokesmen of international Communism have hinted that Communist parties must be created everywhere without delay; others have said that their formation could be postponed indefinitely. The only indigenous Communist journal dealing with all-African problems carried, in a single issue, arguments in favor of creating African Communist parties "in each country," "in each region," and "in the more developed countries."[30] It is likely that Moscow has considered and reconsidered the question several times since 1958. Whatever the answer, the existing Communist organizations have a major role to play in the double task of making the revolutionary masses absorb the "sharp weapon of Marxist-Leninist theory" and of creating "effective mass organizations" throughout Africa.

The South African party is the most obvious one to play such a part, if only because of its older cadres, its established links with the Soviet and European parties, and perhaps its greater reliability; even in South Africa one of its unique advantages is the use of whites to overcome the restrictions put on the Africans.[31] Its organ, *The African Communist*, published since the fall of 1959 (and presently produced in London), has become a major bond among Communists all over Africa.[32]

Moscow and the African Trade Unions. Communists have always regarded the trade-unon movement as a useful "transmission belt" to the masses, an organizing universe beyond the party, and a device for the selection and screening of potential cadres. The weakness of Communist parties in Africa has vastly increased the importance of trade unions.

Historically, Soviet trade-union policy (for the non-Communist world) has vacillated between advocacy of "leftist" dual-unionism (forming Communist unions to challenge the existing moderate ones) and "united labor" alliances. In the Khrushchev era, attempts to create separate Communist unions have been given up in favor of attempts to win the uncommitted elements in the African labor movement.

Soviet attention has been concentrated on problems of national trade-union politics and international labor affiliation, rather than on the mechanics of recruitment, collective bargaining, and strike techniques. Soviet interest has centered on taking over (or at least neutralizing) non-Communist unions "from above." Actually there were very few Communists at the grass-roots level in African labor, but some key leaders, especially in West Africa, were Party members or sympathizers.

To the extent that they were unionized (less than twenty per cent) African workers in the 1950's were divided between unions affiliated with the Communist-run World Federation of Trade Unions (WFTU) and the "Western" International Confederation of Free Trade Unions (ICFTU); but there was an increasing tendency in the nationalist movements to favor a third all-African union federation, separate from both the ICFTU and the "colonialist" French Confédération Générale du Travail (CGT), whose parent body was the WFTU.

The major shift in Soviet "advice" regarding trade unions was analogous to that which led to Communist cooperation with the national bourgeoisie: to back "labor unity" with active WFTU participation. In practice, this meant to create a bloc of the independent African unions with those in the WFTU, isolating or splitting those in the ICFTU. The price Moscow had to expect its followers to pay for this was to consent to the disaffiliation of "leftist" unions from the WFTU—something which, it was made clear, was no more than a tactical maneuver.[33] In the Soviet view, labor unity would give the Communists their best chance to advance within the trade-union center, to keep rivals and renegades in place, to influence government policy, and to screen and indoctrinate men for Communist party work.[34]

The trend toward independent African unions gained momentum when Sekou Touré, as head of the trade-union confederation in French Guinea, created an African CGT autonomous from the French CGT and the WFTU. Initially, Diallo Abdoulaye, the influential pro-Communist Vice President of the WFTU, opposed Touré's move bitterly. But the mass of Guinean labor flocked to Touré. Characteristically, in September 1956 the policy changed: Abdoulaye was allowed to join with Touré in calling for a "unity" conference, with the "pro-Western" Force Ouvrière staying out. Thus the Union Générale des Travailleurs d'Afrique Noire (UGTAN) was launched in 1957 as an unaffiliated African trade-union center—enjoying, however, the active backing of the "left" (Abdoulaye became Vice President of UGTAN). In spite of the overlap of personnel and UGTAN's maintenance of relations with the WFTU, the Communists were facing a formidable difficulty, for (unlike the national-liberation coalitions) here Guinea and Ghana were pursuing rival initiatives, with Touré dominating UGTAN and the Ghanaian Trade Union Congress (TUC) still affiliated with the ICFTU.

After UGTAN was formed, it still took considerable time to bridge the gap between "Black Africa" and "Arab Africa" by sponsoring a common labor organization. At last, in Casablanca in May 1961, an agreement was reached to establish an All-African Trade Union Federation (AATUF). The Soviet press and the WFTU hailed this, despite some reservations, as a success for the "progressive forces." Indeed, the adopted ban on dual affiliation (which a few years earlier would have hit the WFTU hardest) was by 1961 primarily anti-Western in effect, since most leftist unions had already abandoned the WFTU and some of the major moderate groups continued to belong to the ICFTU. In substance, the agreement produced an equilibrium between the ICFTU forces (Tunisian, Kenyan, and Nigerian, among others) and the pro-WFTU elements (with the Guinean and Ghanaian unions holding the balance). This was a partial victory, but no more, for the "unity" forces.[35]

Although they praised the formation of the AATUF as "a great victory," Soviet authorities have remained reserved about its prospects. They recognize the successes of anti-Communist, moderate labor organizations, and the paradox that the most heavily unionized areas in Africa (Nigeria, Congo, the Rhodesias) are almost entirely outside Communist, or even AATUF, influence. A number of leading African trade-unionists have firmly come out against Communist "fronts."[36] Moscow may have also been embarrassed by the wholehearted endorsements of pan-Africanism by Leftist African labor spokesmen, which were made at a time when Soviet officials were seeking to avoid such a clear-cut identification. On the contrary, Communists have tried to explain, unconvincingly, that all-African organizational "isolationism" and "proletarian internationalism" are not in conflict with each other.[37]

The Communists and the WFTU have not, meanwhile, abdicated their own special role. Since 1959 the WFTU has continued to train African syndicalists in its special school in Budapest. Heavy African representation (94 out of 958) at the Fifth World Congress of the WFTU in Moscow in December 1961 no doubt also provided an opportunity to consult and agree on common policies for Africa. In its program, the WFTU fully endorsed the formation of the AATUF and pledged its friendship. Yet the speeches at the Congress also revealed some suspicion, some resentment, and some concern. The report of WFTU Secretary Ibrahim Zakaria allowed for a possible dissolution of AATUF or the deterioration of relations with the "independent" (Ghanaian and Guinean) unions, which were called instruments of the ruling state parties. Several delegations took a harder line regarding the national bourgeoisie and the need for Communist party work. Later, the Inter-African Trade Union Conference, held in Dakar in January 1962, was bitterly denounced as a mass deception of African workers perpetrated by stooges of the ICFTU and the American CIA; the African Trade Union Confederation (ATUC) formed at Dakar was said to be subservient to the ICGTU and the International Confederation of Christian Trade Unions.[38]

The struggle was by no means over. Indeed, Ali Yata, General Secretary of the Communist Party of Morocco, wrote a remarkably frank article (published in the December 1961 issue of the Soviet-directed *World Marxist Review*) spelling out Communist reservations about the AATUF: its objectives are not clearly defined; its chief economic task is overlooked (Moscow resents the support of the African Common Market plan by even radical nationalists); many of the AATUF leaders pursue a "false neutralism" by "indiscriminately placing the socialist and the imperialist countries in the same category." The article added that some union leaders are in danger of "overestimating the role of the trade unions":

> They alone cannot lead the struggle for national and social liberation, for the socialist society to which the working people aspire and the inevitability of which is determined by the laws of social development. The leading role can only be played by an organized, disciplined vanguard of the working class, thoroughly versed in the laws of social development and class struggle revealed by Marxist-Leninist science. The Communist parties are that vanguard.

Nonetheless, Communist workers were called upon to give the AATUF their full support.[39] As a Soviet journal had described the general "Leninist" strategy regarding front organizations, Communists must "take advantage of every—even the smallest—opportunity of gaining a mass ally, even though this ally be temporary, vacillating, unstable, unreliable, and conditional."[40]

The trade-union movement is the most important of several "fronts" on which Soviet policy-makers have relied in Africa. In addition, there is the usual array of federations of youth, teachers, women, students, lawyers, and journalists; most of these have spawned African affiliates and held conferences on African soil.[41]

Finally, there is the growing "Afro-Asian" complex of organizations in the Bandung tradition, with its bevy of solidarity conferences and committees, and the All-African People's Conferences. While the Soviet Union has given generous verbal (and in some instances, financial) support to these organizations, there is no evidence that it controls them or thinks it does. Moscow does not seem to rely on this network except for propaganda purposes and contacts. In fact, these bodies have been the scene of numerous conflicts—between neutralists and Communists, between "Black" and Arab movements, between Africans and Asians, and finally between Soviet and Chinese Communists.

It is true that, over the years, most "Afro-Asian" activities have become more militant in spirit. Moscow can hardly take credit for this. It remembers, no doubt (as Ali Yata's article confirmed), that even the best "front" organizations cannot do the job of Communist parties; this is especially true in Africa, where most governments have successfully gained control of all the public organizations within their state. When faced with a challenge, the governments and their ruling parties (even in the case of Ghana, Guinea, and Mali) can be expected to be far more effective in coping with it than the Communist "fronts."

African Crises and Revisions in Strategy

Until about 1959 Moscow saw Africa as an organic part of the "Afro-Asian" mass. It applied formulas and policies to Africa as best it could, while giving higher priority to other parts of the "emerging" world. A general sense of optimism pervaded Soviet policy, and an expansive identification with the anti-Western "national-liberation movements" ushered in an era of the Communist "soft sell." Only then did Africa come to attract major attention among Soviet policymakers. Potekhin's published reports on the Accra Conference were a landmark, indicating (despite unmistakable reservations) a strong desire to associate the Soviet Union with the African upheavals. Increasingly aware of its African audience, Russia stopped considering itself an outsider. Now Soviet hopes for the speedy, automatic gravitation of new African states toward "the socialist camp" had reached their peak. In retrospect, they were not only excessive but also surprisingly simplistic. Since then a distinct note of skepticism and disappointment has crept into Soviet commentaries about Africa. On top of the general uncertainties regarding Africa (so unusual of Soviet positions in other areas), a partial hardening of the policy line became apparent in 1961–63. This change in Soviet expectations and conduct was due largely to the intervening experiences with Africa as well as the double confrontation with China and the United States.

By 1960 the realities of African politics began to vitiate Moscow's stand. Faced with a succession of confused splits, alliances, and divisions among the new African states, Moscow could no longer in-

voke the myths of Afro-Asian or all-African solidarity; a differenti-
ated policy was needed. Seemingly obliged to pick favorites, Moscow
was often confronted with difficult choices. Could it propitiate both
Ethiopia and the Somali Republic with the two at odds? Could it refrain from identifying either Guinea or Ghana as the most promising
and progressive of African states? Could it avoid taking a stand in
the rivalry between the "Black" African states and the Arab north?

The risks and benefits of taking sides in African struggles were
simpler to calculate once the earlier alignments (e.g., Ghana vs. the
U.A.R.) yielded to new blocs conforming more closely to cold war
patterns and the "two-camp" view; by 1962 such a dichotomy was
apparent in the confrontation of the so-called Casablanca powers
with those of the Monrovia and Lagos conferences. While they remained eager not to antagonize anyone but the "extreme reaction-
aries" among African leaders, the Soviet authorities evidently felt a
greater kinship for the vigorous, "progressive" Casablanca group
than for the alternative grouping, which they considered to consist
largely of puppet regimes and right-wing elites.[42] The choice was
clear, even if Moscow was visibly disturbed by the fact that the "right
wing" had succeeded in doing precisely what the Communists had
sought to make their own monopoly—attract the moderate and uncommitted states (such as Nigeria, Togo, and Somalia). The new
guiding principle was apparently to reward states willing to cut their
ties to the West and cultivate contacts with the Soviet bloc.

There were other causes for concern in Moscow. With independence achieved, the new African states no longer looked on the U.S.S.R.
as a natural ally; their foreign policies—even with Soviet indulgence
regarding neutralism—left much to be desired. Soviet publications
now spoke more frequently of the "collaborationist parties . . .
mushrooming all over the 'decolonized' world"—presumably thanks
to the support of imperialist powers.[43] In United Nations voting on
such issues as the seating of Communist China, the U.N. force in the
Congo, and the condemnation of Soviet nuclear tests, the African
states proved that they were by no means natural allies. Finally, Moscow had to acknowledge that many of the new states were not interested in a total break with the former colonial powers, whose financial,
economic, and technical assistance they needed.[44] And the various

schemes for an African Common Market—popular even among the "progressive" nationalists—were by no means to Moscow's liking, as Khrushchev made clear in various angry tirades in May and June of 1962.

The Congo Crisis. Nowhere were the dilemmas and difficulties of Soviet policy in Africa illustrated as clearly as in the Congo crisis. At first, in July 1960, Moscow sought to identify itself with African nationalism by backing the United Nations action, which it believed to be directed against Belgian colonialism: this looked like a safe, cheap, and consistent move. Then, afraid of being outmaneuvered by the West and the U.N. command, the Soviet Union shifted to give separate support to Patrice Lumumba.[45]

Soviet support for Lumumba was overwhelmingly verbal. When he was ousted, jailed, and finally murdered, Moscow failed to act. Having earlier failed to give his forces military support, it now refrained from intervening; instead, it concentrated on vicious attacks on the United Nations, and on increasing diplomatic and personal exchanges between Soviet and non-Western statesmen such as Nehru and Nkrumah.

Moscow also equivocated with regard to the inchoate successor regime of Antoine Gizenga in Stanleyville. It was apparently deterred from giving it stronger support by a desire not to take undue risks (the intervention of Soviet forces might well have invited a showdown with the Western powers) and a desire not to endorse a losing cause: backing a hopelessly weak friend was not worthwhile if it meant jeopardizing a possibly "correct" relationship with the victor government. For months, Moscow was unable to decide whether to recognize Adoula (whose cabinet Gizenga had temporarily joined) or to oppose and assail him for his failure to fight Tshombé's Katanga regime to the finish.[46]

Finally, on December 2, 1961, the Soviet government received Adoula's consent to the restoration of diplomatic relations. Soon there were rumors of Soviet offers of military assistance to the Adoula regime. Moscow, however, did not even then fully renounce its support for Gizenga. When Gizenga was arrested in January 1962, the Soviet press broke its peace with Adoula and predicted another "Lumumba-style" murder. And yet the Soviet authorities maintained "correct" diplomatic relations with the Congo government.

Moscow derived some benefit from the Congo crisis. It made excellent propaganda capital out of it, especially over Lumumba's murder and the association of the West with the Belgian cause. The Congo affair paved the way (perhaps unexpectedly) to a more ambitious rapprochement between Moscow and Accra by bringing them together in backing Lumumba. On the other hand, the Congo crisis exposed the U.S.S.R. to the African peoples as a power claiming to be their friend in words, prepared to praise Lumumba posthumously as a hero, but ultimately failing to act on behalf of the African revolution it claimed to champion. Moreover, in its corollary efforts in the United Nations, the Soviet Union failed to muster the essential support of most African states.[47]

Moscow was caught by surprise by the Congo crisis. It had not expected revolutionary opportunities requiring direct action on its part. But once it had decided not to commit its own forces and to avoid substantial risks of a showdown with the U.S., the Soviet Union faced the characteristic choice of supporting Adoula—typifying a man in power but basically hostile to the U.S.S.R.—or Gizenga, politically kindred but (as one East European leader put it) "of all our African friends . . . the real pygmy." No African fellow traveler has ever remained a stable and dependable ally of the U.S.S.R.: for Moscow the only safe Lumumba was a dead Lumumba. But after the Congo crisis Khrushchev had to ask himself whether Sekou Touré and Kwame Nkrumah might not prove to be Adoulas, too, rather than bigger and better Lumumbas.

Guinea. By 1961 Guinea, Ghana, and Mali had become identified as the three Soviet favorites in Africa. Among them Moscow had increasingly singled out Guinea as the most advanced. But as so often in Africa, political appearances were deceiving. In September 1961, Conakry announced that 18 Soviet technicians had been arrested for smuggling stolen diamonds (from the nationalized Guinean diamond industry). In October, Soviet Ambassador Daniel Solod was reported as saying that Guineans "did not want to work, were ruining Soviet equipment, and were not to be taken seriously."[48] Touré reportedly refused to receive Solod. In November, Touré's men clamped down on opposition groups. A militant Communist employed by the Guinean Press Agency was killed after being arrested for "economic espionage" on behalf of a foreign embassy.[49]

Finally, a crisis was precipitated when a memorandum criticizing the ruling PDG was circulated by five officials of the Teachers' Union. The union's secretary-general, Keita Koumendian, who had long been active in the WFTU and considered himself Touré's rival in the Guinean labor movement, was arrested along with four others alleged to have been in touch with Guinean Communists in Conakry, Paris, and Dakar. On November 23 the five were sentenced to jail terms ranging from five to ten years. This news in turn triggered public demonstrations and disturbances; after Koumendian's student supporters marched on Sekou Touré's house shouting "Down with the PDG," the government closed all schools.

On December 11, Touré accused the Communists of instigating the student riots and planning to overthrow his government; he further claimed to have evidence of "subversive" contacts with a bloc embassy in Conakry. On December 16 Ambassador Solod left Conakry for "reasons of health"; Guinea had requested his withdrawal.

When a group of Guinean students in Moscow—probably at Soviet instigation—demanded that the teachers be freed and Solod allowed to return, Touré recalled over forty of the students with the comment, "We don't need fanatical propagandists here." According to Colin Legum, Moscow refused to permit their departure until Conakry threatened to send no more students to the U.S.S.R.[50]

For some weeks Moscow went out of its way to deny "libelous inventions" and "exaggerated, false rumors about Soviet interference in the internal affairs of Guinea."[51] Early in 1962 Anastas Mikoyan paid an impromptu visit to Conakry to repeat Moscow's promise not to interfere; he was received with marked coolness and restraint. Solod was replaced as ambassador by Dmitri Degtyar, who was not only a top Soviet expert on the Near East and Africa but also an economist specializing in foreign trade.

Henceforth Moscow made a distinct effort to cater to Ghana first, instead of Guinea. In part, this stemmed from Nkrumah's agreement

with Soviet foreign-policy positions in the fall of 1961; but it was
also doubtless an attempt to create a counterweight to estranged
Guinea. Mikoyan—visiting Ghana, Mali, and Morocco after his trip
to Guinea—said (according to the TASS version of January 12,
1962) that Ghana "had made great progress in building socialism in
the country"—an unprecedented statement. *Pravda* toned this down
somewhat, so that it only praised the Ghanaian "effort to build socialism," but it was clear that the courting of Ghana was on in earnest.
A later Soviet broadcast declared: "The Soviet Union and other
socialist states are always prepared to assist Ghana in its endeavor to
build a socialist regime so that its resources may be used in the best
way for economic development."[52]

African Alternatives. After some temporizing, Moscow felt compelled to clarify its view of several thoroughly uncomfortable trends
in Africa. As for the movement for "African unity," Moscow ap-
proved unity of action, presumably against the West, but not federation. But what about Pan-Africanism? It had been classified in theory
as a petty-bourgeois, potentially racist effort; in practice, however, its
widespread appeal dictated the necessity of finding a *modus vivendi*.
After returning from Accra in 1959, Potekhin wrote that "the ideology of Pan-Africanism has many things which are foreign to our
world outlook. But Pan-Africanism pursues the aim of rallying all
African peoples to fight against colonialism and imperialism for their
national liberation. From this point of view Pan-Africanism deserves
the support of all people of good will."[53] The relativism that had
marked the Soviet response to national movements was thus in evidence again.

In 1960, Potekhin explained: the concept of a "United States
of Africa" was a progressive *slogan,* but the obstacles facing its realization were so formidable that it could not be a practical task. Potekhin argued that regional federations were more feasible and useful;
plans for the Ghana-Guinea-Mali union seemed to be the example he
had in mind.[54] The main consideration, of course, was who would
do the uniting. When in March 1961 the former French possessions
in Africa formed the African-Malagasy Union, the Communists explained that "not all unity is useful and progressive." In brief, a pro-
Communist united Africa was welcome; an anti-Communist Africa

was better divided. That in essence was the Soviet advice to the Addis Ababa Conference of Heads of State in May 1963. Pointing out that the United States had "no objection to a united Africa within the framework, say, of a military bloc under their control or of the Common Market," Moscow concluded: "Africa needs unity, but not just any kind of unity is in the interest of its peoples."[55]

To the Soviet observers, the problems of "African socialism" and other variants of "unscientific" socialist ideas were especially grave. By 1960 Soviet authorities were eager to expose the fallacies of rival varieties of socialism. Potekhin, for instance, went out of his way to give systematic exposés of Léopold Senghor's ideas of Negro (or African) Socialism, Nasser's "cooperative socialism," and Nkrumah's variant.[56] While the single outstanding argument against "unscientific" socialism is its denial of the class struggle as fundamental to the development of society, one gathers that it is the rival appeal of other creeds that is at the root of Soviet concern: Moscow obviously fears the magnetism of viable indigenous alternatives that promise individual, social, and national progress.

African tribal and religious loyalties were somewhat easier to categorize.[57] These were, of course, obstacles to progress, survivals of a primitive past. Potekhin has argued that tribal separatism is "the principal obstacle to a united national front in the colonies. In the countries that have already won their independence (Ghana, Guinea, etc.) tribal chiefs are the main reactionary force."[58] As on other African issues, Soviet experts differed among themselves. In explaining what happened in the Congo, two Soviet correspondents struck an unusually realistic note: Lumumba failed to get the support of Bakongo tribesmen because "belonging to a tribe, to a language group, is often a stronger tie than political convictions."[59] Still, Soviet comments tend to minimize subnational loyalties in Africa, or else to equate them with retrogressive and traditionalist forces that are being successfully opposed by rational, or at least national, trends.

Religious influences are, with very few exceptions, identified as reactionary and divisive. The institutionalized church is usually depicted as a tool of imperialism, and the Vatican is described as a secret member of NATO. Religion becomes a problem only when Moscow or native Communism is confronted with a choice between primitive African religion and "Western" Christianity. In this situation, Moscow has insisted that there can be no return to the savage past and that only the best of earlier African culture must be preserved, while at the same time seeking to propitiate "Black chauvinists" of the type of Jomo Kenyatta. Here again, political utility is the decisive consideration.

Similar equivocation appears in Soviet comments on African borders. The new states have, of course, assumed the political boundaries of the former colonies—boundaries which, more often than not, were arbitrarily drawn without regard to ethnic groups.[60] But while favoring a reshuffling by ethnic criteria "in principle," Soviet statesmen and scholars have not publicly come out in opposition to the existing sovereign units.

In Soviet terms, the process of nation-formation is far from completed in tropical Africa, though the implications of this finding are not spelled out.[61] However, even without the existence of nations, Moscow acknowledges the existence of nationalism there. Typically relativistic, the Soviet view of nationalism in Africa is a peculiar compound of political utility and deep-seated suspicion. It has always been axiomatic that national self-determination is subordinate to class interests.[62] But although in theory nationalism is still put down as ultimately "bourgeois," political expediency has required that national self-consciousness in the emerging nations be styled a "basically progressive" phenomenon. In practice, political zigzags (for instance, regarding Nigeria and Somalia) have canceled the benefits of Soviet manipulation of the national appeal. At the same time, it has become clearer that Communists will oppose nationalism when attempts are made to exploit it for "national egoism and national exclusiveness." Precisely in Africa, such narrow nationalism "represents a serious danger," since it emerges at a time of bourgeois strength, while Marxist groups south of the Sahara "have just begun to be born."[63]

Second Thoughts in Moscow. The Khrushchev policy, having failed to score, found itself under attack. Within the Communist fold, the nature of the national-liberation movement and national-front tactics became matters of intense debate. Even more dramatic was the argument over "direct action," centering around the Chinese discussed in a subsequent chapter) that the Soviet Union dodge all resort to armed struggle. Here as on other issues found itself caught between the fundamentalists in Peking and the nationalists in Africa.

While assailing African pacifism, the Soviet leaders rejected the contention that in Africa "direct action" was the normal means to power. An authoritative survey explained: "With the colonial system approaching its last days, the peoples of the colonies are . . . wherever possible attaining independence by peaceful means." And it went on to declare: "It is characteristic that many countries of Africa have achieved independence without large armed uprisings and bloody conflicts."[64]

Soviet failure to give direct military assistance to the Algerian, Congolese, and Angolan "progressives" is thus revealing of Khrushchev's calculus of risks and gains.

Cameroun. Perhaps the outstanding instance of Soviet failure to support African movements engaged in armed struggle came in Cameroun. The *Union des Populations du Cameroun,* formed in 1947 as a part of the RDA, had early adopted a radical program and had refused to break with the Communists when the rest of the RDA did. The Communist training of some of its leaders and the radicalism of its main supporting tribe, the Bassa, led it to embark on "direct action"—a commitment that became a condition of survival when the French authorities outlawed the UPC in 1955. In September 1958, direction of the movement was assumed by Félix-Roland Moumié, who has been called the first African Communist "professional revolutionary." He travelled frequently to the Communist bloc and was a member of the board of various Afro-Asian Solidarity committees. After years of bitter fighting and the attainment of Camerounian independence in 1960, the remaining cadres of the illegal UPC consisted of terrorists professing to follow the tenets of Marxism-Leninism but too wild to accept fully either the discipline or the ideology of Communism.

The example of the UPC is most instructive in the context of Sino-Soviet rivalry, because Moumié rejected as nonsense the Khrushchev thesis about a peaceful road to power. Although until 1962 the pro-Soviet Communist press never recognized the UPC as Communist,

Moscow had at one time lent it support. But evidently in his conversations with President Ahidjo of the new Cameroun Republic, on January 3, 1960, Soviet Deputy Foreign Minister Firyubin delivered a promise not to help Moumié any more. A *Pravda* correspondent in Yaoundé said Moscow had "at one time" thought Moumié's tactics correct but no longer felt able to support him. According to Camerounian Foreign Minister Okala, who saw Khrushchev at the United Nations in the fall of 1960, Khrushchev did not deny having advised Moumié in the past, but said that Moumié had not taken his advice. Okala quoted Khrushchev as having told Moumié: "No revolution can be organized from outside. . . . Return to Cameroun to suffer with your countrymen and come to power legally through elections!"

By this time Moumié had turned to Peking. He had visited Communist China in the fall of 1959 and returned there in mid-1960. In 1960 the Communist Chinese embassy in Conakry opened a special liaison office with the UPC, and North Vietnam likewise established contact with it there. In an interview with Fritz Schatten in April 1960, Moumié virtually ignored the Soviet Union but kept talking about China. Recalling his personal interviews with Mao, he showed Schatten, "almost triumphantly," a French translation of Mao's writings on guerrilla warfare (1938) with a personal dedication from Mao. Pointing to the book, Moumié remarked: "Here you'll find out what is going to happen in Cameroun."

Moumié was poisoned in Switzerland on November 4, 1960; Swiss, West German, and "Afro-Asian" sources later claimed that the murder was performed by one Wilhelm Bechtel, on orders from the French "Red Hand." The link between the UPC and Peking continued even after Moumié's death: "In 1961, as a result of the arrest of several UPC activists, it was confirmed that the Chinese were training Camerounian rebel cadres in guerrilla warfare technique"; evidently they also provided financial support and modest amounts of small arms.[65]

In almost every instance, Soviet failure to support "direct action" has led the "armed struggle" movement in Africa to seek, and gain, closer ties with Peking. Moscow is bound to view this pattern with some alarm.

By 1961 it was apparent that application of the "Khrushchev

line" had brought no significant breakthroughs. Since then Moscow has obviously lost some faith in nationalism, neutralism, the colonial bourgeoisie, and the African leadership.[66] Potekhin has admitted that ancestor worship is very much alive and that "tribalism is not simply the intrigues of the imperialists" but an organic, indigenous force. He has also shown impatience with African leaders who spread "the illusion that African society is without classes," adding that "fundamentally the peasantry is an uncompacted, atomized mass of small producers, illiterate and politically extremely backward."[67] Since the "peasantry" constitutes some ninety per cent of Africa's population, the prospects for progressive revolution would seem dim.

Correspondingly, Soviet statements have placed greater emphasis on the role of the working class in Africa. In almost "Chinese" tones Khrushchev was moved to recognize (in his Sofia speech, on May 18, 1962):

> Unfortunately, truths which are fully obvious to us Communists, are not always acceptable to many leaders of the national-liberation movement. . . . Under contemporary conditions the national bourgeoisie has not yet exhausted its progressive role. However, as contradictions between the workers and other classes accumulate, it more and more reveals an inclination for agreement with reaction. . . .

> Leaders who really hold dear the interests of the people and of the toiling masses will have to understand sooner or later that only by relying on the working class . . . can victory be achieved. . . . Either they will understand this, or other people will come after them who will understand better the demands of life.

The corollary was increased emphasis on "action." An authoritative Soviet article declared in February 1962:

> Brute force was and still remains a main function of colonial policy. For this reason the national-liberation movement in many countries will still take the form of armed struggle and will turn into national-liberation uprisings and wars.[68]

The most striking evidence of a readjustment in policy was the formation of Communist parties in parts of Africa where none had previously existed. A Tunisian weekly reported from Conakry that the Foreign Section of the CPSU Central Committee had allegedly decided that after 1961 Communist parties were to be formed wherever possible in Africa.[69] For some time a similar "line" had been argued by *The African Communist*, but not until the CPSU had been closely consulted was the existence of a Communist Party of Lesotho (Basutoland) announced in November 1961.[70] The wide publicity given this otherwise fairly insignificant party made it a symbol of the new departure. By mid-1962 the existence of Communist parties in Northern Rhodesia and in Zanzibar was acknowledged.[71] Elsewhere too—from Kenya to Nigeria, and from Angola to Senegal— Communist groups displayed unprecedented overt activity.[72]

For reasons which are not yet entirely clear, this course was not pursued with all the requisite vigor. Here the problem overlapped with broader disputes in international Communism. Thus, in the British Communist Party it was R. Palme Dutt, the veteran of dealings with the colonial Communists, who found that in many African countries "conditions are becoming manifestly ripe for the formation of Communist parties."[73] Typically, it was he who in 1962–63 urged conciliation with the Chinese "line." In fact, there are indications that he has played a unique role as adviser to *The African Communist*.

Likewise, the shift in policy constituted a short-lived victory of the "French" over the "Italian" Communist orientation. Disappointment with the record of the French comrades had contributed to the formula, promoted by the Italian Communists, of working through radical nationalist organizations in Africa. Giorgio Amendola, the leader of the right wing of the Italian party, openly spoke of "the new possibilities of approaching socialism by original roads, even where there is no Communist party."[74]

The French Communists, by contrast, were eager to regain the leading role as middlemen between center and periphery. In 1960 one of their leaders reported to his Central Committee that "the dissemination of Communist ideas in the African countries is at once the duty and task of our party. . . . We should aid the Marxist groups springing up in Africa, help in their educational work and, when the conditions arise, in forming parties."[75] After Sekou Touré's *volte face*, Moscow seems to have endorsed the "French" argument.

Thus the summer of 1962 saw, along with the announcement of new parties, a series of meetings and formal links between the French Communists and "fraternal" parties in West Africa—the PAI in Senegal, the rebel wing of the UPC in Cameroun, and the Sawaba Party in Niger—all three heretofore carefully shielded from the lime-light of Communist endorsements.[76]

Ironically, the example of Cuba suggested that a Communist take-over could succeed without a Communist party—and African Com-munists were examining the lessons.[77] But as a rule the need for a Communist party remained recognized. It was reasserted, for in-stance, for Nigeria in March 1963; and the following month TASS an-nounced the creation of a new Nigerian Socialist Workers and Peas-ants' Party, guided by the principles of "scientific socialism."[78]

It appears that in the first months of 1962 a combination of queries and protests—from Chinese Communists, from some Afri-cans, perhaps from some East European and Soviet specialists—brought to a head a reassessment of Communist bloc strategy in Africa. One well-informed observer claimed to know that African Communists were urgently demanding a change in Soviet strategy.[79]

Evidently as a result of such a general reconsideration of policy, the wisdom of the Khrushchev line was nonetheless reaffirmed. In what may have been the upshot of a conference in Prague, *Rude Právo*, the official organ of the Czechoslovak Communist Party, on March 21, 1962, advised Communists in developing countries to con-tinue to tolerate "national bourgeois" leadership until its utility was exhausted. Reportedly representing "the policy of all the Communist parties in Eastern Europe that support Premier Khrushchev," the article sharply denounced the "dogmatic" and "adventurist" course identified with Peking. Curiously enough, the same piece attacked the "revisionist" view according to which the non-capitalist develop-ment is "practically socialist" and which assumes that it is therefore possible to reach socialism under national bourgeois leadership.[80]

The Cuban crisis of October 1962 seemed to induce a further Soviet retreat from risk-taking, in the face of increasing skepticism about the African revolution. In 1963 a Soviet analyst who three years earlier had seen opportunities on all sides, thus reassessed the emerging world of new nations: "Lack of organization and awareness on the part of the masses . . . and their inability to grasp fully the objective situation and real possibilities still retard the development of many newly independent countries and nations. There is no jumping out of this phase." Stressing the great variety of circumstances that give rise to unforeseen forces abroad, the article concluded on a gloomy note:

> It will naturally take some time before the peoples get their bearings and learn to distinguish wheat from chaff, sheep from goats. To oust the forces of internal colonialism from politics is the domestic affair of the nations concerned.

And it acknowledged with more than customary frankness: "The path is not smooth and not easy. The lights of complete freedom sometimes still appear far away."[81]

Indeed, by 1963 all Communist parties in Africa were illegal, and none seemed to be faring well. Among Moscow's erstwhile friends, Sekou Touré had effectively bridged the gap between the Casablanca and Monrovia powers and restored businesslike relations with the West. President Keita of Mali warned in January 1963 against "ideological assimilation" by the Communists. A month later, the President of Tanganyika, Julius Nyerere, warned fellow Africans of the prospect of a "second scramble for Africa" with the Communist powers. At the Third Afro-Asian People's Solidarity Conference in Moshi, not only did the Sino-Soviet conflict erupt into Chinese Communist lobbying to bar Russian and East European Communist "whites," but Moscow was constrained to admit that some African leaders "would like to direct the solidarity movement not against imperialism, colonialism, and its agents, but against all white people."[82]

Moreover, economic ties between the African states and the West increased, contrary to Soviet admonitions. At the United Nations, Soviet intransigence over the budget marked, according to some observers, the "end of a honeymoon" with the African member states.[83] Incidents involving African students in the Soviet Union multiplied; no longer able to deny them, Alexei Adzhubei, editor of *Izvestiia*, remarked in explanation that "Russians are human beings like everyone else."[84]

Yet the record of failures and frustrations did not keep Khru-shchev from trying again and again. What he considered fruitful themes was illustrated in the official message he sent to the heads of all African states in response to the resolutions of the Addis Ababa conference of May 1963: championing general and complete dis-armament, making Africa a nuclear-free zone, removing foreign troops and bases from the continent, boycotting the states guilty of racial discrimination or colonialism, and expanding trade relations were all causes which permitted the Soviet Union to identify itself with the African states.[85]

Soviet Prospects in Africa

In its attempts to appeal to Africa, the Soviet Union possesses certain distinct assets. It was never part of Africa's colonial past and can easily identify itself with the peoples of Africa against the colonial powers. The Soviet Union's own experience provides a powerful ex-ample of rapid modernization, economic development, and efficient controls. Unlike the "capitalist" West, which also can support the new nationalism in Africa, the Soviet Union is further identified with social revolution and with the struggle against discrimination and prejudice. As a bitterly disillusioned Togolese student wrote after leaving the Soviet Union, he had gone there believing that it was the champion of anticolonialism and racial equality and the living em-bodiment of scientific socialism—according collective and individual freedom, making rapid strides in material progress, and aiming at general welfare for all.[86]

Particularly to the young intelligentsia, trade unionists, and "ac-tivists" of the new Africa—themselves in part susceptible to an elitist, authoritarian, and manipulative outlook and impatient for rapid and dramatic change—the Soviet experience must loom as an admirable accomplishment. Totalitarianism in itself cannot be expected to arouse moral or political indignation in Africa as it may in the West. Furthermore, tropical African states lack counterweights in the form of professional armies that could assume anti-Communist or anti-Soviet positions.

Finally, many Africans are inclined to deny the necessity of choosing up sides in the East-West struggle, which to them is a squabble among the white "outsiders." If they also make light of the dangers of Communism, it is partly because they have no experience with it, and partly (as Fritz Schatten has suggested) because they meet the Soviet Union at its best. Limited in their contacts to the post-Stalin era or even more recent years, younger Africans do not recall the years of greatest terror and suffering in the U.S.S.R. Moreover, they encounter the Soviet Union and its allies primarily as dispensers of economic and technical assistance, cultural events, free publications, and mass rallies.

On the other hand, the obstacles to Soviet success are numerous and formidable. The Soviet Union and the abortive nuclei of native Communists must operate in a setting of overwhelming illiteracy, tribalism, religious and racial differences, and in societies where the "proletariat" is tiny and reliable Communist organizations are non-existent. They seek to stimulate complex and disciplined political activity in a situation marked by political volatility, personalism, and instability. Moscow must operate from a considerable geographic distance, at considerable expense. It was relatively easy for Moscow to make a convincing argument for the community of Communist and nationalist goals against a common foe, the colonial powers; but it has proved far more difficult to find a positive bond between the Communists and the uncommitted Africans in domestic and international relations alike. The willingness to see an ally in Moscow has decreased rather than increased as African states have gained independence.

Moreover, the West has certain inherent advantages in being able to tolerate an "African personality" in a pluralist family of nations. If Africa uses material accomplishment as a criterion in seeking support, the United States should stand higher than the U.S.S.R. Sensing this, Communist writers have gone out of their way to warn that such an approach is "most dangerous, if only because technology has acquired such prestige in our age that it may well prevent many from seeing that in the hands of the imperialists technology is utilized to exploit the riches of this or that country in the interest of those same imperialists."[87] Furthermore, economic and technical aid is furnished by the West in far greater amounts than by the Soviet bloc.

It would be fallacious, however, to think of the Soviet effort in Africa as merely one of competing with the West: Moscow must also vie with the Chinese challenge and with indigenous appeals. Communism and Soviet power have an attractiveness for leaders of the radical young intelligentsia; but these men—the lack of appropriate labels has given rise to unfortunate designations such as "Afro-Communists" or (more correctly) "Afro-Marxists"—may well be determined to use Soviet power and Communism to further *their* ends just as Moscow has tried to use them.

Here for Moscow the obstacle is the sense of African uniqueness—in "experience" and in "personality"—so strongly held by many nationalist intellectuals. In 1956 Richard Wright wrote:

> Black people primarily regard Russian Communists as *white* men.
> Black people primarily regard American, British, and French anti-Communists as *white* people.

He went on to add something particularly significant in the light of more recent trends in Africa:

> The Negro, even when embracing Communism or Western democracy, is not supporting ideologies: he is seeking to use instruments (instruments owned and controlled by men of other races!) for his own ends.[88]

To Moscow's chagrin, this insight has been amply borne out in Africa. Sekou Touré, for instance, though a man of "Marxist" background and leanings, in 1960 repeated his refusal to allow members of his party to become Communists: Communism, he said, was not the way for Africa. Even he rejected such basic tenets of the creed as the necessity of the class struggle, the reactionary nature of spiritual and religious values, and the dictum that pan-African ideals are inescapably "bourgeois." Typically, he has praised the utility of Soviet organizational experience; he will accept anything that can be usefully adapted to African conditions. As for the ideology, he has said: "The philosophy does not interest us. We have concrete needs."[89]

Clearly, indigenous radicals have a distinct advantage over those of the Soviet stripe. Moscow can try to appeal to socialist, anti-colonial, and authoritarian leanings. Local radicals can appeal to all these but also to the sentiments of Africanism, in their tribal, racial, national, and Pan-African forms. In Africa today what carries appeal is not doctrine but techniques: prescriptions for rapid modernization and political control; means, not ends.

Few Africans have remained Communists, with doctrinal and organizational loyalties, for any significant length of time. Bolshevism, fathered in another era for another world, has difficulty competing with forces and attitudes such as nationalism and Africanism, which Moscow has been inclined to consider easily manipulable, or to write off as romantic and petty-bourgeois, or to assail as trojan horses of imperialism. African nationalists may adapt Communism, but they will not adopt it. Communism could perhaps become "nativized" in Africa, but Communism africanized would not yield a Muscovite Africa. The prospect therefore seems to be: Soviet appeal, yes; Soviet control, no.

In the long run, Moscow, and Communism, cannot settle for Africanism or African nationalism as a sufficient cause. They must fear its emergence as an alternative to Moscow, not as a compromise with it. Having learned their Soviet lessons, the new African leadership may look with particular suspicion on Communist efforts to unseat the incumbents.

Nationalism can be a barrier to Communism or a stepping-stone to it. At present Moscow appears to be realistic enough to anticipate at least some possibility that an independent Tanganyika or Nigeria becomes a better bastion against Communism than a colonial Angola or Southern Rhodesia.

The absence of Soviet efforts at military or political conquest in Africa reinforces the hypothesis that Soviet interest there is not primarily material, economic, or even strategic. It is misleading to think of present Soviet interests in Africa in terms of a geographic penetration from contiguous Communist areas. Speculation about Soviet plans to use Egypt, Algeria, or Somalia as "footholds" or "bridges" misses the point of the Khrushchev strategy: to win without fighting.[90] This does not mean that Moscow is unaware of the geopolitical position of Africa. It has stressed the continent's potential riches, especially in ores (such as uranium and cobalt) and diamonds. It is conscious of its own handicap of distance; in fact, in explaining the failures of Communism a recent Soviet statement adds, "The distance of tropical Africa from the major centers of the world revolutionary movement also had its negative effect."[91] Moscow's primary interest has been to deny military bases and the use of natural resources to the West; the offer to make Africa a nuclear-free zone (in addition to its propaganda function) reflected this.

For the time being, attempts at direct Soviet control have been consciously laid aside. The Soviet Union no longer claims that the African revolution is essential to spark revolution in the West. Nor does it claim that imperialism can be defeated only by depriving it of its colonies. It simply takes it for granted that eventually Africa is bound to gravitate toward "the socialist camp."

Everything considered, Africa has not held a high priority in Soviet commitments. Moscow will not, in its present mood, gamble its peace and safety for the sake of bringing the benefits of its own system to the peoples south of the Sahara—however much it would welcome the establishment of African "Cubas" in the future.

In fact, the disillusionment with African developments, coupled with the Sino-Soviet rift, may well bring an end to the protracted effort of the Kremlin to avoid choosing between East and West. Khrushchev himself described the revolutionary opportunities of our age as lying first and foremost in the colonial world. Paradoxically, he now finds himself impelled to move in the opposite direction—a direction, moreover, which Soviet popular attitudes would seem to prefer.

If and when, on the other hand, the failure of the new order in Africa becomes serious and manifest, Communism could commend itself as a plausible alternative. And this possibility must not be ruled out. Indeed, if Communism is viewed as a malady of modernizing societies, its appeal in Africa is likely to increase as tensions and dislocations increase. If, then, African governments accumulate a record of failure, corruption, and stand-pattism, frustrated intellectuals and bureaucrats may begin to look for a new cause and a new organizational base. It is most doubtful whether African Communism would then be identified with the U.S.S.R. But, at any rate, the Communists may be right in saying that for Africa "the biggest battles are yet to come."[92]

2

THE SOVIET UNION: ECONOMIC ACTIVITY

Alexander Erlich
Christian R. Sonne

In this study of Soviet economic policies toward sub-Saharan Africa, the first section discusses changes in the "Marxist-Leninist" attitude to the problem of economic underdevelopment. The second section attempts to pull together available data on the trade, credit, and technical assistance relationships between the Soviet Union and the new African states. A brief summary and tentative prognosis are given in the concluding section.

There are several reasons for starting with matters of ideology. Such a procedure closely corresponds to the actual sequence of events. In the course of Soviet relations with the underdeveloped world, the export of ideas preceded the export of goods, and sub-Saharan Africa was no exception; as will be seen later on, the scope of purely economic exchanges is still limited. Moreover, although the crudely manipulative nature of the Soviet official doctrine makes it an exasperating subject for analysis, it is this very manipulativeness that explains why the gyrations of "Marxism-Leninism" can be a helpful guide to the actual intentions of Soviet leaders. By following the twists and turns of official theorizing we can obtain more information on motives and likely prospects of Soviet economic policies toward the new Africa than we could hope to deduce merely from trade and aid statistics.

The authors are grateful to Louise E. Luke for invaluable assistance.

Soviet Views on Underdevelopment

The major components of the Soviet ideological syndrome are familiar enough. They are, first of all, the "Marxist-Leninist" theory of imperialism, which dates from Lenin's tract of 1916; second, the concept of a "non-capitalist pattern of development" enunciated by Lenin in 1920; and, third, the "demonstration effect" of Soviet industrialization during the Five-Year Plan era. The interlocking seems perfect, and easy to grasp: the first element holds colonialism largely responsible for the grinding poverty of dependent areas and for the relative opulence of the metropolitan countries; the second points to the possibility of achieving modernization without falling prey to class inequality, profiteering, and the waste of productive energies during periodic depressions; the third shows that this has already been done with resounding success in the largest underdeveloped country on earth. Superficially, this argument suggests monolithic and undeviating orthodoxy. But, in fact, the "Marxist-Leninist" appeal to the underdeveloped world carried real strength not because Soviet leaders unyieldingly stuck to the initial premises of the doctrine, but because they made massive departures from it and took advantage of compensating errors in the early predictions.

As for imperialism, everyone knows that Lenin described it as capitalism in the stage of decay, marked by the proliferation of monopoly and the parasitic *rentiers*. It is less generally realized that Lenin put in a strong *caveat* at this point: he said not only that "this tendency toward decay does not rule out a rapid growth of capitalism," but that "capitalism as a whole is growing immeasurably faster than before."[1] Finally, and most significant in the context of our present discussion, he insisted that "capitalism grows fastest in the colonies and in overseas territories."[2] The way in which he went about proving the point was impeccably "orthodox": the rate of profit was bound to be higher in backward countries than in advanced countries because of the scarcity of capital, the relatively low price of land, the low wages, and the cheap raw materials;[3] the capital inflow thereby attracted would result in "tremendously accelerating" the development of capitalism in backward countries.[4]

History has not dealt kindly with these predictions. The backwardness in huge areas of Asia, Africa, and Latin America did not prove self-correcting; capitalism did *not* "grow fastest in the colonies and in the overseas territories" (except the so-called "areas of recent settlement" like Australia and North America, which were, as Lenin and many others failed to perceive, in a class by themselves). In fact, the backward countries as a whole fell further behind the West than they had been in 1916; their willingness to acquiesce in this state of affairs, however, declined drastically, and political independence has reduced their patience still further. It is therefore hardly surprising that Lenin's sanguine view of the potentialities of capitalist development in the colonies was quietly discarded.

In overhauling the theory of imperialism, Soviet ideologists emphasized that foreign investments had as a rule made a negligible contribution to the growth potential of the colonial economies (a point that quite a few non-Marxian Western economists would accept although they would argue it differently) and that Western governments had frequently lent support in backward areas to reactionary ruling groups opposed to economic progress. Moreover, imperialism was blamed for deliberately obstructing the development of the dependent areas in order to perpetuate its economic domination and prevent the rise of dangerous competitors: "The monopoly capital of the imperialist countries, taken as a whole, cannot go in for the industrialization of underdeveloped countries because this would deprive it of high profits, realized through selling its commodities to underdeveloped countries at high monopoly prices."[5] Even by Stalinist standards of theorizing, this was a singularly weak and forced argument. Its inadequacy was all the more glaring because Western economists had meanwhile advanced cogent explanations of why capital exports tended to flow to advanced countries rather than to Africa and Asia, and why it was wrong to assume that greater scarcity of capital inevitably entailed higher returns to investment. But as propaganda the Soviet interpretation was quite effective. It is easier to inflame passions and gain sympathy by blaming economic backwardness primarily on the manipulation of hated foreigners rather than on such impersonal phenomena as a shortage of "social overheads," the small size of the market hindering application of modern capital equipment, and a limited ability to absorb and generate new technology. Thus the notion of a sinister capitalist conspiracy has been allowed to stand; it was reiterated in the 1961 program of the CPSU, which declared that "contemporary capitalism . . . is holding down the industrial development of the underdeveloped countries."[6]

But this charge could be dangerous if overstated. The "Marxist-Leninist" cause in the underdeveloped countries would be ill-served if Soviet ideologists were to insist, as they had under Stalin, that the newly won independence of these countries was nothing but a sham, and that their leaders were either stooges of the imperialists or plain dupes. This "sectarian" policy is now being roundly condemned. And in accordance with the proclaimed intention to put an end once and for all to the "deadening stereotypes" inherited from the time of the "personality cult," another doctrinal shift seems in the making, notably in respect to Africa. While the propaganda barrage against Western aid and economic influence continues, a leading Soviet Africanologist, I. I. Potekhin, has conceded that "the nationalization of foreign-owned enterprises is not yet possible everywhere" and that it is necessary to attract foreign investment because "national capital in most of the [African] countries is negligible in size and extremely scattered."[7] The change of tone in these statements, which have been seconded by others, is particularly significant in conjunction with unorthodox pronouncements in other problem areas.

Like his theory of imperialism, Lenin's concept of a "non-capitalist" pattern of development for the "backward nations" has undergone a good deal of change. At first glance, it appeared to be incompatible with the notion of colonial countries developing their capitalism faster than the rest of the world. Moreover, it seemed to conflict with Lenin's strongly held view that socialist revolution presupposed a certain minimum level of capitalist development, which, according to him, had been attained in Russia by 1917 but not in the dependent areas. In fact, however, there was no contradiction: the backward nations, Lenin argued, could skip over the capitalist stage of development "if the victorious revolutionary proletariat will carry on systematic propaganda in them and if Soviet governments will come to their assistance with all means at their disposal."[8] At the time, this statement certainly did not appear fantastic. The swift advance of the Soviet armies toward Warsaw in July 1920 raised hopes for the imminent victory of communism in much of Europe. Hence it was logical to assume that while capitalism in underdeveloped countries may have been growing fast, the European revolution was advancing even faster and that support extended by the victorious proletarian regimes would provide the peoples of Asia and Africa with the possibility of a short cut toward socialism. But after these hopes were dashed, the concept of stage-skipping was put aside, and emphasis was restored to the contribution that "national revolutionary movements" could make to the downfall of the world capitalist system.

These readjusted predictions, too, fell wide of the mark. As the old empires dissolved, the capitalist system in the West showed no signs of breaking down, and the comparatively high living standards of the Western workers, which allegedly depended on surplus profits earned in colonies, did not drop as predicted. More important—in the context of the present discussion—the economic policies of the new nations proved difficult to categorize. The governments of the new states were decidedly non-Communist; in Soviet parlance, they represented the "national bourgeoisie." Yet most of them firmly committed themselves to the idea of development planning and proceeded to create sizable state-owned enclaves within their nonagricultural sectors. While imponderables and considerations of equity undoubtedly played their part, the main reason behind this decision was strongly pragmatic. The new leaders did not rush headlong into nationalizing all of the existing privately owned enterprises, but they did feel that constructing bulky "social overheads" and launching, or greatly expanding, certain large-scale basic industries would be too heavy a burden and too high a risk for private enterprise in their countries, which suffered from a shortage of capital, a low level of skills, and small domestic markets. However, when various African and Asian leaders spoke of their countries as moving toward a "socialist pattern of society," Soviet ideologists winced; the appellation "socialist," in their view, was to be reserved exclusively for nationalization programs carried out by Communist-controlled governments, and the loss of exclusive rights to the name could be ideologically and politically damaging. (The 1961 party program, it might be noted, is sharply critical of the "theories of national-type socialism" advanced in Asia, Africa, and Latin America.) In order to cope with these irregularities, the old concept of "state capitalism" was revived. First advanced by Engels and used by generations of Communist theorists from Lenin on, "state capitalism" was a convenient label for situations in which a "bourgeois" state owns some of the means of production and transportation or a "proletarian" state exercises control over facilities owned by (or leased to) private individuals and groups. Depending on the need, the "state capitalism" in question could be classed as either reactionary or "historically progressive." Since the mid-fifties the state-owned enterprises in the new Asian and African economies have been firmly placed in the latter category—a further step away from the "dogmatism" of Stalin's day; indeed, recent publications no longer speak of "state capitalism" in Africa, but use the more flattering term "state sector" instead.[9]

This is not the only instance in which the "uniqueness" of the African economies is acknowledged. In most states south of the Sahara, agriculture is organized along the lines of the village "commune." Leaders of the new states feel, as Modibo Keita of Mali put it, that "it would be a bad policy to break down this traditional pattern of collective life; on the contrary, . . . it should be improved so that it can take its place in the pattern of the present-day evolution."[10] In early Soviet writings a fairly dim view was taken of the ability of African "communes" to survive; they were expected to disintegrate, with rich peasants emerging victorious. But recently there has been a complete about-face in this respect: efforts to sustain and modernize the "commune" are strongly backed, and Marx is being invoked as a witness in support of this stand, on the grounds of his references to the *mir* as a possible point of departure for socialist reconstruction in Russia.[11]

It remains for us to consider the third basic shift in Soviet theorizing. The "demonstration effect" of Soviet economic growth most certainly had a profound impact on the thinking of the leaders of nationalist movements in the backward areas. But to be impressed does not necessarily mean to be converted. Obviously, one need not be a very orthodox "Marxist-Leninist" or a particularly heterodox "bourgeois economist" in order to agree with the following baldly stated propositions: (1) a rapid increase in the rate of economic growth in backward countries, which is indispensable in order to break out of the vicious circle of near stagnation, calls for a marked increase in the saving-investment effort; (2) economic development is bound to involve industrialization at a rather early stage, and also, before long,

a relatively rapid growth of domestic capital-goods industries coming both in response to and as an added stimulant of the accelerated
pace of over-all expansion; (3) the availability of a sufficiently large
volume of foreign investment and sufficiently extensive foreign trade
connections cannot always be taken for granted; (4) since superior
productive technology in developed countries represents both a challenge and a threat, the new state would have to intervene more actively to promote and protect economic development than was necessary in older industrialized countries during comparable periods of
their history.

Yet an agreement on these general propositions surely leaves
room for a wide range of choices, depending on the particular conditions of the country in question and on the planners' "rate of impatience." It is by no means inevitable that the decision be in favor
of the Stalinist pattern: huge expansion in the volume of heavily
mechanized industrial equipment at the price of stagnation in agriculture and a painfully slow increase in housing and transportation,
combined with a policy of self-imposed insulation from the world
market. In a typical underdeveloped country with negligible sur-
pluses of food, a minute manufacturing sector operating largely on
the basis of handicraft technology, and only embryonic elements of
"social overheads," such a program would threaten disaster. It could
founder on the impossibility of clamping the required rate of saving
on a wretchedly poor agricultural sector, on the shortage of the capacity necessary to produce the planned addition to capital stock
within the stipulated time, or on the lack of organizational and managerial skills needed to absorb these additions.

The Soviet economy was able to avoid these dangers in spite of
a few extremely close calls only because it was not an economy of a
typical underdeveloped country.* It had a comparatively high man-

---

* In discussing the advantages of their model, Soviet spokesmen frequently
refer to the experience of the backward regions of the Soviet Union rather than to
the Soviet economy as a whole. Rapid economic growth has indeed taken place in
those regions, but chiefly because integration with the more advanced, and vigorously
developing, surrounding areas made possible joint "external economies" (such as
new railroad lines), specialization without risk, particularly in agriculture (for example, cotton-growing in Central Asia), and large-scale exchange of skilled personnel
and trainees between the center and the periphery. The irrelevance of this to small
African states, thousands of miles distant from the Soviet Union and catering in their
trade to its rather marginal needs, should be evident.

to-land ratio, an exceptionally variegated resource endowment, and a large population which made possible economies of scale in many industries at the same time, although the per-capita income was low. Its urban sector, while employing a relatively small share of the total work force, had been gaining ground rapidly over the last three decades before the Revolution, with the capital goods industries leading the way and displaying in some of their key areas a high degree of technological modernity; during the same period the railroad network had been expanding by leaps and bounds and showing a strong tendency to push ahead of current demand for its services rather than to fall behind it. It was in such circumstances that the Stalinist "up by the bootstraps" exercise could bring about a development that was very rapid by comparative standards, even if extremely unbalanced and costly. As Oleg Hoeffding put it, "When the Soviets started, they already had the boots, and the straps to pull on, whereas contemporary Asia is, relatively speaking, still barefooted."[12] The same, obviously, would hold true of Africa. Kwame Nkrumah once stated:

> The problem of unemployment in rural areas must be solved by creating industries in the rural areas, for example, the growing, processing, and preserving of food, local handicrafts including textiles, the manufacture of sugar, salt, and soap, and the expressing of edible oils. . . . The concentration of labor in industrial areas and modern factories requires large capital investment which the resources of most underdeveloped countries cannot bear. . . . Transport by rail, by road, and by civil aviation will be given high priority. . . . [It is] our desire to start industrialization of our country at the same time as we increase the productivity of our agriculture."[13]

These words were spoken in 1955. Yet at that time, as well as in the years that immediately followed, official Soviet spokesmen continued to hew to the old line. An economist specializing in underdeveloped areas asserted that "increasingly large masses in the countries of Asia, Latin America, and Africa" understand the necessity for "basic transformation of the national economy on the basis of development of heavy industry."[14] "What is the chief criterion of sincerity in giving aid to underdeveloped countries?" asked another writer, and promptly replied, "Obviously, aid in developing a national industry—most particularly, heavy industry."[15] The writings of the sixties sound a very different note, however. In 1958, for example, Potekhin declared, while commenting on Western accounts of the economic development of African colonies, that "any industrialization in the true meaning of the word is out of the question because in the African colonies there are no machine-building plants and their construction is thus far not envisaged."[16] Yet two years later the same author was less dogmatic. Industrialization in Africa, he informed his readers, "is for the time being not a matter of the production of machinery and machine tools but of developing light industry serving the consumption needs of the people. For African countries this is an absolutely necessary stage of economic development. . . . For the time being, conditions for establishing an industry producing tools and machinery do not exist there." Nor is this all; the increase in the productivity of agriculture, particularly in tropical regions, was emphatically declared to be "a task which cannot be postponed."[17]

However, the most striking hints at a major revision of theory can be found in an article that deals not specifically with Africa but in general with "regularities of the non-capitalist pattern of development." After the predictable and repetitive quotations of the familiar texts, there is a reference to an obscure, and seemingly minor piece— a letter of greeting from Lenin to the newly formed Soviet republics in the Caucasus.[18] Actually, the letter is most revealing; it emphasizes that the Caucasian republics need "a slower, more cautious, and more systematic transition to socialism" than central Russia (a statement quoted by the author of the article), and offers specific injunctions as to the proper policies for promoting the economic development of small and predominantly agricultural regions with valuable mineral resources and open access to the world market. These injunctions (not quoted by the author) sound like heresy incarnate: their point is that a Communist leadership in such regions should do everything in its power to attract foreign investment and to promote exports while concentrating its own efforts primarily on raising the productivity of agriculture.

These recommendations are deeply subversive not only with regard to what has passed until recently for sound advice to the underdeveloped nations of Asia and Africa, but also with regard to policies that have been foisted upon certain Eastern European "People's Democracies." One might speculate further about the possible impact of a frank and exhaustive discussion of Lenin's other writings of the NEP period, which suggest the usefulness of small-scale production in times of acute capital shortage, the possibility of "peaceful coexistence" between the private and public sectors, the use of marketing and credit cooperatives to raise the efficiency of individual peasant farming, and the importance of "concessions" to foreign capitalists. Most certainly, these ideas would not appear *passé*. But this is precisely why an open discussion of them could be ideologically explosive and why it does not seem likely to occur in the immediate future.

No doubt, after all is said and done, the "demonstration effect" has been the most powerful component of the Soviet message to the underdeveloped parts of the globe: the image of a backward country lifting itself to the level of the second mightiest industrial and military power in the world continues to exert fascination. But the new states could not live by vision alone. The tension between the real and the desired in their economies was high. In order to keep it within limits of tolerance, large-scale aid from more developed countries was needed; as the Soviet economic potential kept growing and as the war damage was made good, the excuses for not providing "assistance with all means at the disposal of the Soviet governments" appeared more and more lame. For obvious reasons, the fact that leading countries of the West had been engaged in foreign aid activities since the end of World War II made Soviet action on the longstanding promise still more imperative. Stalin's successors had fully recognized this as early as 1953. Let us see how this recognition was manifested in their economic policies toward the new African states.

Soviet Trade and Aid

Traditionally the Soviet Union has had few economic dealings with Africa south of the Sahara.[19] Between 1918 and 1940 only 0.5 million rubles of exports and 1.8 million rubles of imports were recorded, and trade took place with only two countries—the Belgian Congo and Madagascar.[20] It should be remembered that some trade went on through the metropolitan countries; for example, the Soviet Union imported cocoa from the Gold Coast through London for many years. The only aid activity on the African continent prior to the mid-fifties was a hospital at Addis Ababa founded by the Russians at the end of the nineteenth century and staffed with Soviet doctors. And until the past decade this hospital seems to have received only intermittent support; in 1952 it was reportedly obliged to charge for services.[21]

Table 1 shows the rapid growth of Soviet trade with the countries of sub-Saharan Africa. Continued expansion of this trade seems reasonable to expect for two reasons. First, the trend thus far shows no sign of abating. Second, there are now 20 more independent countries to be added to the list of Soviet trading partners. Moreover, other countries presumably will receive independence in the not too distant future.

The most striking facts shown in Table 1 are the large imbalance experienced by the Soviet Union in its trade with these countries through 1960 (which reached a high of 35,800,000 rubles in 1959) and the dramatic reversal of the U.S.S.R.'s adverse balance of trade in 1961. The reason for the imbalance seems fairly clear: the African countries are exporting primary products such as cocoa beans, coffee, and groundnuts for which the Soviet Union has no domestic substitutes. For many of these products which are clearly needed, the Soviet Union has paid with convertible currencies, usually sterling. As the London *Economist* put it in 1960 during negotiations between Great Britain and the U.S.S.R. for a new trade agreement:

> Russia always treats its trade with Britain as part of its total trade with the sterling area, with which it claims to run a substantial deficit. . . . Russia argues that to improve its trade balance, it must sell more to Britain.[22]

The 1961 statistics, however, show the effects of the increasing demand of the new nations for such products as machinery, motor vehicles, and aircraft, which can come only from an industrialized country. The equalizing effect on trade of the bilateral trade agreements of the type that the Soviet Union set up with Guinea, Ethiopia, and the Sudan in 1959 was already apparent in 1960, and the impact of deliveries under credit arrangements with Ghana and Guinea is clearly visible in 1961. The U.S.S.R.'s favorable balance of trade should be maintained as more such deliveries are made; for instance, Ethiopia's 90 million ruble credit does not appear to have been drawn upon at all through 1961.[23] While it might be argued that Soviet demand for such tropical products as cocoa beans would increase with the rising Soviet standard of living, the controls of the centralized economy seem more than adequate to keep whatever balance the central planners deem proper. For instance, the U.S.S.R. is reported to have bought 9,000 tons less of the Ghanaian 1961-62 cocoa crop than originally agreed.[24]

It is useful to view the raw figures of Soviet trade with the tropical African countries against the background of over-all Soviet trade, and especially in relation to the U.S.S.R.'s trade with the less-developed non-Communist countries. The latter was more than five times greater in 1961 than in 1955, while total trade did not quite double during this period. From Table 2 it can be seen that the trade with sub-Saharan Africa is insignificant to the Soviet Union, at least in any quantitative sense: it amounted to less than one per cent of total turnover in 1961, and as a proportion of the total trade with the non-Communist underdeveloped countries, it was still only 6 per cent in that year. Conversely, for the four African trading partners of the U.S.S.R. which have released their national statistics, the trade with the entire Communist bloc has never exceeded 13 per cent of their total trade turnover.[25] However, although official Guinean statistics are not available, it has been reported that the Sino-Soviet bloc took 22.9 per cent of Guinea's exports and provided 44.2 per cent of its imports in 1960—undeniably a significant economic involvement with the Communist world.[26]

Trade with the tropical African countries has generally taken place without formal agreements, with payment presumably being made in convertible currencies. However, since 1959 the Soviet Union has been pursuing a program of formalizing trade relationships with agreements, and up to December 31, 1962, had signed twelve trade or trade-and-payments agreements with ten countries: Cameroun, Ethiopia, Ghana (2), Guinea (2), Mali, Niger, Senegal, Somalia, the Sudan, and Togo. The exact role of such agreements—as stimuli to trade, as means of equalizing the trade balance, or as

TABLE 1.—TRADE OF U.S.S.R WITH INDEPENDENT COUNTRIES OF SUB-SAHARAN
AFRICA, 1955–61 (EXCL. UNION OF SOUTH AFRICA)[a]

(Values in millions of rubles)

Country	1955			1956			1957		
	Exp.	Imp.	Tot.	Exp.	Imp.	Tot.	Exp.	Imp.	Tot.
Cameroun	—	—	—	—	—	—	—	0.1	0.1
Ethiopia	0	—	0	0	0.2	0.2	0.2	2.5	2.7
Ghana	0	10.4	10.4	0	7.4	7.4	—	17.0	17.0
Guinea	0	—	0	—	—	—	—	—	—
Ivory Coast	—	2.3	2.3	—	1.8	1.8	—	2.2	2.2
Mali	—	—	—	—	—	—	—	—	—
Nigeria	0	—	0	—	—	—	—	0.2	0.2
Sudan	0.2	—	0.2	0.4	—	0.4	0.6	2.6	3.2
Togo	—	—	—	—	—	—	—	—	—
Uganda	—	—	—	—	—	—	—	—	—
Total	0.2	12.7	12.9	0.4	9.4	9.8	0.8	24.6	25.4
Trade Balance ...			−12.5			−9.0			−23.8

Country	1958			1959			1960		
	Exp.	Imp.	Tot.	Exp.	Imp.	Tot.	Exp.	Imp.	Tot.
Cameroun	0	5.9	5.9	0	7.6	7.6	—	0.2	0.2
Ethiopia	0.6	0.9	1.5	0.5	0.6	1.1	0.8	0.4	1.2
Ghana	—	2.4	2.4	0	7.4	7.4	5.0	19.5	24.5
Guinea	—	—	—	0.8	0.7	1.5	5.2	2.0	7.2
Ivory Coast	—	—	—	—	6.9	6.9	—	4.9	4.9
Mali	—	—	—	—	—	—	—	—	—
Nigeria	—	0.3	0.3	—	6.6	6.6	0	6.3	6.3
Sudan	0.3	0	0.3	3.5	4.5	8.0	4.9	5.2	10.1
Togo	—	—	—	—	—	—	0	—	0
Uganda	—	—	—	—	6.3	6.3	—	4.4	4.4
Total	0.9	9.5	10.4	4.8	40.6	45.4	15.9	42.9	58.8
Trade Balance ...			−8.6			−35.8			−27.0

Country	1961		
	Exp.	Imp.	Tot.
Cameroun	—	—	—
Ethiopia	0.8	8.6	1.4
Ghana	13.9	6.1	20.0
Guinea	24.5	3.8	28.3
Ivory Coast	—	—	—
Mali	7.7	3.4	11.1
Nigeria	0	0.1	0.1
Sudan	8.4	9.4	17.8
Togo	0.1	—	0.1
Uganda	—	3.7	3.7
Total	55.4	27.1	82.5
Trade Balance ..			−28.3

[a] Exp., Imp., and Tot. stand for exports from the U.S.S.R., imports to the U.S.S.R., and total value of goods exchanged; a dash indicates no trade, and a zero indicates trade of less than 50,000 rubles.

Sources: U.S.S.R., Ministry of Foreign Trade, *Vneshniaia torgovlia Soiuza SSR za 1955–59 gody: statisticheskii sbornik* (Moscow, 1961), pp. 14–15; U.S.S.R., Ministry of Foreign Trade, *Vneshniaia torgovlia SSSR za 1960 god: statisticheskii obzor* (Moscow, 1961), pp. 9–10, and U.S.S.R., Ministry of Foreign Trade, *Vneshniaia torgovlia SSSR za 1961 god: statisticheskii obzor* (Moscow, 1962), p. 11.

TABLE 2.—SOVIET TRADE WITH SUB-SAHARAN AFRICA (S.-S.A.) AS PERCENTAGE OF
TOTAL SOVIET TRADE AND OF SOVIET TRADE WITH LESS DEVELOPED
NON-COMMUNIST (L.D.N.-C.) COUNTRIES[a]

(*Values in per cent*)

Trade Category	1955	1956	1957	1958	1959	1960	1961
Exports to S.-S.A. as % of total exports.....	0	0	0	0	0.1	0.3	1.0
Imports from S.-S.A. as % of total imports..	0.4	0.2	0.6	0.2	0.9	0.8	0.5
Trade with S.-S.A. as % of total trade......	0.2	0.1	0.3	0.1	0.5	0.6	0.8
Exports to S.-S.A. as % of total exports to L.D.N.-C. countries	0	0	0	0	1.7	4.9	8.9
Imports from S.-S.A. as % of total imports from L.D.N.-C. countries	6.2	3.1	5.4	2.1	8.9	8.1	6.9
Trade with S.-S.A. as % of total trade with L.D.N.-C. countries	4.2	2.0	3.4	1.2	6.0	6.9	6.0

[a] Zero indicates a percentage less than 0.1.
Sources: U.S.S.R., Ministry of Foreign Trade, *Vneshniaia torgovlia Soiuza SSR za 1955–59 gody: statisticheskii sbornik* (Moscow, 1961). Also U.S.S.R., Ministry of Foreign Trade, *Vneshniaia torgovlia SSSR za 1960 god: statisticheskii obzor* (Moscow, 1961); and U.S.S.R., Ministry of Foreign Trade, *Vneshniaia torgovlia SSSR za 1961 god: statisticheskii obzor* (Moscow, 1962).

possible instruments of political manipulation—is difficult to assess and can be evaluated only in the particular context of each agreement.

To date, the complete texts of only five trade agreements with African countries have been published, and they seem to conform to a fairly standard pattern. A most-favored-nation clause is generally inserted, as is a gold-content clause to protect the trading partners against devaluations. Although lists of goods to be exchanged are appended or listed in separate protocols, other goods may be traded, and there is no set amount guaranteed for export or import. In fact, even in those cases in which agreements have set commodity quotas—a common practice in Soviet trade with Western European countries—there have been wide gaps in fulfillment. In short, these agreements can be viewed as statements of intention to trade, as guarantees of government interest, and as means whereby bilateral clearing accounts are set up.

In two of the cases examined—Guinea and Mali—swing credits were granted. Until 1961 Ghana did not need a short-term credit to cover a deficit in the trading account. The effect of the trade agreements with Cameroun and Senegal, which were signed in 1962, cannot yet be assessed, but it is likely that the trade of these countries with the U.S.S.R. will follow the pattern of the earlier trading partners. However, it is possible that the Soviet Union may become the debtor. Mikesell and Behrman, in their thorough study of Soviet bloc trading practices, cite several instances in which bloc countries have run up debit balances in the clearing account by the rapid importation of raw materials, thereby forcing the trading partner to accept goods it might otherwise not have taken, or at least to extend credit to the U.S.S.R.[27] However, the growing need for capital goods in the African countries is likely to make such imbalances temporary; as the 1961 trade statistics indicate, this has happened in the case of Ghana, Guinea, and Mali.

Soviet aid policy is, in theory and in fact, closely connected with trade. Many Soviet writers have insisted that the importance of aid should not be overstressed and that radical social change and "mutually advantageous" trade are more effective ways to promote growth.[28] Frequently both trade and economic and technical cooperation agreements are signed at the same time. Most important, Soviet aid takes the form of credits almost exclusively, usually at 2.5 per cent repayable in local goods after the delivery of Soviet goods or technical services over a twelve-year period. Grants are rare and usually consist of specific items such as aircraft for government leaders, radio stations, or hospitals. (See Table 3.)

Known Soviet credits to tropical Africa totaled some 244 million rubles ($272 million) by the end of 1962, and further credits of unknown magnitude were extended to Cameroun, Ghana, and the Sudan. Although there is no way of estimating the amounts actually used, they must have been small through 1960, because no significant increase in Soviet exports during that period is reflected in the statistics. This seems especially true in the case of Ethiopia, whose 90 million ruble credit makes it the largest Soviet aid recipient in the area. In 1961 significant amounts of earlier credits do seem to have been used, for the first time, by Ghana, Guinea, and Mali. By way of comparison, it should be pointed out that the Soviet credits offered (although not necessarily used) through June 30, 1961, equal almost exactly American grant and loan disbursements to tropical Africa during the same period. (See Table 4.)

TABLE 3.—SOVIET AID AND TRADE AGREEMENTS WITH AFRICAN COUNTRIES SOUTH OF THE SAHARA

Country	Trade and Payments[a]	Economic and Technical Assistance	Credit (million rubles)	Terms	Miscellaneous
Cameroun	Trade, 9/24/62.	Agreement, 9/24/62	Unk.	Unknown	
Ethiopia	Trade, 3 yrs., MFN, 7/11/59.	Understanding, 7/59; agreement on technical school, 3/8/60; protocol on oil refinery, 3/25/60.	90	Favorable	Ilyushin-14 aircraft, 2/60; 2000 tons wheat sent by Soviet Red Cross to Tigre, 10/23/59.
Ghana	Note exchange starting direct trade, 6/10/59; trade and payments, MFN, 8/4/60; long-term trade and payments, MFN, 11/4/61; protocol listing goods for 1962, 4/18/62.	Agreement, 8/4/60; protocol listing projects, 12/23/60; widened cooperation, 11/4/61.	36+ Unk.	Favorable	Permanent exhibition hall for Soviet goods, opened 9/60.
Guinea	Trade and payments, MFN, 2/13/59; long-term trade and payments (1961–65), MFN, 9/8/60; protocol listing goods for 1961, 1/9/61.	Agreement, 8/24/59; protocol listing projects, 3/1/60; protocol on widened cooperation, 9/8/60.	31+	2.5%, 12 yrs., local goods	1961: 100 kw radio station; grants for medical equipment, autos, mobile cinema; part of library, agricultural machinery; promised opportunity for Guineans to study in U.S.S.R.
Mali	Trade, MFN, 3/18/61.	Agreement, 3/18/61.	40	Favorable	

Country					
Niger	Talks, trade agreement, 1962				
Nigeria	Talks, indefinite conclusion, 6/6–9/61.	Talks, U.S.S.R. offered economic and technical aid, 6/6–9/61.			U.S.S.R. prepared to take Nigerians for study.
Senegal	Trade, 6/14/62.	Agreement, 6/14/62, no credit mentioned.			
Somalia	Trade and payments, 6/2/61.	Agreement, 6/2/61.	47	Favorable, for trade over 5 yrs.	Grant for building 2 hospitals, high school, printing shop, radio station, and for aid in training medical cadres, 6/2/61.
Sudan	Trade, 3/16/59; protocol listing goods for 1960, 4/16/60; protocol for 1961, 1/9/61; long-term trade, protocol for 1962, MFN, 11/61.	Agreement, 4/56.	Unk.	Repayable in local goods	
		Agreement, 11/21/61.	Unk.	Unknown	
Togo	Trade, 6/12/61; protocol giving U.S.S.R. right to place trade mission in Togo, 6/14/61.				
Totals	Trade, 10 countries; agreements, 8 countries; credits, over 244 million rubles; payments, 3 countries; offers, 1 country.				

a MFN indicates inclusion of a most-favored nation clause.

Sources: Official Soviet publications; State Bank of Ethiopia, Report on Economic Conditions and Market Trends, No. 44 (Nov. 1959); United Nations Document E/3556, October 4, 1961; Raymond F. Mikesell and Jack N. Behrman, *Financing Free World Trade with the Sino-Soviet Bloc* (Princeton, N.J.: Princeton Studies in International Finance No. 8, 1958); *The New York Times*, February 21, 1960, and June 15, 1962.

TABLE 4.—SOVIET AND UNITED STATES AID TO INDEPENDENT COUNTRIES OF SUB-SAHARAN AFRICA THROUGH JUNE 1961

(Thousands of U.S. dollars)

| Country | Population (Thousands) 1961 est. | Soviet Credits Extended[a] | | U.S. Aid Used | | | U.S.S.R. Aid/cap ($/cap) | U.S. Aid/cap ($/cap) |
		Amount	Date	Grants	Credits	Total		
Cameroun	3,322.7	—		319		319	—	.10
Chad	2,737.8			2,206		2,206	—	.81
Congo[b]	14,388.8			21,914	1,550	23,464	—	1.63
Dahomey	1,819.8			821		821	—	.45
Ethiopia[c]	15,120.0	100,000	7/59	94,943[d]	11,985	106,928	6.61	7.07
Gabon	430.1			21		21	—	.05
Ghana	6,902.5	40,000+	8/60	5,326		5,326	5.80+	.77
Guinea	2,669.5	35,000	8/59	2,187		2,187	13.11	.82
Ivory Coast	3,327.6			307		307	—	.09
Liberia	1,337.8			22,496[e]	55,592	78,088	—	58.37
Malagasy Republic	5,533.1			1,395		1,395	—	.25
Mali	3,926.4	44,400	3/61	415		415	11.31	.11
Mauritania	709.5			106		106	—	.15
Niger	2,704.8			27		27	—	.01
Nigeria	34,767.3			4,755	1,338	6,093	—	.18
Senegal	2,469.5			207		207	—	.08
Sierra Leone	2,400.0[f]			584		584	—	.24
Somalia	1,990.0[g]	52,170	6/61	8,100	81	8,181	26.22	4.11
Sudan	11,304.0	Unk.	4/56	27,018	6,804	33,822	Unk.	2.99
Togo	1,146.8			1,068		1,068	—	.93
Upper Volta	3,964.6			74		74	—	.02
Total	122,972.6	271,570		194,289	77,350	271,639	2.21	2.21

a Excluding grants to Ethiopia, Guinea, and Somalia, and aid to the Congo in 1960. b Léopoldville government. c Including Eritrea. d Includes $49,200,000 military aid. e Includes $1,200,000 military aid. f U.N. est, mid-1959. g U.N. est, mid-1959, for former Italian Somaliland only.

Sources: Population: P. N. Rosenstein-Rodan, "International Aid for Underdeveloped Countries," Review of Economics and Statistics, Vol. XLIII, No. 2 (May 1961), Table 2-B, p. 123. Soviet aid: Vneshniaia torgovliia, 1956–61. United States aid: United States, Department of Commerce, Office of Business Economics, Foreign Grants and Credits by the United States (June 1961).

Soviet writers hold that the "distinctive feature of these credits is that they are designated to develop key branches of the economy."[29] Actually, through 1960 only 26 per cent of Soviet exports to the countries under analysis were capital goods. (See Table 5.) Although the proportion of capital goods in Soviet exports to the African countries increased sharply in 1960 and 1961, most of this increase reflects massive deliveries of aircraft to Ghana, Guinea, and Mali which may be a non-recurrent phenomenon. The share of other machinery and equipment in Soviet exports to these countries (with the exception of Guinea) is thus far relatively small. An attempt is made in Table 6 to classify Soviet projects planned for the area by sector of the economy. Out of 57 projects, only ten can be classified as relating to heavy industry, and of these, five are cement factories; only two are in light industry. Most significantly, 32 of the projects listed relate to agriculture, agricultural processing, education, medicine, and services (communications, housing, etc.), and nine are in the fields of power and transport, reflecting the primary needs of underdeveloped Africa. In the rough and somewhat arbitrary classification of projects into "heavy" and "light," the former reach a proportion of 40 per cent of the total—higher than the pattern of American aid to Africa reveals,[30] but not enough to substantiate the early Soviet claims of support for heavy industry, especially since only 18 per cent of the projects can be placed under that heading.

In a number of cases (seven out of 57), geological prospecting or feasibility studies by Soviet technicians are planned. However, the Soviet Union does not require the elaborate program and project planning associated with the American aid-giving process. Although this may perhaps have resulted in poor performance in some cases, the lack of detailed reporting and accounting procedures, and also the fact that the projects need not be proposed by the receiver as part of a general development program, may be attractive. The American requirements proved to be stumbling blocks in the year-long negotiations between the United States and Guinea for an aid agreement, and Guinean negotiators spoke favorably of Communist aid-giving techniques, stating that the Communist countries proposed projects and did not put the recipients into the position of having to beg.[31] Soviet experts do not seem to be involved in over-all development

TABLE 5.—SOVIET EXPORTS TO INDEPENDENT COUNTRIES OF SUB-SAHARAN AFRICA,
BY TYPE, 1956–61[a]

(*Thousands of rubles; totals in millions of rubles*)

Country	1956				1957				1958			
	A	B	C	Tot.	A	B	C	Tot.	A	B	C	Tot.
Cameroun	—	—	—	—	—	—	—	—	—	—	90	0.1
Ethiopia	15	—	14	0	23	118	19	0.2	11	137	467	0.6
Ghana	—	—	6	0	—	—	—	—	—	—	—	—
Guinea	—	—	—	—	—	—	—	—	—	—	—	—
Mali	—	—	—	—	—	—	—	—	—	—	—	⌐
Nigeria	—	—	—	—	—	—	—	—	—	—	—	—
Sudan	2	2	351	0.4	142	244	308	0.6	72	—	195	0.3
Togo	—	—	—	—	—	—	—	—	—	—	—	—
Total	17	2	371	0.4	165	362	327	0.8	83	137	752	1.0

Country	1959				1960				1961			
	A	B	C	Tot.	A	B	C	Tot.	A	B	C	Tot.
Cameroun	—	—	91	0.1	—	—	20	0	—	—	—	—
Ethiopia .	8	161	269	0.5	102	372	392	0.8	56	392	406	0.8
Ghana ..	5	5	2	0	3,452	541	965	5.0	12,007	326	1,296	13.9[b]
Guinea ..	34	94	770	0.8	577	1,108	3,317	5.2[b]	18,917	3,302	3,525	24.5
Mali	—	—	—	—	—	—	—	—	5,951	266	1,393	7.7
Nigeria ..	—	—	—	—	—	—	2	0	—	—	4	0.7[b]
Sudan ...	85	1,783	1,707	3.5	164	1,602	3,087	4.9	103	1,756	6,546	8.4
Togo	—	—	—	—	—	—	—	—	—	—	2	0
Total	132	2,043	2,839	4.9	4,268	3,623	7,783	15.9[b]	37,034	6,042	13,172	56.0[b]

Country	Total 1956–61			
	A	B	C	Tot.
Cameroun	—	—	201	0.2
Ethiopia ..	215	1,180	1,567	3.0
Ghana ...	15,437	872	2,269	18.9[b]
Guinea ...	19,528	4,137	7,612	30.5[b]
Mali	5,951	266	1,393	7.7
Nigeria ...	—	—	6	1.0[b]
Sudan	568	5,387	12,194	18.1
Togo	—	—	2	0
Total	41,699	11,842	25,244	79.4[b]

[a] Types of exports are identified as follows: A indicates capital goods, including trucks, tractors, and diesels; B indicates semi-manufactures and industrial raw materials, including cement; C indicates foodstuffs, printed matter, and consumers' goods, including passenger cars.
[b] Discrepancy in Soviet statistics.
Sources: Same as for Table 2.

planning in the countries being surveyed, although the announcement of the agreement with Ghana of November 4, 1961, speaks in broad terms of aid in "performing project-research work."[32]

Data concerning education and technical training are scant. The Soviet Union has not failed to respond to the urgent desires of the new African countries for assistance in these areas, although the number of strictly educational projects so far is not impressive (five out of 57). Soviet writers stress the contributions of Soviet technicians in training "national cadres," or supervisory and skilled personnel, on the job in the projects undertaken with Soviet aid, and criticize Western-supported projects as deficient in the training of indigenous personnel. The formal institutions of learning contemplated under aid agreements with the Soviet Union are modeled after the polytechnical schools of the donor; the largest one planned so far is in Guinea and is to have facilities for 1500 students. A small but rising number of Africans are doing university work in the U.S.S.R., many at the new Patrice Lumumba Friendship University in Moscow; others are receiving specialized technical training in institutes and factories. For instance, in 1962 over 200 citizens of Ghana and Mali were said to be training in the U.S.S.R. to fly and service the Soviet aircraft sold to those countries for their national airlines.[33]

The methods used by the Soviet Union in implementing technical aid should not be overlooked. Soviet technical aid can best be compared with the work done by many Western firms under so-called "turn-key" arrangements, whereby a firm builds a plant, imports the necessary equipment, puts the plant in operation, trains indigenous personnel, and then turns over the operating unit to the recipient firm or government for a fixed fee. Soviet organizations perform the same "start-to-finish" operations. According to recent testimony in the Senate by a senior official of the United States Agency for International Development, Soviet technicians "appear businesslike and competent, although too narrowly specialized." They keep to themselves, living apart from the local population and, perhaps because of language difficulties, very rarely mix socially. However, they have acquired reputations as hard bargainers and frugal tippers. Some evidence of friction with local authorities has also been reported: apparently several Russian technicians were caught smuggling dia-

TABLE 6.—SOVIET PROJECTS CONTEMPLATED IN AFRICA SOUTH OF THE SAHARA, 1962

Field	Number of Projects	Field	Number of Projects
Agriculture	7		
Agricultural processing	5	Mining	4
Education	5	Power	1
Medicine	5	Transport	8
Services (4 in communications)	10	Heavy industry	
Consumer goods industry	2	(5 cement factories)	10
Subtotal	34	Subtotal	23

Grand total: 57 projects

Source: *Vneshniaia torgovlia*, 1958–61, January–June 1962.

monds out of Guinea in coffee bags.[34] It appears, then, that the Soviet experts, like their American counterparts, are doing a reasonably good job despite human failings.

The brief survey of the economic relations of the African countries with the Soviet Union which follows reveals that a limited range of tropical primary products is exported to the U.S.S.R. in return for some capital goods, but predominantly for semi-manufactures, raw materials, and consumer goods (cotton cloth, matches, soap, and so forth). The trade history is typically erratic; in Ghana and possibly the Sudan, large purchases seem to have been made for political advantage, and, in Guinea, it can be said that political purposes prevail over economic ones. The history of official contacts seems to follow a typical pattern: diplomatic recognition, a visit of African leaders to Moscow for talks, announcement of a trade agreement—often in conjunction with an economic and technical cooperation agreement and a cultural agreement. After that, there are negotiations on protocols listing goods to be traded and projects to be undertaken, agreements on arrangements between the banks involved, and regular trade contracts between Soviet foreign trade organizations and the African government foreign trade organizations or private firms.

Cameroun. Cameroun, which became independent in 1960, traded with the Soviet Union without any formal arrangements until September 1962, when a trade agreement was signed. Apparently hoping for closer relations, the U.S.S.R. had made large purchases of coffee and cocoa in 1958 and 1959 but cut back sharply in 1960, and did not trade at all with Cameroun in 1961. Small amounts of cotton cloth were bought from the U.S.S.R. An unknown amount of aid was proffered at the time the trade agreement was signed.

Ethiopia. Soviet imports of coffee and skins from the empire of Haile Selassie rose sharply in 1957 but declined somewhat through 1960, when Ethiopia's imports of a variety of Soviet goods exceeded its exports to Russia. In value, consumer goods exceeded semi-manufactures and industrial raw materials over the period 1956–61, while capital goods ran a poor third, amounting to less than 10 per cent of the total. (See Table 5.)

During a visit by the Emperor to Moscow in July 1959 a trade agreement, an aid agreement with a credit of 90 million rubles, and a cultural exchange agreement were signed. (The combined effect of these economic and diplomatic moves seems to have had political ramifications; a study of United Nations General Assembly voting in 1959 shows a definite shift in Ethiopia's vote to the Soviet position on several issues.[35] However, it is by no means certain that economic assistance, rather than the Emperor's view of a changing world situation, was the motive force behind Ethiopia's actions.) By December 31, 1962, the only project actually planned under this large credit was the $12 million oil refinery at the Red Sea port of Assab with a planned capacity of 500,000 tons a year, which far exceeds Ethiopian domestic needs.[36]

Ghana. Ghana has been a traditional supplier of cocoa beans to the Soviet Union, but until 1959 they were bought through London. Two sets of trade and aid agreements have been signed, in August 1960 and in November 1961. The 1960 trade agreement set up a clearing form of payment, which, together with the credits, made it possible for Ghana to sustain the reversal of its traditional surplus in trade with the U.S.S.R. It is perhaps significant that only matches were imported by Ghana in 1955 and 1956, and that there were no imports whatsoever in 1957 and 1958; small amounts of machinery, petroleum products, and other consumer goods were introduced for the first time in 1959. The promotion of Soviet goods has been enhanced by the opening, in November 1960, of a permanent exhibition hall in Accra.

The sudden increase in Soviet buying in 1957 might be attributed to a Soviet attempt to make a good impression on the newly independent state, but it should be noted that there was a sharp cutback in 1958. According to the Economist Intelligence Unit, the Soviet Union "took the opportunity of favorable prices to build up very substantial stocks, which enabled it to withdraw almost entirely from the market in 1958."[37] Nevertheless, in four of the six years between 1955 and 1960 the Soviet Union was Ghana's fifth largest customer in cocoa.

Within four months of the first aid agreement a protocol listing projects, including a hydroelectric plant on the Black Volta, was negotiated. Although most of the other projects appear to be in agriculture and agricultural processing, the 1961 agreement includes plans for a lathe-building factory and a textile plant.[38]

Guinea. In Guinea Soviet bloc penetration is reported to be the greatest; the bloc accounted for 9.3 per cent of Guinea's imports and 16.2 per cent of its exports in 1959, and 44.2 per cent of imports and 22.9 per cent of exports in 1960.[39] Soviet relations with Guinea began with diplomatic recognition two days after its citizens voted to reject de Gaulle's association plan. On December 4, 1958, President Sekou Touré received a Soviet delegation.[40] On February 13, 1959, a trade and payments agreement was signed. During 1959 trade began almost from scratch, and a favorable balance on current account for the Soviet Union was immediately established. Sugar, crabmeat, and cement were the main Soviet exports in 1959, but capital goods increased in quantity in 1960, and in 1961 appeared to comprise the bulk of Soviet exports to Guinea. Guinea exports coffee, bananas, and pineapples.

In 1960 a long-term trade and payments agreement, with a provision for a swing credit of $600,000, was signed. Unpaid balances remaining twelve months after expiration of the agreement are to be paid in convertible currency or by means acceptable to both parties.[41] This may provide an opportunity to apply political pressure or to win propaganda kudos by granting forgiveness of debts. Settlement of accounts that run over the maximum swing credit is provided for by permitting the creditor to suspend or revoke export licenses; furthermore, at the request of either party a mixed commission to discuss problems must meet. Only future practice will reveal whether these avenues are used for propaganda or pressure.

In Guinea, familiarity with Soviet purposes and practice may be breeding contempt. While the specific accusations against Soviet Ambassador Solod, which led to his dismissal in December 1961, were that he had been instrumental in fomenting a teachers' strike, a growing fear of dependence on one country or group of countries seems to have played a role. This can be inferred from the remarks of Anastas Mikoyan, who accompanied the new Soviet ambassador to Guinea. He reportedly emphasized the lack of interference in the internal affairs of other countries that characterized Soviet policy, and stressed that no ideology is for export and that "each state is sovereign."[42]

Furthermore, dissatisfaction with the Soviet handling of aid projects and with Soviet equipment, which is often unsuitable for tropical conditions, has been reported. The greatest single failure has been the 700-hectare state rice farm at La Fié, which so far has yielded no results despite the expenditure of a large part of the planned investment.[43]

Another instance of Soviet bungling might be mentioned. Apparently a ship with a cargo of cement bound for Conakry was routed to Monrovia because of inadequate unloading facilities at the Guinean port. There it arrived just before the rainy season, and the cement was unloaded and left uncovered on the docks. The rains came. When the Czech trucks sent to fetch it arrived, only pyramids of hardening cement were to be found.[44]

Ivory Coast. The Ivory Coast exports cocoa beans to the U.S.S.R., with payment presumably being made in convertible currency. Soviet purchases began in 1959 and ceased in 1961; no evidence of previous Soviet imports of this commodity through France since World War II can be found.

Mali. A trade agreement with Mali was signed on March 18, 1961, and trade began in that year.[45] Clearing accounts were set up, and a swing credit of 500 million Mali francs was granted. In the agreement, the Soviet negotiators were careful to tie the Mali franc to the United States dollar.

Aid and cultural agreements were signed at the same time as the trade pact, when Prime Minister Keita was in Moscow; the aid agreement included a credit of 40 million rubles.[46] The most significant project, on which surveying has already begun, is the railroad from

Bamako, the capital, to Kouroussa in Guinea (200 miles), which has a rail link to the port of Conakry.[47]

Nigeria. Nigeria, the largest country of the region, has only minimal trade with the Soviet Union and only slightly more with the Soviet bloc as a whole. Talks on economic relations were held in Moscow during June 1961, at the time of a visit by a mission led by the Nigerian Minister of Finance. After expressions of good will and a Soviet offer of economic and technical assistance, the parties stated that they would decide the question of concluding a trade agreement "in the near future."[48] Undoubtedly political considerations in Nigeria, the most conservative of the new African countries, have led it to proceed with caution in establishing relations with the Soviet bloc countries. Under the contemplated agreement, oilseeds, cocoa beans, cotton, and hides would be exchanged for capital goods, tractors, pharmaceuticals, cement, textiles, and other consumer goods.

Senegal. On June 14, 1962, Premier Mamadou Dia of Senegal signed the usual three agreements with the Soviet Union at the end of a state visit to Moscow. No credit was mentioned in the communiqué issued.[49] Senegal was the first country of the so-called Brazzaville Group (African-Malagasy Union) to enter into agreements with the U.S.S.R. It has been followed recently by Cameroun and Niger. It is still too early to ascertain whether the recent removal of Dia will have any effect on the planned trade relations between Senegal and the U.S.S.R.

Somalia. No trade between Somalia and the Soviet Union had been recorded through 1960. However, after negotiations in Moscow during June 1961, with the Somalian delegation being headed by the Premier of the country, trade, assistance, and cultural exchange agreements were signed. In the trade agreement a five-year special credit of 7 million rubles was granted in addition to the regular credit of 40 million rubles, making Somalia the largest per capita Soviet aid recipient. Exchange of Somalian raw leather, cotton, bananas, and oilseeds for Soviet farm machinery, industrial equipment, and consumer goods is contemplated under the trade agreement.[50] It is not clear precisely what the special trade credit is and how its terms differ, if at all, from those of the major credit. Included in the announcement of the agreements were references to several grants to be used for building two hospitals, a high school, and a radio station.

The Sudan. Trade with the Republic of Sudan has increased substantially since early 1959, when a trade agreement was signed. (See Table 1.) The Sudanese appear to be prompt and assiduous in negotiating the protocols listing goods to be exchanged, as these have been announced for 1960, 1961, and 1962. A close examination of the distribution of Soviet exports to the Sudan from 1956 to 1961 shows that consumer goods predominate; their total value is roughly twelve times the total value of capital goods and more than twice the total value of semi-manufactures and industrial raw materials put together. (See Table 5.)

Soviet entry into the Sudanese cotton market on a significant scale took place for the first time in 1957, when the Sudanese faced difficulties in marketing their long-staple (sakel) cotton, which comprises most of their exports. The Soviet Union bought 2.6 million rubles' worth at a price 30 per cent above the average paid by other importers of Sudanese cotton. In 1958 no cotton at all was purchased, apparently because the Sudanese refused to enter a bilateral trading arrangement; after they acquiesced in March 1959, Soviet purchases began again, with prices falling as volume increased.[51]

Besides the credit of an unspecified amount cited in Western sources in 1956, the Sudan received in November 1961 another credit of undisclosed amount for a variety of projects under an economic assistance agreement of that date. Ten light industries are to be constructed with Soviet assistance.

Togo. The first Soviet trade agreement was signed with the Republic of Togo on June 12, 1961; in contrast to most, the instrument was signed in Lomé, Togo's capital, rather than in Moscow. The usual exchange of primary products (coffee, cocoa beans, cottonseed oil) for machinery, textiles, and building materials is contemplated.[52] Only a token amount of trade had taken place by the end of 1961, and no aid agreement was signed.

Uganda. Uganda has exported copper to the U.S.S.R. since 1959 but thus far has bought no Soviet goods and has no formal trade arrangements with the Soviet Union.

The above outline suggests some general characteristics of Soviet-African economic relations. One of the most pressing needs of the

TABLE 7.—SOVIET IMPORTS OF FOUR COMMODITIES FROM AFRICAN
AND NON-AFRICAN COUNTRIES, 1955–61

Country of Origin	1955	1956	1957	1958	1959	1960	1961
COCOA BEANS (*thousand tons*)							
Cameroun	—	—	—	6.9	9.1	0.4	—
Ghana	11.7	12.2	37.6	3.4	10.5	36.6	15.7
Ivory Coast	2.4	2.9	4.3	—	9.5	8.1	—
Nigeria	—	—	—	—	9.0	11.6	—
Non-African	—	1.3	2.2	0.1	1.7	1.4	4.8
Total imports ...	14.1	16.4	44.1	10.4	39.8	58.1	14.9
COFFEE (*tons*)							
Cameroun	—	—	100	—	1,150	—	—
Ethiopia	—	200	1,650	100	621	—	300
Guinea	—	—	—	—	310	1,604	520
Non-African	1,520	3,054	3,339	3,978	11,173	17,541	27,863
Total imports ...	1,520	3,254	5,089	4,078	13,254	19,145	28,683
COTTON (*thousand tons*)							
Sudan	—	—	2.0	—	6.3	5.4	9.9
Non-African	465	485	591.0	552	184.0	185.9	131.7
Total imports ...	465	485	593.0	552	190.3	191.3	141.6
SMALL HIDES (*thousand pieces*)							
Ethiopia	—	—	846	937	161	450	—
Nigeria	—	—	229	387	84	311	360
Non-African	7,468	10,553	17,551	18,858	18,560	19,151	15,501
Total imports ...	7,468	10,553	18,626	20,182	18,805	19,912	15,861

In trade with the African countries, the following general characteristics may be noted: there were 15 annual rises of more than 50 per cent (not including the initial trading years); 16 annual drops of more than 50 per cent; and a total of 40 annual changes.

Sources: Same as for Table 2.

new African states is a stable market for their primary products. The insistence of Soviet publicists that planned economies can avoid the fluctuations of the free market is not borne out by the record, even allowing for the newness of Soviet-African trade relations. As is shown in Table 7, 22 of the 30 annual changes in the amounts of exports from the seven African trading partners of the U.S.S.R. were greater than 50 per cent. Such violent fluctuations are common in bilateral trading and appear in most Soviet trading accounts.[53] The Soviet claim that capital goods are the most important contribution of the Soviet economy to the emerging nations must also be heavily discounted as a description of the present state of affairs, for reasons indicated in an earlier part of this section, but it may prove correct in the future.

There is some reason to believe that the exchange of technicians and simple capital goods for primary agricultural products, at a level not substantially above the present, yields a small net gain to the Soviet Union, even after the uneconomically low interest rates of the credits have been allowed for. It has been argued with some force by Joseph S. Berliner that there has been a very definite shift over the past decade in the comparative advantage of Soviet capital goods and manufactures in relation to agricultural products and raw materials.[54] Soviet demand for the exports of Africa may also be expected to remain at least at present levels. Although it is true that the Soviet Union got along for over 40 years with a minimum of tropical foodstuffs, the growing needs of the "consumer's paradise" promised at the Twenty-Second Party Congress may be more difficult to suppress in the future.

TABLE 8.—COMPARISON OF SOVIET PRICE PAID FOR GHANAIAN COCOA BEANS WITH
THEIR AVERAGE PRICE, 1955–60; SHARE OF U.S.S.R. IN GHANAIAN
COCOA BEAN EXPORTS

Year	Soviet Price (£/ton)	Average Price (£/ton)	Amount (£/ton)	Per cent	Soviet Rank as Buyer	Exports to U.S.S.R. as % of Total Exports
1955	319.9	318.4	+ 1.5	+ .5	5	6.2
1956	227.9	217.8	+10.1	+ 4.6	5	3.8
1957	172.5	195.5	−23.0	−11.8	5	13.9
1958	290.7	315.8	−15.1	− 4.8	14	0.7
1959	254.2	274.8	−20.6	− 7.5	6	3.1
1960	211.2	219.4	− 8.2	− 3.7	5	11.4

Sources: Ghana, Office of the Government Statistician, *Annual Report on External Trade of Ghana and Report of Shipping and Aircraft Movements and Cargo Loaded and Unloaded* (Accra): 1957, Vol. I, p. 176; 1958, Vol. I, p. 179.

Ghana, Office of the Government Statistician, *Monthly Accounts Relating to the External Trade of Ghana and Report of Shipping and Aircraft Movements and Cargo Loaded and Unloaded* (Accra): 1959, Vol. IX, No. 12, p. 108; 1960, Vol. X, No. 12, p. 116.

Furthermore, an examination of Soviet pricing policy on goods traded with sub-Saharan Africa reveals no obvious noncommercial motives. For instance, the analysis of cocoa-bean trading with Ghana contained in Table 8 reflects initial bonus pricing, presumably to establish a trade relationship, and subsequent hard bargaining. Generally the Soviet Union has paid African exporters prices commensurate with those paid to bloc exporters and slightly lower in most cases than those paid to other non-Communist countries—a practice that probably reflects the lesser quality of the African product rather than any studied bias against the Africans. On the other hand, African buyers of Soviet exports seem to be favored with lower prices than bloc importers, paying about as much as other non-Communist countries for Soviet products. However, the price disadvantage to bloc importers is more likely to be the result of a "customs union effect" within the bloc than a reflection of a policy of favoritism toward African buyers.[55]

Conclusions

The "specific African realities" to which Soviet writers have recently been referring certainly do exist. Some underdeveloped countries are indeed more underdeveloped than others; and, perhaps more important, they are underdeveloped in different ways. True, in terms of per capita income, sub-Saharan Africa compares not unfavorably with the bulk of Asia; in fact, some individual countries like Ghana and Nigeria have a per capita income well in excess of the all-African average of $100 and, a fortiori, of the lower all-Asian average. Yet there are strong compensating factors on the other side of the ledger. The relatively small size of individual countries (Nigeria and Ethiopia are the only ones with populations over 15 million) sets a rigid limit to the economies of scale that can be attained in manufacturing. There is no "disguised unemployment" in agriculture in tropical Africa as a whole (in spite of some local pockets here and there); in fact, there is labor scarcity, which renders inappropriate the familiar policy of moving large numbers of people from agriculture to industry. The fact that agriculture is the main earner of foreign exchange, and that extensive land-improvement programs increase the demand for limited manpower still further, would make such a shift even less rational. Lastly, while income per capita is not lower than in older underdeveloped countries, it is much more evenly distributed—and this applies most emphatically to agriculture. Soviet writers are not exaggerating when they note that "a feudal class and a rural bourgeoisie are absent." As a result, the resources that can be diverted from luxury consumption by voluntary or forced saving and directed toward the expansion of productive capacity are exceedingly limited. It goes without saying that the persistence of the village "commune" has been a potent force operating in favor of equalitarianism.

It is perfectly clear, of course, that the "objective facts" of the situation and their reflection in the minds of men do not, taken by themselves, tell us much. Facts can be brazenly denied, and wishes of the local population ignored; the history of Soviet behavior abounds in examples. But so long as the policy of courting the friendship of the present African leaders is adhered to, it would be preposterous to spoil it by making a do-or-die stand on matters about which the Soviet Union can do next to nothing for the present, much as they may offend its ideological sensibilities. One might go further and argue that these sensibilities are now somewhat less touchy than they used to be. The Soviet leaders do seem to have learned a few things from "mistakes and distortions" made during the period of forced Stalinization of the Eastern European "People's Democracies," and their faith in the easy transferability of the original Soviet model must have suffered quite a jolt from Poznań, Warsaw, and Budapest. The recognition of these "mistakes," incidentally, has already found a reflection in the latest edition of the authoritative text on political economy.[56] Moreover, there is evidence that some aspects of Stalin's economic policies prior to 1934 are no longer "off-limits" for criticism.[57] True, all these adjustments are made most cautiously, with a watchful eye on "revisionist" hotheads, and there is definitely no desire to tear down the house in order to mend a leaky roof. Moreover, no effort is spared and no distortion is considered excessive in attempts to blur important differences of opinion among "bourgeois" economists and political leaders by presenting all of them as irrevocably opposed to public ownership in backward countries and to a development policy that would not have the maximization of private profits as its main goal. But all this is fully in keeping with the qualified and carefully hedged nature of the new policy of "softness" on Africa.

If our last point has validity, the Soviet moderation in questions of African economic policy is not merely a matter of old-fashioned diplomacy at its best. It might be objected, of course, that the analogy with the East European developments of 1956 could be easily overdone. If the new African countries could be talked into pursuing a Soviet-type industrialization policy, and if such a policy should end in an impasse or worse, the local government rather than the Soviet Union would be blamed. While this is likely to be the case, the risks involved would nevertheless remain grave. The breakdown of an ambitious industrialization program would set off a full-scale political and social crisis, and it is, conservatively speaking, far from certain that the benefits would accrue to the Moscow-controlled local Communists; an explosion of tribal warfare and a spread of militant and ruthless racialism seems a more probable outcome. It is certainly neither an accident nor plain eyewash that the last program of the CPSU sounds a solemn warning against "anti-white" nationalism. There is always a danger that the forces of this nationalism, by pushing too strongly and too fast, may play havoc with Khrushchev's "long-pull" policy and provoke an international conflagration.

This danger is all the graver because of China. It is one of the most momentous developments of the last decade that the Soviet model now has not only a number of competitors to the right, but also one formidable rival to the left. The Chinese Communist leadership has been trying for years to solve the stupendous problems attendant upon the rapid industrialization of one of the most underdeveloped countries of the world by extending the mobilization of manpower and the control over the lives of its subjects to lengths never attempted by Stalin; moreover, it has harnessed into the service of this campaign the fiercest brand of anti-Western nationalism. The Chinese experiment has been recently undergoing a grave crisis, but it would be rash in the extreme to ignore its actual and potential impact on the underdeveloped world. A switch toward the Chinese brand of Communism would certainly represent one of the heaviest blows the Soviet Union could now suffer in Africa. And since the

Chinese chances of gaining a firm hold there would be likely to increase in case of social upheaval, the premium put by the Soviet leaders on relative tranquillity is bound to be raised correspondingly, and a peaceful "growing into Khrushchevism" must appear even more desirable than it would if Mao Tse-tung had never existed.

It might be objected that this conclusion, while not implausible, is based on severely incomplete premises. Although it is perfectly true that the collapse of ambitious industrialization programs in African countries might have dramatic repercussions, why assume that the mighty Soviet Union and the other more advanced countries of the "socialist camp" could not be relied upon to provide a sufficient volume of economic and technical assistance? This is undoubtedly a legitimate question to raise, and it leads us straight to our last point.

Curiously, it is Lenin's text of forty-odd years ago that can provide us with a good clue not only to the motives behind the present Soviet policy of economic aid but also to its limitations. It will be recalled that when Lenin made his statement about assistance to the underdeveloped, the victory of the European revolution seemed within easy grasp; the "Soviet governments" that he hopefully expected to extend the assistance would have represented the industrial heartland of the West. Even if the United States were temporarily excluded it would not be fatal, because a socialist Western and Central Europe would surely be more than a match for the transatlantic capitalist colossus.

The governments of the "socialist camp" of the sixties advance the promise of "powerful support" in an altogether different situation. In spite of large forward strides in industrialization over the last decades, they are by and large "in-betweens"—vastly superior in their economic potential to the underdeveloped world, but greatly inferior to the West. Since no revolutions in the West are within sight, and wars are no longer counted upon to bring them about, the further narrowing of this gap as rapidly as possible ("catching up and overtaking") is now a more crucial task than ever—a situation Lenin certainly could not have contemplated in 1920. True, in an important sense this task is now easier to accomplish than it was during the early Five-Year Plans, since the capacity for expanding the productive plant and the ability to absorb new technology are much larger. But on the other hand, the claims of the military sphere have increased immensely, and the consumer can no longer be treated as high-handedly as before; moreover, the large reservoir of "superfluous" rural manpower is very nearly exhausted, and certain areas of the economy that were badly neglected under Stalin happen to have very high capital requirements (for example, chemicals and housing). It is only natural that the present Soviet long-range plans which attempt to meet these demands while maintaining a high rate of expansion are extremely tight and, in the agricultural field, border on the adventurous.

The bearing of this situation on economic aid to underdeveloped countries is clear: a modicum of "mutually advantageous" trade can be useful, although the Soviet consumer can, in a pinch, do without cocoa. Likewise, a strictly limited amount of investment aid is not likely to hurt; it can be a good way of getting rid of obsolete machinery still being produced in Soviet machine-building plants, or of employing low-level technicians. However, investment aid on a substantial scale would absorb resources badly needed for the expansion of Soviet productive and military potential and for going at least a part of the way toward meeting the "revolution of rising expectations" within the Soviet Union. The calculation, while tough, is not unrealistic; even if an underdeveloped country were prepared to go Communist tomorrow as a result of Soviet aid, a ruble of investment in it would mean a smaller increment in the economic and power potential of the Communist bloc—the law of higher returns to investment in more advanced countries knows of no exceptions. (There is, incidentally, nothing hypothetical about this case; as Paul A. Baran has pointed out, the Hobson's choice between more Soviet growth and more assistance to the Asiatic "People's Democracies" is a very real source of dissension within the international Communist movement.) [58] It is therefore hardly a slip of the pen when Soviet writers, while extolling Soviet generosity, still try to prove that "mutually advantageous trade" is a vastly better form of assistance than aid, and that aid, when supplied on a very large scale, is in fact harmful.

We have spoken thus far about limitations on Soviet economic aid in general. The situation with regard to the new African states is, in principle, not different. For the time being, the volume of Soviet-

African trade represents such a small share of the Soviet total turnover that it should not be very difficult to keep increasing it substantially, or even (if an urgent need should arise) dramatically. On the other hand, the absorption capacity on the receiving end is likely to remain small for quite a while. But as time wears on, the situation will become more difficult on both counts. We would therefore expect that the increase in the flow of Soviet aid will slow down substantially before it has been able to satisfy more than a fraction of the need. The effect on the Soviet Union's standing is more difficult to predict; that will almost certainly depend, in large measure, on the action—or inaction—of the West in the future.

EASTERN EUROPE

Robert and Elizabeth Bass

The "People's Democracies" of Eastern Europe—Czechoslovakia, Poland, the German Democratic Republic, Hungary, Bulgaria, and Rumania—have played an active role in the broad Communist endeavor to establish viable and lasting connections in Africa south of the Sahara. Although their interests in Africa still appear to be largely parallel to those of the Soviet Union, they have not acted simply as Moscow's pawns in an elaborate African strategy. Relations between the various Communist parties and governments have changed considerably since 1956, and as a result the East European states have been able to give some practical consideration to their own interests in Africa, to respond to political and economic incentives quite distinct from any pressures conceivably emanating from the Soviet Union.

Politically, each of the East European governments has sought ways to affirm its own legitimacy. The present party and government leaders have not been blind to the value of international relationships and commitments as a mark of prestige, both within the world community and in the eyes of their own peoples. This prestige is most urgently sought by East Germany, but it is just as real for post-1956 Hungary and for Communist Czechoslovakia, which enjoyed a long tradition of acceptance in the Western cultural and commercial community before 1948.

The East European countries, much more than the Soviet Union, also have a genuine interest in expanding their international commercial ties in Africa. The era of forced industrialization and agricultural collectivization, which began in the late 1940's and culminated in heavy pressures during the Korean war, left all the "People's

Democracies" with top-heavy economic structures. Their new industrial plants lacked both the raw materials needed for full operation and the markets that would consume their products. The post-Stalin "New Course" and the subsequent efforts to achieve a moderate but continuing increase in the standard of living set in motion a search for supplemental foodstuffs. In addition, because they have not been able to compete successfully or on an adequate scale in Western markets, they suffer from currency exchange problems similar to those of the younger nations.

These considerations have made the East European states keenly alert to new opportunities in Africa and in developing areas in general. In view of these real needs and opportunities, East European trade and technical assistance cannot be stereotyped as unprofitable "economic aggression" pursued solely for ideological or propaganda purposes and at the direct behest of the Soviet Union.

It is also widely recognized that doctrinal dissensions are in the process of transforming some fundamental relationships between members of the Communist world and perhaps undermining the pivotal position of the Soviet Communist Party. Seen in this context, Africa, as much as the other uncommitted continents, provides varied opportunities for independent action in several fields. This is clear to the Chinese Communists, and the East European states are presumably aware of their attractive status as small countries, with no colonial past, and posing no direct threat to the aspirations of the new nations. And the Soviet Union is unlikely to discourage any spontaneous initiatives by its East European partners so long as it needs support in its ideological duel with China.

There is another perspective from which specific East European activities in Africa during the past three to four years should be viewed. Taken together, the existing trade ties, delegation exchanges, training programs, broadcast schedules, and contacts between semi-official organizations of trade unionists, journalists, youth, and sporting groups are impressive. Nevertheless, we have no real evidence that the East European states, any more than the Soviet Union or China, have devised an effective formula for identifying the aims of international Communism and the aspirations of African nationalism.

The impression, perhaps stronger in America than elsewhere, that the Soviet Union and the East European states have certain charismatic qualities for Africans clearly remains to be demonstrated.[1] This tendency to overestimate the appeals of Communism springs in part from a sensitive awareness of the colonial record of several West European countries. Probably it is also fostered by the apparent absence in Africa of an "anti-Communism" of the sort understood within the Atlantic alliance; this, in turn, has engendered apprehension whenever Africans have shown interest in the ability of the Communist world to satisfy certain immediate African needs through prescriptions radically different from those favored by the West.

Certainly there exists a school of Afro-Marxist thought to which a number of prominent African personalities subscribe and which extends to a generation of younger men schooled in France or Eastern Europe who undoubtedly keep in touch with their former mentors. On the other hand, there are few African Communist parties and none notable for numerical strength, efficient organization, or widespread influence. Nor is there any convincing proof that Afro-Marxism can be equated with contemporary Marxism-Leninism.[2]

Thus it would be fair to say that the growing number of contacts between the East European states and the new African countries does not prove any substantial degree of ideological commitment by Africans. Nor can it be assumed that communication is very much easier for East Europeans than for others: the "People's Democracies" must surely strike most visiting Africans as highly industrialized societies that are necessarily rather remote from Africa's most urgent problems.[3]

It cannot be ignored, however, that the East European states can draw on considerable experience to fortify their present position in sub-Saharan Africa. Some East European states, notably Czechoslovakia, can revive commercial contacts established before the Second World War; all of them have been active in Asia, the Middle East, and northeastern Africa at least since 1955, and therefore have gained experience in conducting diplomacy, trade, and propaganda in less developed areas.[4]

By 1956 individual East European states had concluded formal trade agreements with Lebanon, Syria, Afghanistan, Saudi Arabia and Yemen, India, Burma, Ceylon, Indonesia, and Pakistan, as well as Egypt, the Sudan, and Ethiopia. Czechoslovakia and Poland had each participated in a number of international trade fairs, and Czechoslovakia had established its Technoexport Corporation, which specializes in the sale of entire industrial installations and promotes the acceptance of Czechoslovak goods in the developing countries.[5] Likewise, in 1955 and 1956 Egyptian technicians were already receiving industrial training at Gottwaldov, though their presence was overshadowed by that of the military pilots who had been invited by the Prague government. Czechoslovak personnel were dispatched to Egypt soon after the ill-fated attack on the Suez Canal.[6]

By the mid-fifties something had also been learned about the value of trade and technical assistance as vehicles for disseminating political publicity. For example, the Polish government discovered among its own nationals a Moslem engineer who, in the course of his professional assignment in Damascus, received favorable public attention after a cordial interview with the Syrian Grand Mufti that ranged over the wide field of Polish Middle Eastern relations.[7] This sort of dexterity in catering to the particular sensitivities of the uncommitted, generally anti-Western neutralists was, in fact, an early feature of East European activity outside the Communist sphere. A characteristic example may be found in an English-language publication of the Czechoslovak Ministry of Foreign Trade dating from early 1956:

> In bilateral negotiations, especially with regard to countries with underdeveloped economies, Czechoslovakia expresses her willingness to negotiate adjustments to stabilize prices, and firmly supports the interests of the countries producing raw materials and encourages their sensible endeavors for agreements to protect themselves against the chaotic oscillations on the world markets. With due respect to the national pride of her trading partners in these countries, which have made great progress in the development of their own economies, Czechoslovakia is following and will continue to follow only mutual economic interests.[8]

By 1958, well before substantial new opportunities arose south of the Sahara, East Europe's trade with Asia, the Middle East, and some parts of Africa was already greater than that of the Soviet Union; it had more than doubled since 1954 and amounted to approximately five per cent of the area's total trade.[9] Some of this commercial activity, of course, was no more than a partial return to normal trade patterns that had been interrupted by the war and later inhibited for political and ideological reasons. Yet the very fact that old patterns existed and could be resumed was important, since the arrival of East European traders and governmental representatives in Africa did not appear to the new states as a novel or menacing overture, but rather as a natural resumption of established policies.

Trade and other types of economic relations are, perhaps, the most tangible sign of Eastern Europe's growing interest in sub-Saharan Africa. It would, however, be entirely unrealistic to discount the relevance of ideology in the conduct of any Communist state, whether large or small. If, therefore, there is comparatively less public discussion of the ideological foundations of East European action in the developing countries of Africa, this is probably only because a substantial body of Soviet literature was already in existence well before the East European states could give practical consideration to their own role in this field. Much comment is, in any case, channeled through the authoritative *World Marxist Review*, which is published in Prague, and in other widely circulated publications of the international Communist front organizations, whose headquarters are generally in Eastern Europe. Nor is it likely that the Soviet Union has done much to encourage discussion on a subject of major importance to its own long-range policy objectives, especially in view of the independent initiatives already taken by Chinese emissaries in Africa and elsewhere.[10]

East European Communists have, accordingly, fashioned their ideological outlook largely on the Soviet model. The November 1957 Declaration of the Conference of Twelve Communist Parties (including, of course, those of the East European bloc) reaffirmed the need for a Communist party, a planned economy, public ownership of the means of production, collectivization of agriculture, and working-class solidarity in any state to which the Communist world could give its unqualified support.[11] This rather inflexible position—not yet substantially modified—reflects neither the reality of contemporary African development nor the actual policies pursued by the East European states and the Soviet Union in recent years.

In these circumstances, the "People's Democracies" have tended, during the past three or four years, to censure the leadership of the new African states on ideological grounds while at the same time continuing to broaden areas of contact with them. Thus certain African governments have been characterized as "unstable" and "conciliatory toward imperialism and feudalism."[12] African statesmen and politicians have been charged with "lack of determination to break with imperialists . . . because, in their desire to serve their people, they overestimate the difficulties entailed [in such a break]."[13] Attention has been called to "the so-called 'neutralists' who, under the pretext of preoccupation with internal affairs and adherence to the principle of non-interference, actually aid the colonialists" at a time when "class differentiation is at the initial stages and the progressive organizations are weak." Even worse, "In some African countries . . . the state leadership has passed into the hands of vacillating, conciliatory elements, and even direct agents of the imperialists."[14]

These comments sound a note of frustration. While revealing Communist hopes and intentions, they indicate the difficulties of formulating an effective and ideologically sound policy toward sub-Saharan Africa. In practice, however, theoretical reservations have not proved a serious obstacle to action. Economic ties of all types have been established, and all the East European states are engaged in a determined effort to influence the younger African political elite that will eventually inherit power.

There have been two theoretical bases for this activity. First, economists and journalists in the East European states echo the Soviet view that political independence for Africans means little without real emancipation from the capitalist economies of the West; and this, it is said, can only be assured by substantially increasing trade with and technical assistance from "the socialist camp."[15] It is frankly asserted that these economic relations will encourage "the dissemination and more or less conscious assimilation of Marxism, or at least of some of its basic principles—for example, its definition of imperialism, . . . ways of solving the land question, forms of nationalization, and the building of an independent economy."[16]

The apparent justification for action in non-economic spheres was set forth in the Statement of the Conference of World Communist

Parties, issued in Moscow in December 1960. This document announced that "like-minded Marxists continue to unite in the countries that have thrown off the colonial yoke and taken the path to independent development."[17] In a conscientious effort to increase the number of these "like-minded Marxists," the East European states have played host to an increasing flow of African government delegations, students, trade unionists, journalists, and industrial trainees, and they have also become active in the various international front organizations in sub-Saharan Africa.

The East European states have also found it convenient to invoke the concept set forth in the 1961 Program of the Soviet Communist Party, which characterizes the new African countries as "states of national democracy." This means that although they retain many features of bourgeois society and the capitalist system, which makes them quite different from the "People's Democracies," they are still in a transitional phase of development. In Czechoslovakia it has actually been suggested that the African states are entering an evolutionary period similar to the postwar period in Eastern Europe. Obviously referring to the events of 1948, commentators writing about present-day Africa suggest that the "national democratic" state will eventually produce a "national front," which will in turn become the springboard for launching a truly socialist society, conceivably even through parliamentary methods.[18] In the meantime, the "national democracy" concept makes it possible to stress the size and significance of the public sectors of the African economies and to emphasize the need for aiding their further development. This idea also makes it easier to construe the independent and unpredictable attitudes of Africa's present leaders as a challenge rather than an obstacle to further action.

Economic Relations

The major trade activities of the East European states are still centered outside Africa. According to the available information, Africa south of the Sahara accounted for less than ten per cent of the Communist world's exchanges with underdeveloped areas during 1960, with Czechoslovak exports and Soviet imports the only exceptions.[19] Communist trade with all developing countries, in turn, barely exceeded ten per cent of the total trade of Czechoslovakia, which is easily the largest international trader among the East European states.

Thus it is clear that the remarkable percentage increases reported and forecast for East European trade with Africa since 1960 actually proceed from a very low base. We read that new agreements "will double the flow of Polish trade with the African continent," but Poland's total trade turnover with Africa was a bare $19 million in 1960.[20] It should also be remembered that the East European states are reporting marked percentage increases in their trade with Asia and Latin America, and that their commercial efforts in these continents are perhaps more successful than in tropical Africa.

What is striking about East European activity in Africa is that it seems to rival that of the U.S.S.R., as shown in Table 1. Czechoslovakia, for instance, has for several years been a much more substantial exporter than the Soviet Union, even though not as large a buyer, and this pattern is repeated throughout the East European bloc, all of whose members sold more in Africa than they bought in 1960. The U.S.S.R., on the other hand, has been a much better buyer; she can apparently satisfy her foreign exchange requirements more adequately in Western markets, and she does not face the problems that forced industrialization has created in Eastern Europe. It is true that Eastern Europe's total trade turnover with sub-Saharan Africa has not been much larger than the Soviet Union's, but this is because its collective purchases were perhaps half those of the Soviet Union while its exports for 1960 were at least three times as large. Recent trends suggest that the "People's Democracies" are beginning to increase their purchases, but it is hard to be certain whether greater quantities of goods are actually involved or whether the reported increases are purely statistical and therefore artificial. The figures may simply reflect the fact that purchases are now made and reported directly in the independent African states instead of through British, French, and other European firms, which was the usual practice in earlier years.[21]

The growth of trade—particularly by Czechoslovakia, East Germany, and Poland—with Guinea, Ghana, and Mali, although rela-

TABLE 1.—EAST EUROPEAN AND SOVIET TRADE WITH SUB-SAHARAN AFRICA, 1948-60*

(Millions of U.S. dollars)

	1948	1950	1952	1954	1956	1958	1960
Imports							
Eastern Europe	10.2	4.2	5.1	3.8	9.4	10.4	19.4
Czechoslovakia	5.2	2.1	2.6	1.2	2.7	5.6	9.1
Poland	4.7	2.1	2.2	1.9	4.6	2.9	4.4
Others	.3	—	.3	.7	2.1	1.9	5.9
U.S.S.R.	10.0	4.9	11.7	26.0	9.8	19.5	48.2
Exports							
Eastern Europe	23.8	13.7	20.3	28.1	37.1	36.7	45.4
Czechoslovakia	20.3	12.4	16.7	16.5	23.6	23.8	24.6
Poland	1.4	.5	1.7	6.4	3.3	4.0	4.0
Others	2.1	.8	1.9	5.2	10.2	8.9	16.8
U.S.S.R.	.1	—	.1	.6	1.0	.9	15.5
Turnover (imports plus exports)							
Eastern Europe	34.0	17.9	25.4	20.3	46.5	47.1	64.8
U.S.S.R.	10.1	4.9	11.8	26.6	10.8	20.4	63.7

* The East European figures are those reported by African countries, and this coverage is not complete. Guinea, for instance, was not among the reporting countries. Also, trade with the Union of South Africa accounted for a relatively large share of the totals: East European imports from that country totaled 2.3 million in 1956 and 5.1 million in 1960, and East European exports to it totaled 7.4 million in 1956 and 8.2 million in 1960. It should also be noted that the East European figures may especially understate Eastern Europe's imports by omitting purchases made through West European intermediaries. As presented here, import values are f.o.b. country of origin and export values are f.o.b. country of destination.

Source: United Nations, *Direction of International Trade*, Annual Summary issues, Vols. VI–IX.

tively modest in absolute terms, has attracted much attention in the West because of the broader political context in which it has taken place. But these three are by no means the only African countries where contacts are being actively developed. East European traders have recently given much attention to the sixteen African states whose association with the European Common Market was subject to reconsideration at the end of 1962. Poland has working agreements with Nigeria, Togo, Senegal, and Liberia, and plans to establish trade centers in those countries.[22] Ethiopia, Somalia, and even the Niger Republic have trade agreements with East European countries. A limited agreement has been reported between Sierra Leone and the Polish Cooperatives' Trade Association, and a pact between Bulgaria and the Malagasy Republic was signed in Paris in 1961. Rumania's agreements extend to twelve African countries, including the Ivory Coast, Dahomey, Cameroun, Chad, Upper Volta, and the Central African Republic—a rather esoteric collection apparently resulting from an earlier master agreement with France.[23] However, this relatively rapid expansion of trade with the "new" countries does not seem to have affected trade with the Union of South Africa, which, in 1961, remained Eastern Europe's oldest and third largest trading partner in Africa—and this despite the political attacks leveled at her by all the Communist states.

It is difficult to say whether the economic ventures of the East European states in Africa are characterized more by national competition or bloc cooperation. Scores of East European delegations traveling in Africa cross paths with remarkable frequency, and they offer scholarships and technical assistance almost as often as trade pacts.[24] It is probably safe to say, however, that there does exist a certain amount of ordinary commercial competition, with each country seeking supplies and markets more or less independently through its own specialized foreign trade organizations.[25]

Two accounts of Czechoslovakia's commercial methods which have appeared in Soviet journals, perhaps to be held up as models, note that local sales and purchasing agents are carefully selected from among established indigenous firms with good credit standing; Czechoslovak representatives are used only when there are no suitable local firms. In some instances, such local firms handle the majority of business details and work on a profit rather than a commission basis within a framework of general policies on pricing, servicing, and so on, established in Prague. Advertising, which is considered extremely important, is sometimes also handled locally under the broad supervision of a foreign trade advertising organization subordinate to the Ministry of Foreign Trade in Prague. This suggests that at least some of the larger Czechoslovak export firms conduct their African business dealings with an eye to avoiding bad credit risks and attaining a maximum in local good will.[26]

It is unlikely, however, that any of the other East European states has as much experience and flexibility. In Warsaw, for instance, there have been complaints that Poles "are still novices on foreign markets" and that their foreign trade organizations "frequently come out second best in competition with well-known firms which have been there for years."[27] This implies not only some clumsiness in manner but also insufficient sensitivity to the need for adopting suitable techniques when competing in countries that are bound to compare every proposition from Eastern Europe with others emanating from the United States or Western Europe.

A measure of competition, however, does not rule out the likelihood of increased coordination in the future. Since internal and external prices in all Communist countries are independent of each other, and because it is difficult for planners to judge the costs or profits of their foreign trade, it is probable that there are some provisions already in operation to safeguard against the possibility of virtual price wars between the East European states. On the positive side, some joint economic efforts have already been undertaken: Poland and Czechoslovakia have collaborated on a sugar refinery project in Ceylon, and it has been announced that East Germany, Poland, and Czechoslovakia are jointly operating a shipping company called Uni-Africa, serving West African ports.[28] Finally, the commission on foreign trade of the Council for Economic Mutual Assistance (CEMA) is doubtless working to integrate exchanges within the bloc and resolve problems created by the continuing absence of an extensive and flexible basis for multilateral payments. At present, East European agreements with African states remain strictly bilateral— and if there is in fact an "unseen hand" at work here, it is not likely to be Moscow's.

So far, however, there exists no broad division of effort among the East European states in Africa, even though such a division is logically implicit in attempts to coordinate economic planning within the bloc.

Apart from their role as traders, the East European countries account for a significant share of Soviet bloc aid to sub-Saharan Africa. Between 1954 and 1961 they supplied $116 million of the approximately $480 million in grants and credits committed by the Communist states. In 1961 alone they offered at least $73 million out of some $210 million, or more than a third of the Communist total.[29] These commitments, of course, are promises, not actual disbursements or deliveries of goods on credit. Furthermore, they involve rather small sums when compared with the actual disbursements of long-term funds from non-Communist Western and multilateral sources to non-Arab Africa, which averaged nearly $400 million annually in the years 1957–1959 and are still increasing.[30]

To the African recipients, however, bloc aid is important, because the East European countries have supplemented rather than offset the tendency of the U.S.S.R. to give large amounts of assistance to a few countries. Thus, by the end of 1961, identifiable East European grants and credits had gone to only five countries—Ethiopia, Ghana, Guinea, Mali, and Somalia. Among these, Ghana and Guinea together accounted for nearly seventy per cent of the total, and one Hungarian source has claimed that bloc credits will supply eighty-five per cent of the external capital required under Guinea's current development plan.[31] New credits to Mali, Ghana, and Guinea and negotiations with Nigeria were reported in 1962, and more may be anticipated.[32] Still, the fact remains that the great majority of East European credits have been offered outside Africa. The Middle East and Asia accounted for nearly ninety per cent as of 1961, and this aid continues to expand simultaneously with what is being offered to Africa, although the balance is likely to shift somewhat in Africa's favor.

As yet there is no distinctive pattern to Eastern European aid to Africa south of the Sahara. The earliest aid commitment to the area, agreed upon in 1958, was Czechoslovakia's $2 million to Ethiopia to equip and assist hospitals. The bloc's credits to Guinea started in 1959, the first commitment to Ghana dates from 1960, and the bulk of allocations to date were made in 1961. Details on the terms, or even the exact purposes of most of these, have yet to be revealed, and signatures on credit agreements appear to be only the beginning of a protracted procedure involving additional protocols and contracts. Ghana and Poland, for instance, signed a credit agreement in April 1961 covering a variety of industrial projects, but the first specific contract does not appear to have been finally concluded until March 1962.[33]

In most respects, East European aid to Africa is following patterns already established in Asia and the Middle East. Virtually all assistance is in the form of interest-bearing loans, rather than grants or interest-free credits (such as those offered by Communist China). All loans are tied to concrete projects, and thus take the form of delivery of specific goods and services for which payment is deferred, rather than the allocation of money which the recipient may dispose of for limited purposes. One African source has even indicated that credits do not normally cover the cost of the East European technical personnel who invariably arrive with the equipment; it is said that "assistance is given in the form of plants and machinery, while the receiving state provides all expenditures in connection with civil engineering. In practice, the equipment supplied works out at a third, which means that the state bears two-thirds of the cost involved."[34]

From what little is known of Eastern Europe's agreements, they still appear less generous than those of the U.S.S.R., although there is evidence that this may be changing. Whereas credit offered by the Soviet Union is usually repayable over twelve years at 2.5 per cent interest, relatively "capitalistic" terms have been asked by East European creditors: periods of three to five years at two to four per cent interest were cited as Czechoslovakia's standard policy in 1958, and rates of four and seven per cent were reported for Czechoslovak and Polish loans to Indonesia in 1959 and 1960.[35] Information on agreements with African countries remains fragmentary, but periods of four or five years are most frequently cited for the East European countries. Czechoslovakia may be a possible exception; it is reported to have granted ten-year loans to Ethiopia and Guinea. East European interest rates may also be dropping to the Soviet level, judging by reports of 2.5 per cent interest rates on Hungarian, Polish, East German, and Czechoslovak credits to Guinea.[36]

The East European countries also tend to sponsor comparatively small undertakings and to supply complete plants in a variety of light or secondary industries. Propaganda to the contrary notwithstanding, East European credits cover an astonishing number of projects that cannot reasonably be considered heavy industries. A sugar refinery that Poland is supplying to Ghana on credit will be complemented by a candy factory and molasses distillery.[37] Ghana's agreements with Hungary provide for an electric light bulb factory and a pharmaceutical plant.[38] Czechoslovakia's credit agreement with Mali, signed in June 1961, may potentially cover a textile plant, a flour mill, a broadcasting station, a hospital, and an assembly line for agricultural machinery.[39] Czechoslovakia's $10 million credit to Ethiopia in 1960 provided for a canvas shoe factory and assistance in the development of cotton and sugar plantations.[40] A full list of existing agreements would, of course, include undertakings in the producers' goods sector, such as foundries and electrical equipment plants.[41] But in general, the projects to be undertaken on East European credits are more reminiscent of allegedly "neo-colonialist" prescriptions for development than of any Communist formula.

In contrast to the theoretical views held by the exponents of orthodox Communist principles, the East European states appear to be pursuing an open-minded policy of supplying whatever the African states think they need and the creditor can effectively deliver. Since the receiving African countries have many needs, project initiation becomes easy—especially because the creditor states are happy to assist in basic surveys, design, and planning.

A case in point is Poland's December 1961 agreement with Ghana, involving $28 million. Apparently this expands an earlier accord of April 1961 totaling $14 million to cover some twenty industrial plants, only a few of which are specifically mentioned. Accra, however, has described the agreement as "preparing the ground for a study" of all Ghanaian industrial projects to determine which of them would benefit from machinery and equipment that Poland's industries are able to supply, adding that a joint committee was meeting "to establish a program for the utilization of Polish credits."[42] Similarly, an announcement in May 1961 of a Czechoslovak credit to Ghana for "plant and equipment" has been followed by a series of more specific agreements whose nature suggests that implementation is barely out of the planning stage: Czechoslovakia's Technoexport Corporation was to conduct surveys to locate suitable sites for hydro-electric power plants during 1961, subsequently to assist in designing them, and eventually to provide and install the equipment. Likewise, the Skoda works are to supply to Ghana the machinery for a sugar refinery whose site was to be surveyed by Czechoslovak experts during 1962, with delivery and installation scheduled for 1963.[43]

One innovation worth special mention is Poland's formation of a joint fishing company with Guinea. This form of capital transfer, distinctly new in bloc economic relations with the developing countries, could prove quite effective, since it appears on the surface even better suited to satisfy national pride and the desire for "economic independence" than the usual "long-term credits on a basis of mutual equality." The arrangement, so far as we know, assigns to Guinea fifty-one per cent of the shares, with the understanding that the entire remaining Polish holdings will be purchased by the receiving country over a period of time. Poland, meanwhile, supplies boats, managerial and technical personnel, and much of the refrigeration, canning, and repair equipment. This project became effective in January 1961 and there has been talk of a similar arrangement with Ghana and of African countries conceivably participating in an East European shipping line.[44]

Technical assistance, more than trade or loans, is clearly an important vehicle for the bloc's effort to influence elite opinion in Africa. Not only can advisers and technicians help popularize Marxist concepts and Communist institutions; they can also impress leading African groups with the capabilities and methods of East European states. Technical aid thus typically includes projects of high publicity value, such as Czechoslovakia's equipment and medical staff for nearly a dozen hospitals in Ethiopia, or Bulgaria's more modest provision of midwives to Guinea.[45] But even medical aid may carry a message, as when Poland sent doctors to organize health cooperatives in Ghana.[46] The steady flow of Polish and Czech teachers to Ghana and Guinea promises many contacts with the coming generation of educated Africans. Warsaw has filled an economics chair at Accra University with a professor from the Central School of Planning and

Statistics. Three historians—a German, an African, and an American Negro—each trained at the University of Leipzig, were on the staff of Nsukka University in Nigeria during 1962. Likewise, and apparently notwithstanding the events which led to the expulsion of the Soviet ambassador to Guinea in December 1961, East European teachers continued to predominate in teaching technical and scientific subjects in that country's secondary schools during 1962.[47] East Germany and Czechoslovakia have also been conspicuous in helping Guinea and Ghana to expand their mass communications facilities, not only by training and advising journalists but also by supplying printing presses and radio transmitters.[48]

The numerous surveys of African natural resources conducted by bloc technicians have been explicitly coupled with charges that the West seeks to maintain a stranglehold on Africa's extractive industries. It has even been alleged that Western experts deliberately refrain from searching for and making known new resources as part of a "neo-colonialist" conspiracy to perpetuate African underdevelopment.[49]

But the "People's Democracies" do not seem to regard their assistance program solely, or even chiefly, as a convenient means of scoring propaganda points. Their hope is that technical advice to governmental and managerial echelons will influence and possibly guide institutional development in the new African states. Bloc action to fill the vacuum left by the French departure from Guinea in 1958 did achieve immediate international notoriety, but its real significance was that it established a precedent now being followed elsewhere. Though less spectacular, it is significant that in the fall of 1961 Poland made available a group of industrial experts whose job was to gather data and prepare reports for use by Ghana's planning authorities, and that Czechoslovak experts are drafting and supervising Mali's current economic plan.[50] It is equally interesting that Czechoslovakia has created a special agency, known as the Polytechna enterprise, to coordinate Czechoslovak technical assistance activities and act as a general servicing organization catering to the needs of developing countries.[51]

These efforts are accompanied by the inevitable flow of technical personnel preceding and accompanying all deliveries of equipment and engaged in the study of tropical conditions, the discussion of designs, installation, and training native personnel. Exact numbers are not available, but since the East European states are the principal exporters in the Communist world, it is likely that their representation in Africa is correspondingly large and growing rapidly. As recently as 1959 there were only a handful of Soviet technicians stationed at the Russian hospital in Addis Ababa. By 1961, on the other hand, various press reports estimated the number of Communist experts in sub-Saharan Africa at approximately seven hundred, and in May of that year one African source went so far as to suggest that there were twelve hundred in Guinea alone.[52] What does seem certain is that opportunities for increasing the flow of East European technical advisers remain substantial and the deterrents few. The Republic of Guinea, for instance, retained East European advisers even after the expulsion of the Soviet ambassador to Conakry in December 1961. The team of Czechoslovak, Hungarian, Polish, and Soviet technicians who had been invited to Guinea before the troubles that led to the removal of the Soviet ambassador apparently arrived early in 1962 to take over the operation of an expropriated Western bauxite firm and to construct an aluminum plant.[53]

Political Action

Communist goals in Africa are predominantly political, not economic, in character. The primary aim of the entire bloc is to bring about specific institutional and ideological changes in the young African states; particular economic benefits, whether they accrue to the East European or the African countries, remain of secondary importance in the Communist calculus of preference. Trade and other economic relations are therefore related to and generally coordinated with other programs, notably the training of African students, contacts between trade unions and professional organizations, diplomatic initiatives, and propaganda work.

Leaving aside the almost uninterrupted exchange of soccer teams, bicycle champions, and track stars, which can be explained by a common interest in certain types of sport, Eastern Europe's recent relations with tropical Africa abound in displays of what Thorstein Veblen once called "resolute conviviality."

A few examples, picked at random, will suggest the diversity of these efforts. A sculptor commissioned by the East German Labor Federation (FDBG) is at work on a "statue of liberty" for the trade union headquarters in Conakry; in Hungary, another sculptor is laboring on a likeness of Patrice Lumumba for eventual presentation to the Congolese people.[54] Folk dancers from Mali, invited to tour Poland, have used Czechoslovak commercial air services from Bamako, Conakry, and Dakar.[55] A research center for tropical veterinary medicine has been established in Leipzig.[56] The East German cruise ship "People's Friendship" has stopped in Guinea with over five hundred vacationing sightseers aboard.[57] The Czechoslovak Embassy in Addis Ababa has obtained local publicity by contributing funds to a Red Cross festival.[58]

Naturally, some such actions are less effective than others. None are substantial projects in themselves, but most of them are calculated adjuncts to sustained and massive programs of major importance to virtually all the East European governments.

Among these major programs, none is more important than the training of African students. The drive to enlist young Africans for study in Eastern Europe has been made by all bloc countries, the greatest number so far having gone to Czechoslovakia and the German Democratic Republic. Counting industrial trainees and others in non-university programs, African students in the "People's Democracies" represent 21 African countries and number in the thousands.[59] This is impressive, since educational institutions in Eastern Europe are far smaller and less numerous than in the West, or even in the U.S.S.R.

Communists may express much ideological impatience with African politics, but they probably entertain few illusions about the prospects of short-term political action south of the Sahara. Guinean students, after all, were recalled from Czechoslovakia after the expulsion of the Soviet Ambassador from Conakry in December 1961, and subsequent discussions with President Touré involved not only the Soviet Union but the other Communist diplomatic representatives.[60] Current East European thinking about Africa is therefore likely to take a longer perspective—as suggested by the support urged for non-Communist parties in all developing countries by an authoritative Czechoslovak daily.[61] There is doubtless also an awareness that "like-minded Marxists" may not appear on African soil either rapidly or in significant numbers, and that much time and effort will be required to swell their ranks through scholastic and technical training programs inside the Communist world.

Effort alone, however, is no guarantee of success, as direct exposure to life in a Communist state may well lead Africans to reject Communist goals for reasons having little to do with the quality of the training they have received. The type of problem encountered by the East European authorities has been illustrated dramatically on several occasions. In August 1962 a small riot occurred in Sofia, apparently after African students were assaulted by Bulgarian youths for seeking white dancing partners in a public restaurant. Early in 1963 an Ethiopian student who had abandoned his studies in Brno, Czechoslovakia, explained his departure largely in terms of his resentment at having been used as an instrument of propaganda at recurrent political demonstrations and rallies. On February 12, 1963, massive disorders again took place in Bulgaria in the wake of official attempts to suppress an All-African Student Union, which had been organized without government sanction in December of 1962. Some 200 Africans protested the official ban and were dispersed by riot police, who made numerous arrests. Subsequently, more than 100 African students—almost a third of those then in the country—were either expelled or left the country, some voluntarily and some at the behest of their own governments. In May 1963 violence also flared up in Prague, where African students were beaten in broad daylight, apparently without intervention by the police, on one of the city's principal thoroughfares; the cause was said to be resentment against the allegedly privileged status and preferment accorded African students by university authorities.

Despite such incidents, official expectations seem little changed, and all educational programs for Africans launched since 1959 are being carried forward with zeal. The Wilhelm Pieck Youth College at Bogensee, East Germany, established in 1961 and specializing in ideological training, continues to admit African students to its courses of study, which include the social sciences, politics, journalism, as well as Russian language, history, and literature.[62] Since 1961 Poland has offered an increasing number of "Lumumba scholarships" and has established two grants for the study of nuclear physics by young Africans.[63] It would also appear that Warsaw has been able to avoid racial incidents, and that Africans have received a more cordial reception there than elsewhere in the bloc.

The aspirations of every East European functionary with responsibility for foreign student matters are still those set forth in 1959 by an official of the Czechoslovak Ministry of Education:

> The resolutions of the Eleventh Congress of the Communist Party of Czechoslovakia are the basic directives for the foreign relations of our colleges. . . . We shall . . . endeavor to make our work an effective component of Czechoslovakia's efforts to strengthen the socialist camp, to enhance the progressive forces throughout the world, and to preserve peace. At the same time we shall see to it that the foreign relations of our colleges adequately support the political and educational activities of the Communist Party. . . . We shall increase our political and ideological demands in the evaluation of every foreign operation, so that anything we organize will by its content and method have distinct socialist character. . . . We want our foreign guests to return to their countries not only as outstanding experts, but also as Czechoslovakia's dedicated friends and adherents of socialist ideas. To attain this object it is necessary to create an adequate milieu and atmosphere . . . and gain influence over the foreign student.[64]

Somewhat belatedly, steps were taken to create this "milieu." In September 1961 the Czechoslovak government decided to establish an "institution of higher learning which will accommodate foreign students and Czechoslovak experts interested in careers abroad"; this was to be "further proof of the help which our state grants to countries that have freed themselves or are freeing themselves from colonial domination."[65] This school, known as the University of November 17,* began operation with an enrollment of approximately one thousand, and it now also administers several preparatory schools located between Slovakia and eastern Bohemia.[66] Following the pattern established at the Friendship (Lumumba) University in Mos-

---

* Nazi occupation forces closed the Czechoslovak universities on November 17, 1939.

cow, all the African students in Prague are concentrated in this one institution.[67] There is, however, a significant and ingenious difference: the student body in Prague is said to include a substantial number of carefully selected Czechoslovaks who are destined for foreign assignment—presumably about the time their African schoolmates return home and assume positions of some authority.

The training received by Africans in Eastern Europe appears to be mostly in the natural and applied sciences. Courses in electrochemistry and instruction in diesel and railroad engineering are offered to Mali students in Czechoslovakia. A group from Togo has studied medicine in Poland, Ghanaians have studied geology in Hungary, and courses in tropical and subtropical agriculture are being offered to African students at the University of Leipzig. More recently, students from Mali, Guinea, Angola, Cameroun, Uganda, and Sierra Leone have attended various language schools at Lodz, Poland, and similar institutions in Czechoslovakia. The Rumanian government is awarding postgraduate medical scholarships in gerontology and also has played host to Somali and Togolese students of oil and gas geology.[68] There is some evidence that the study of physical education is popular among African and other foreign students; but with very few exceptions (notably the Youth College at Bogensee) courses in the social sciences and other liberal arts disciplines are not offered to Africans by the host establishments of Eastern Europe.

In the related but nonacademic sphere of youth exchanges, there has also been much activity, most of it either sponsored or encouraged by the International Union of Students (IUS) and the World Federation of Democratic Youth (WFDY) with the active participation of national youth organizations.[69] Generally, the emphasis has been on arranging visits to Eastern Europe by organization leaders from Africa, with the Free German Youth Organization playing a conspicuous role, for reasons to be discussed later on.

The kind of prize most eagerly sought by East Germany and other "People's Democracies" is a visit from a youth leader—such as the Research Officer of the Ghana "Young Pioneers," who attended a two-month course in "youth organization" in East Germany, or the Director of the Kwame Nkrumah School for Youth Functionaries, who stopped briefly in Berlin to discuss improved and expanded means of cooperation.[70] Men in such positions are clearly able to influence developments in their own countries, and direct exposure to the East European model is considered important. Almost all the bloc countries have also sponsored summer trips by groups of African youngsters to the youth camps of Eastern Europe and have sent delegations of their own on good will and friendship missions south of the Sahara.

As might be expected, the headquarters of the WFDY in Budapest and of the IUS in Prague have also served as favored reception centers for visiting youth officials. Moreover, the international character of these organizations and the affiliation of several African youth groups has made it easy to hold executive meetings of these bodies in Africa, at which delegations from the bloc countries are naturally able to participate.[71] As a result, regular liaison between African and East European youth organizations has become a well-known and widely advertised feature of Eastern Europe's broader concern with the independent states of Africa and has probably yielded some tangible rewards.

Africans generally have an intense interest in their young people, and they are probably impressed by Czechoslovakia's model children's clinics, recreational centers, and similar facilities. The Czechs, in turn, naturally hope that a personal visit to these institutions may prompt African officials to adopt certain East European models for the youth organizations in their own states.

The motives guiding East European action in the labor field are similar to those behind the student and youth exchanges. Student training, however, is a long-term investment, whereas trade union cooperation may offer more immediate rewards. Although organized wage earners still represent a small segment of African society, they are politically influential in several of the younger sub-Saharan states. In these states in particular, the African labor leader is worth cultivating.

For the East European states, the special significance of trade union contacts is related to their search for recognition as legitimate governments. The first training center for African trade unionists, although sponsored by the WFTU instead of an East European state, was opened in Budapest in September 1959—an opportune moment to begin dispelling any qualms felt by African and Asian labor leaders after the suppression of the 1956 Hungarian revolt. Nor is it surprising that the most extensive facilities for African labor leaders are centered in East Germany, where the Federation of Free German Trade Unions (FDGB) seems to enjoy greater freedom of international action than does its government, which lacks official diplomatic recognition in Africa. The German Democratic Republic has at least three institutions that offer training and guidance to African labor functionaries: the Fritz Heckert Trade Union College in Bernau, the Hochschule fuer Gewerkschaften (High School of the Trade Unions) in East Berlin, and a labor college attached to the University of Leipzig.[72] During the summer of 1961 a similar training institution was opened by the Czechoslovak Revolutionary Trade Union Movement (RTUM) in Prague.[73]

Unlike the International Confederation of Free Trade Unions (ICFTU) and the national unions of the West, the Communist states see an advantage in the close relations between African trade unions and their respective governments. In the younger African nations, the government is often the largest employer of wage labor, and this has tempted the East European labor schools to inject more political content into their trade union programs than is feasible in other areas of contact.[74]

At Budapest great emphasis is openly placed on questions of "colonialism" and the role of the trade unions in the "continuing struggle" for national independence. The political purpose of the new Czechoslovak trade union school has been discussed in considerable detail and with much candor by the Director of the Central School of the Czechoslovak Trade Unions, and may serve as an illustration of the technique employed elsewhere in the bloc. According to his account, the school was planned for about a year and received assistance from the staff of the Fritz Heckert Labor College at Bernau. The course of instruction falls into three parts and is conducted in French and English.

At the start, the prospective African trade unionist is lectured on the "development and experience" of the Czechoslovak "socialist republic," "the development of human society," "imperialism," "the significance of the world socialist system," and "the fundamental principles of capitalist and socialist economics." He is then taught the role of trade unions in a capitalist society and their "struggle for economic rights, for social progress and peace." Subsequent lectures deal with the history of the WFTU and other international trade union organizations and stress the need for African trade-union unity and for the "disintegration of the world colonial system." Other topics include "the world socialist system and the nature of the assistance given by it to the economically less developed countries; the problems of agriculture in Africa . . . and . . . an analysis of class forces and their role in the national liberation movement." In the final portion of the course students are lectured on the role of trade unions during the construction of a socialist society, the principles of national economic planning, and the role of unions in organizing production.[75]

In addition to this type of indoctrination, Czechoslovakia has established direct liaison with labor organizations in Ghana, Nigeria, Senegal, Mali, Cameroun, and Guinea.[76] The Labor College at Conakry, established in 1960 under the sponsorship of the Union Générale des Travailleurs d'Afrique Noire (UGTAN), receives support from East German and probably from other bloc trade unions. The East German FDGB alone spent some $1,250,000 during 1960 on various forms of assistance to foreign trade unions, and allotted more than half this amount to Africa.[77] This suggests that the total expenditures of the entire bloc and of the WFTU were substantially larger. These sums have doubtless been increased since the Fifth Congress of the WFTU in Moscow in December 1961.[78] Almost one hundred African representatives attended the Congress to hear Soviet, Chinese, and other spokesmen forcefully reject suggestions for cooperation with non-Communist trade unions and greater autonomy for member organizations (as advanced by Agostino Novella, the Italian President of the WFTU). Instead, the new program for Africa, as described by Ibrahim Zakaria, a Sudanese secretary of the WFTU, called for "the development of trade-union action and solidarity in the fight against colonialism," and spoke of "mustering the masses" to support Communist-oriented policies in the new countries.[79]

Increased East European activity is also likely to result from the formation of the African Trade Union Confederation (ATUC) in January 1962, in Dakar. The sympathetic support given to the new confederation by the ICFTU has been assailed from Communist and African quarters alike. The ATUC has been characterized as a "rival body" to the AATUF and as subservient to the ICFTU, which, while it "flies the workers' flag, carries out political tasks in the interests of colonialism and neo-colonialism."[80]

What the ultimate reward of all these indoctrination programs and lavish expenditures will be is doubtful. Even in Ghana, overt action by the WFTU or any Communist trade union is viewed with as much suspicion as any Western initiative would be.[81] Soviet insistence on the right to continue nuclear testing, personally reaffirmed to the WFTU delegates in Moscow by Khrushchev in December 1961, probably weakened the standing of East European labor programs; African circles were unanimous in condemning French atomic experiments in the Sahara and in expressing dismay at the resumption of Soviet tests in the autumn of 1961. Nor is an occasional statement by African laborites on the ambiguous status of East Germany a valid indicator of African trade-union opinion, since the issue of East German recognition is quite irrelevant to African problems. Finally, despite some factors favoring the growth of the Communist unions, the rigid East European model of trade-union organization may yet prove neither as relevant nor as attractive to Africa as its sponsors imagine.

East European diplomacy and propaganda are the cement that gives cohesion and direction to the institutional programs launched by the East European states in the past several years. Characteristically, in the mid-1950's there was only one Czechoslovak consular mission in the Union of South Africa. As of 1962, Czechoslovakia maintained diplomatic relations with Ethiopia, the Sudan, Somalia, Ghana, Guinea, Mali, Togo, Nigeria, and Tanganyika, and was continuing to expand its official representation. The other "People's Democracies" are following the Czechoslovak lead.

These diplomatic missions are important for a number of reasons. Since there are few Communist parties or indigenous front organizations in tropical Africa, there is a real need for centers from which to guide Communist information and exchange programs and to supervise the increasing number of East European technicians, traders, and organized delegations that are visiting the African states. The existence of accredited missions is also a prerequisite to the welcome rituals connected with the reception in Eastern Europe of African heads of state and governmental delegations. The Emperor Haile Selassie and Presidents Touré and Nkrumah have each toured the bloc on state visits, as have large numbers of lesser African officials.[82] Finally, there is the usual role that any embassy or legation is asked to play in trade promotion and the definition of technical assistance agreements.

East European diplomatic representation in Africa profits substantially from the membership of the "People's Democracies" in the United Nations, which enjoys great prestige among the younger nations. Their U.N. delegations afford the East European countries extensive opportunities for social and personal contact with African representatives. Perhaps more important, East European delegates have raised or supported issues almost certain to appeal to African popular and diplomatic sentiment. Nor is it only in general debates that their voices are heard; East European delegates sit on various committees and commissions, where the slavish ritual of reiterating official Soviet positions is less apparent than in the General Assembly because East European delegates are frequently the only Communist spokesmen on a committee.

During the Fifteenth Session of the General Assembly, for instance, Bulgaria insisted in the Trusteeship Council that insufficient Western pressure had been exerted on Portugal and Spain to grant independence to their overseas territories, and Czechoslovakia demanded the transmission of full and accurate information on political conditions in those areas. During the general debate on colonialism, the Polish Deputy Foreign Minister pleaded for the immediate end of all colonial rule and characterized the presence of Western military bases in newly independent countries as a form of neo-colonialism.[83] Czechoslovakia introduced a resolution urging "maximum support of efforts of newly emerging states to strengthen their independence." Poland protested against French atomic tests in the Sahara, and was joined by Hungary, Bulgaria, and Czechoslovakia in attacking as "collective colonialism" United States and West European support for French policy in Algeria.[84] Somewhat later, at the the World Health Organization Assembly in New Delhi, the Czechoslovak representative asked that a greater proportion of senior posts be made available to African and Asian nationals.[85]

Clearly, the line between diplomacy and propaganda is a thin one. It is precisely through diplomatic channels that the "People's Democracies" have been able to denounce Western economic aid to Africa as "neo-colonialism" and to say that NATO is a military alliance seeking to involve African states in aggressive policies. East European representation in Africa, as in the United Nations, is an important vehicle for propaganda activity.

For reaching a broader African public, radio broadcasting remains a standard technique. Most short-wave programs intended for tropical Africa originate in East Germany, Poland, and Czechoslovakia, but even Bulgaria is now making a token contribution to the total effort. Spurred, perhaps, by concern over the effective use of this medium by the Chinese People's Republic, the number of hours devoted to African broadcasts appears to have increased sharply since 1959, reaching more than fifty hours a week for the entire East European bloc in 1961, and continuing to rise by perhaps as much as 50 per cent during 1962.[86]

In part, the content of East European broadcasts is adapted to the assumed interests of African listeners, who are asked to address questions to the various East European radio networks and who sometimes hear messages and greetings from their countrymen who are visiting or working in the "People's Democracies." Occasionally, radio contests result in a free vacation trip to Eastern Europe for the winner.

On broad international issues, however, East European comment does not seem to differ substantially from domestic output. To take a few examples of the material broadcast during the Congo crisis in mid-1960 and subsequently on the death of Patrice Lumumba, in February 1961:

> The real cause of the armed aggression against the Congo is the fact that Belgian, British, American, and West German monopolies . . . refuse to give up their political and economic position in an effort to prevent the immense wealth of the Congo from

getting into the hands of the Congolese people. . . . As a result, the tension in the country is increasing, the occupation troops are terrorizing the people of the Congo, massacring Congolese citizens, and even threatening the lives of the leading citizens of the Congolese state.[87]

The fact that the colonial powers could not apply armed intervention in the majority of newly established states, and that in cases where they did dare, they suffered defeat, is the best proof of the strength of the national liberation movement, as well as of the power of the socialist system, whose very existence fetters the movements of imperialism.[88]

With the aid of the UN Secretary General . . . Hammarskjold, the colonialists first of all stirred up disorder in order to prevent any subsequent attempt to restore legal order, and ended by assassinating Patrice Lumumba and his comrades, these great heroes of the liberation struggle of the Congolese people and of other African peoples.[89]

In addition to broadcasting, many other conventional propaganda devices have also been employed. These include African showings of East European feature films, trade fairs, various kinds of exhibits, and the distribution of illustrated magazines and periodicals intended for export and regularly printed in English- and French-language editions.[90]

However, the current aim of the "People's Democracies" seems to be not so much to increase the flow of material from Eastern Europe as to generate essentially pro-Communist sources of news and comment in the independent African states. To this end, several of the East European states have collaborated with the International Organization of Journalists (IOJ) to provide money, equipment, and technical personnel—notably to Mali and Guinea—in order to establish or to enlarge press and radio facilities. Very clearly, their hope is to wean the small number of practicing African journalists and broadcasters from reliance on Western press agencies and to train a new generation of writers and commentators who will be not only anti-Western by inclination, but propagandists by training.

To this end, Czechoslovakia has been supplying radio transmitters to Guinea. East Germany has supplied modern printing equipment to Guinean newspaper plants, and Czechoslovakia has concluded agreements to provide both Guinea and Mali with Czech news agency and photo services.[91] The National School of Journalism, organized by the Guinean Press Agency in February 1961, has two Czechoslovak faculty members, and its best graduates "will be given the opportunity to complete their training and extend their horizons in friendly countries such as Czechoslovakia, where they will work in the press agencies, broadcasting stations, or editorial offices of the larger newspapers."[92] The first meeting of an all-African association of journalists, which was held in Bamako in May 1961, was attended by representatives of the IOJ and of the International Radio and Television Organization. Speakers from the two groups pointed out that Czechoslovakia had provided the equipment for the national headquarters of the Union of Mali Journalists and was furnishing a high-speed rotary press, and that the Union of East German Journalists had collected 750,000 marks to help the cause of African press and radio development.[93] The East European television network (Intervision) has considered extending technical assistance to broadcasting facilities in East Africa.[94]

It should be noted that the German Democratic Republic, although an active participant in the wide variety of initiatives and activities we have described, is the one East European state to which all the newly independent African countries have denied official diplomatic recognition—a unique and obviously uncomfortable position.

The East German reaction to this anomaly has been curious. On the one hand, attempts are made to act as if the problem did not exist. Walter Ulbricht dispatches official messages of greeting to the heads of African states, and Dr. Lother Bolz, the Foreign Minister, addresses communications to the United Nations Security Council on the East German attitude toward the Congo.[95] Ostentatious recognition is accorded to individual African countries as they receive their independence, and in 1962 even a change in the premiership of Tanganyika was officially acknowledged.[96]

On the other hand, much purely negative and vituperative propaganda has been released to stimulate African interest in the German question. An elaborate theoretical framework has been devised for this purpose, more so in East Germany than in any of the other "People's Democracies."[97] The colonial powers, it is asserted, have had to abandon the application of force, once the classical method of colonialism. Instead, they now pursue an indirect policy intended to enfeeble the national liberation movements of Africa by preventing the formation of truly independent states and by crippling the development of truly viable economies with deceitful offers of economic assistance. The German Federal Republic is usually identified as the chief architect of this pernicious design and one of its most active promoters. Together with the United States, it is accused of acting as a screen for the other members of the Atlantic alliance and the European Economic Community by feigning a spurious disinterest in its relations with the nations of Africa. In fact, however, West German monopoly capitalism is said to be most active, and its economic assistance to African countries to be expressly designed to undermine the public sector of states attempting to free themselves from Western imperialism.

Nor is the racism of the National Socialist era a thing of the past. The ideologists of the German Federal Republic are credited with the invention of an entirely fictitious "black racism" which, in turn, provides the pretext for Western intervention in Africa's internal affairs. Even the Roman Catholic Church is alleged to have been pressed into action by Bonn in order to cloud the real isues and bewilder the African intelligentsia. By an extension of these arguments, East Germany, more consistently than the other "People's Democracies," has led an attack on the European Common Market as the instrument of a new type of "collective colonialism" of which the United States is ultimately to be the chief beneficiary and whose real character is revealed in the aggressive aims ascribed to NATO.

These official attitudes pervade not only East German periodicals, theoretical journals, and the various educational establishments attended by visiting Africans: they are also expressly propagated by two major semi-official organizations. The first of these, the East German Committee for Solidarity with Africa, founded in July 1960, has organized fund-raising drives in support of several African causes and has sponsored the exchange of delegations and publications. It furnished medical supplies valued at 100,000 marks to the Congo in

December 1960, and provided emergency relief funds to Somalia in 1961 after severe storms had struck the country.[98] Aside from these activities, the Committee's chief aim has been to direct a stream of attacks and warnings against the "neo-colonialist" character of the developmental assistance that the German Federal Republic is providing to the African states.

An almost identical function is performed by the German Africa Society, which was launched in March 1961 under the presidency of Professor Walter Markow. Its sixty charter members include not only prominent East Germans but also several African personalities; its stated purpose is to broaden friendly relations with the peoples of Africa and to assist in the job of eliminating colonialism and neo-colonialism from the African continent.[99] It has repeatedly protested against the right of official representatives of the Federal Republic to speak for all Germans in Africa, and its president was invited to Nigeria in January 1962 to help expand the historical faculty at the University in Nsukka and to lecture on world history.

This apparent duplication of effort may be read as an indication of the intense concern that the East German authorities have about their own international image and standing. Their precise expectations, however, are unclear, since it is difficult to decide whether their propaganda is directed specifically at African audiences, more obliquely at Western audiences, or at both simultaneously. In any case, it is certain that the East German economic commitment in Africa is not commensurate with its verbal concern with the alleged motivations of Western aid—and whether in African eyes the second will prove a satisfactory substitute for the first may well be awaited with skepticism.

Conclusions

What the "People's Democracies" will eventually achieve in Africa is impossible to forecast; but the prospects for success are not bright. African curiosity about Communism has not led to much actual acceptance of Communist methods and principles, and ideological consistency will probably continue to be viewed in Africa as an irrelevant and potentially dangerous luxury. Given an intelligent, generous, and farsighted policy by the Western democracies, the shibboleth of "colonialism" and "neo-colonialism" upon which the spokesmen for all the East European states rely so heavily should eventually lose its potency. On the other hand, African determination to resist external pressures—from the West as well as the Communist world—will not diminish, and may very well increase.

Furthermore, there is no evidence that the "People's Democracies" have conducted themselves with such skill as to escape all criticism and suspicion. Their lack of subtlety in attempting to indoctrinate African visitors and students in Eastern Europe, for instance, or the use of their personnel and arms in clandestine operations within Africa, can hardly be expected to endear them to Africa's leaders.[100]

Inevitably, the new African states will make certain decisions that may give a temporary advantage to individual members of the Communist bloc or to the "People's Democracies" as a group. But such decisions will have little bearing on the long-term development of Africa's own distinctive society and institutions, and it would be a mistake for the East European states—as it would for the West—to greet them as evidence of an African surrender to the blandishments of Communism.

4

YUGOSLAVIA

William E. Griffith

Had it not been for Stalin's insistence in 1945–48 on total Soviet domination of the Yugoslav Communist Party, security police, and army, Africa might still be of little interest to Yugoslavia.[1] After the 1948 Moscow-Belgrade break, Tito was confronted with serious domestic and foreign policy problems. Just as today Albania looks to China to avoid again falling under the domination of Yugoslavia or Russia, so after 1948 Yugoslavia looked to the West for protection against the Soviet Union. And just as Albania today is trying to improve relations with Italy, Austria, and other Western powers in order not to be left with only Chinese support, so in 1948 Yugoslavia was unwilling to depend solely on the West, a group of powers ideologically hostile to it. Shortly after the 1948 break, Tito undertook not only a cautious soliciting of economic and military aid from the West but also a more ambitious, world-wide approach to the nonaligned powers. He hoped to establish and legitimatize himself with the nonaligned nations in order to obtain from them more effective political support for his independent position in the Balkans and to spread his version of Communism among them.

Tito's timing in this effort turned out to be most propitious. Such newly independent powers as India, Burma, and Indonesia feared the Chinese in much the same way that Tito feared the Russians but were at the same time deeply suspicious of the "Western neocolonialist imperialists." Many of them shared Tito's desire to avoid international war at almost any cost. Their power, they knew, was anything but military; it arose rather from the desire of both the West and the Communist states to obtain their good will and to influence them, if possible.

In the early fifties tropical Africa (with the exception of Ethiopia and Liberia) was still under the domination of European colonial powers, which ruled out political and economic penetration by Yugoslavia. The political and economic patterns of current Yugoslav activity in Africa were thus developed in Asia and the Middle East. Tito took pains to establish good personal relations with Nehru, U Nu, Sukarno, and above all with Nasser. This he did by visits, by constant cultivation of the neutralists in the United Nations, by consistent Yugoslav support for the anticolonial cause, and by offering such token amounts of economic and technical assistance as he could afford.

Tito's efforts faced fewer obstacles after the death of Stalin in 1953, when both the Soviet and (temporarily) the Chinese general line toward underdeveloped nations became more conciliatory. Such developments as the Bandung Conference in April-May 1955, the Geneva Summit Conference in July 1955, and the general international *détente* in the latter year were also favorable. Most important, however, was Khrushchev's initiative of May 1955 toward a rapprochement with Belgrade and his public acknowledgment of the doctrine of "various roads to socialism." This relieved Tito of worries about Soviet or Chinese countermeasures against his activities in Asia, and even suggested that he could profit considerably from Soviet operations in Africa. By 1958, when the second Moscow-Belgrade break occurred, Tito had improved his position: the Asian neutralist statesmen and some of the emerging African leaders, in the flush of their first disillusionment about Soviet and Chinese efforts to influence them, were prepared to listen somewhat more favorably to Belgrade than to Moscow or Peking.

Yugoslavia has one great advantage over both the United States and the Soviet Union in dealing with the Afro-Asian bloc: her small size. As with Israel, the Asians and Africans need not fear that Yugoslavia will dominate them or attempt—as do the United States and the Soviet Union—to force them to take sides between East and West on international issues. Yugoslavia and Israel do not demand of the Afro-Asians the discipline of involvement, but they can offer some modest economic and technical aid and some allegedly proven solutions to pressing domestic problems. It is not surprising, therefore, that both countries have been quite successful in Africa.

The Yugoslav Economic and Political Base

At least until 1961, the increasingly favorable Yugoslav domestic economic base also made it easier for Tito to further his aims toward the underdeveloped countries. The 1948 break with Stalin and consequent termination of Soviet aid to Yugoslavia provoked a serious economic crisis. But by 1951, in large part because of the sophisticated handling of the situation by the United States, Yugoslavia had already begun to receive and accept substantial American economic and military aid. At the same time, Tito and his Yugoslav associates, particularly Edvard Kardelj, had realized that their pre-1948 hyper-Stalinist domestic economic policy was both economically and politically irrational: it was largely responsible for depriving them of mass popular support, which, without a Soviet guarantee of their continued power, they now increasingly felt they needed. As a result, forced collectivization of agriculture was abolished and Yugoslav agriculture became and has remained to this day overwhelmingly one of private peasant proprietorship. (However, private peasants' farms were legally limited to ten hectares; it was hoped—largely in vain—that this measure, combined with heavy taxation on peasant properties and produce, would drive peasants toward the few remaining agricultural collectives.) The Yugoslav regime also decentralized industry, sharply scaled down and decentralized the industrialization program, re-established a rational price system, established workers' councils as a means of improving labor morale, and considerably liberalized foreign trade.[2]

By the mid-fifties these changes, and the increasing volume of economic aid from the United States, had begun to improve Yugoslavia's economic position. At the same time—and this is perhaps the special Yugoslav achievement—the political supremacy of Tito and the centralized Communist party remained intact. The apparent challenge of Djilas in 1953 proved only ephemeral.

In 1959 the Yugoslav economy suddenly surged ahead. The neo-entrepreneurial capitalist activities of the managers of the decentralized factories began to be profitable; domestic petroleum output had jumped from 150,000 metric tons in 1952 to 940,000 in 1960; and the introduction from Italy of artificial fertilizer factories and better seed grains gave a boost to agricultural production. Indeed, the 1959 harvest was so good that for the first time since the Second World War Yugoslavia had an export surplus of grain. Yugoslavia's foreign trade balance improved, her rate of economic growth was only exceeded by Japan, and industry was providing her with an export surplus of manufactured goods, which, although not of sufficiently high quality to meet great success in the Western market, were ideal for trade with underdeveloped countries.

By 1959, when new African nations began to become independent in large numbers, Yugoslavia was in a position to launch a modest political and economic offensive in Africa. It was no longer totally dependent upon the West for food or other economic aid; it had an increasing export surplus in manufactured goods, which would very well complement the imports it could hope to receive from African countries; and it had an increasing number of political, economic, and technical specialists who could be made available for service in Africa. Yugoslavia's anticolonial record in the U.N. had made it the "white" state of which most Africans were perhaps the least suspicious, and Tito had established friendships with the Asian neutralists, the Algerian FLN, and, particularly after the 1956 Suez crisis, with Nasser.

Furthermore, some of the new African states appeared particularly amenable to Yugoslav influence. Nkrumah in Ghana and Sekou Touré in Guinea had developed patterns of rule that had much more in common with Tito's. Tito, Nkrumah, and Touré had all combined one-party and one-man rule with national planning and a non-Soviet variety of authoritarian "socialism" characterized by a private peasantry plus economic decentralization within a market economy. These three also shared a curious combination of nationalism and internationalism that seems to be characteristic of small, new, and ethnically complex states that wish to play a role in international affairs.

Finally, there is another factor which gives the three states common experiences, problems and (to some extent) policies: Tito, Nkrumah, and Touré have each been engaged in the delicate and difficult task of creating a unified state out of territories formerly rent with ethnic hostility. This is a problem common to almost all emerging African states, many of whom are made up of areas initially quite arbitrarily delimited by the conflicting ambitions of the European colonial powers. The interwar history of Yugoslavia was dominated by ethnic strife, and the hundreds of thousands who perished in the fratricidal Serb-Croat struggle during the Second World War were only the greatest demonstration of its fury. The pre-1941 Yugoslav Communist Party, the nucleus of the postwar Yugoslav ruling elite, had very nearly been wrecked by factional strife, a considerable part of which was along ethnic lines. However, the common wartime partisan struggle forged an increased degree of multi-ethnic unity.[3] The genuine allegiance of the Yugoslav ruling elite to the idea of the Yugoslav state and also to the internationalist ideals of communism represents a remarkable departure from the traditions of the southern Slavs. The existence in Yugoslavia of religious hostility, of economically backward regions within one state (Bosnia and Herzegovina, Montenegro, Macedonia, and the Kosmet), and of a growing religious and cultural pluralism is potentially attractive to African leaders. The attraction is greater because, with the exception of Albania, Yugoslavia is the only European country with a strong Moslem minority (in Bosnia, Herzegovina, Macedonia, and the Kosmet), a survival of the centuries of Ottoman rule. Particularly for such a Moslem as Nasser, but also for many Moslem leaders in tropical Africa—as well as those who for other reasons of religion object to Communist atheism—this relative political and cultural tolerance, plus the rapid economic development of the backward Moslem areas of Yugoslavia, is probably a most attractive example.

Yugoslav Policy in Africa

The Yugoslav aim in Africa is, and will probably remain, much the same as it has been in Asia: to achieve a degree of political influence and economic penetration that will provide new allies and mutual assistance in foreign policy, to obtain more non-European sources of raw materials and markets for its manufactured goods, and to further the spread of communism. So far, the most important Yugoslav achievement on the continent of Africa is probably the establishment of very close relations with Nasser in Egypt and the FLN in Algeria. In many ways, Nasser's new "Arab socialism" has clearly been modeled on Yugoslav ideology and practice, and Yugoslav advisers were reported to have played a major role in drawing up the Egyptian program.[4]

Yugoslavia's ambitions are primarily focused on North Africa, largely for reasons of its geographic proximity; but the Mediterranean littoral of Africa, which is outside the geographic concerns of this chapter, is not without influence on tropical Africa. Nasser and King Hassan II of Morocco have had some influence in the south through their formation, along with Guinea, Ghana, and Mali, of the "Casablanca group." Although Yugoslavia is not officially a member of this group, it has made clear its strong support of it: one influential Yugoslav author recently called it the "core of independent Africa."[5] Yet during 1962 the influence of the Casablanca group declined sharply, and it may well be on the way out entirely.

Another major political benefit that Tito has obtained from his relations with the newly independent tropical African states was their participation in the neutralist "summit conferences" in Belgrade in September 1961 (which had been arranged, in part, during Tito's African tour the previous spring).[6] At Belgrade, with only Nigeria absent, Yugoslavia received more sympathetic understanding and support from the independent African states than did India. Tito's speech took the Soviet position on disarmament, on the Soviet resumption of arms tests, on the German question, on the European Economic Community (against the threat of whose discrimination he urged a conference of nonaligned states to plan joint defensive action), and (implicitly) on decreasing the power of the U.N. Secretary-General. Like all the other speakers, he demanded greater representation for the nonaligned states in the Security Council, the Economic and Social Council, and the Secretariat. While none of the African states came out directly against these proposals, and the more radical of them echoed part of Tito's position concerning the U.N., only Nkrumah endorsed Tito's positions on Germany, the Soviet resumption of atomic tests, and the EEC—and even he (like all the others) did not propose any limitation on the Secretary-General's powers. (Not surprisingly: for Asians and Africans the Secretary-General represented a powerful protector in times of need.) The Conference's final resolution urged a nonaligned conference on economic affairs but did not refer specifically to the EEC.

The Yugoslavs considered the Belgrade Conference a major success for their general policy of furthering and gaining influence in a neutralist group of nonaligned nations. But in fact Tito's speech identified him so firmly as a supporter of Soviet positions that he was increasingly isolated from all but the most radical African opinion. Furthermore, Nehru's personal distaste for sharing the limelight with Tito, Nasser, and Sukarno at Belgrade gave way in late 1962 to profound disillusionment over the lack of nonaligned support for India against China. In retrospect, the 1961 Belgrade Conference appears a transitory rather than a permanent symbol of Yugoslav prestige and influence among the nonaligned powers.

But the Belgrade Conference was not the only Yugoslav success in Africa. Another and lesser one resulted from the Yugoslav maneuvers during the Congo crisis.[7] The Congo question was the first great African problem in which the new African states themselves were able to play what seemed to them a significant role in international politics. For the African states, their experience in the Congo was like eating the fruit of the tree of knowledge: they lost their political innocence, acquired a taste for international diplomacy, and came to realize that they must take support where they find it. The Soviet political propaganda, economic actions, and military posture toward the Congo disillusioned even the more radical of the newly independent African states. For although Soviet support of Lumumba and Gizenga was favored by the Casablanca group, Khrushchev's cynical use of the Congo crisis as a pretext to attack the U.N. itself—the only international forum in which African votes outweighed African political weakness—lost for Moscow considerable prestige and influence in Africa.

The Yugoslavs, on the other hand, were not considered by the African states to be interested in or capable of dominating any one of them. Furthermore, the Yugoslav delegation at the U.N. managed to avoid becoming identified entirely with the Soviet position. To be sure, the delegation consistently supported the radical African position; it gave full support first to Lumumba, then to Gizenga, and, finally to Adoula; but it avoided the Soviet error of taking a totally anti-U.N. position on these problems. Whether or not this Yugoslav divergence from Soviet Congo policy was in accordance with an agreed division of roles with Moscow is uncertain. On balance, this seems rather unlikely. In 1961 Soviet and Yugoslav Congo policy (support of Lumumba and Gizenga) was identical, and by the time the Yugoslavs turned to Adoula the Soviets had lost so much good will that they were in no position to object to, and perhaps even favored, the Yugoslav switch.

Yugoslav economic policy toward the new African nations, as authoritatively set forth by Dr. Janez Stanovnik, begins with the premise that the relatively "well-developed state economic sector" in new African states, once directed entirely "toward supporting foreign investors," must now be put in the service of developing economic independence. This requires "sufficient accumulation [of capital] for expanded production," "orientation toward the home market," and direction of "economic development toward the key, or basic, branches of the economy." It follows, Stanovnik continues,

> that these objective imperative demands of economic develop-
> ment call upon the underdeveloped countries to take appropriate
> steps to restrict private capitalist tendencies, particularly in the
> foreign "capitalist sector," no matter what the ideological beliefs
> of the national political leadership.

Attacking the "counteroffensive of private capital," Stanovnik maintains that the creation of an "investment climate," as recommended by a 1954 United Nations General Assembly resolution, would mean "the abandonment of a resolute policy of economic development." Stanovnik's conclusion represents the Marxist-Leninist analysis on which Yugoslav activity in Africa and other underdeveloped areas is based:

> An analysis of the dual character of colonial economy leads to
> the conclusion that capitalism which marches forward in the
> colonialist form is met and opposed by a more or less unified
> front of the native economy and native society containing within
> itself its specific stratification (sometimes by caste, often by
> tribe, and seldom by class in the exact meaning of the term).
> Even in cases where colonialism had been compelled to make
> concessions to the natives and where it allowed the entry of the
> natives into the sector of modern production which conditioned
> the formation of the national bourgeoisie, in most instances this
> bourgeoisie was not an agent of imperialism but rather a sup-

porter of the native, that is national, element against foreign colonization.

Workers, however, represent in all colonies the most active part of the society in the struggle with colonialism. Workers are in the most immediate conflict with colonialism, a social and national enemy. Although the workers are often not too numerous insofar as their forces are concerned, nor is their class consciousness on a very high level because the process of proletarianization is still incomplete and the links with the native village remain strong, this stratum represents the most organized social force in the underdeveloped colonial countries.

Although the anticolonialist revolution is decisively anticapitalist, it does not represent primarily the struggle of hired labor against capitalist exploitation, but the rising of nearly all elements of the exploited national economy against the foreign exploiter, who appears simultaneously also as the bearer of the capitalist relations in production. That is, capitalism in the colonies has begun to develop capitalist relations in production within the limits of the capitalist economic sector, but has not started at the same time also the process of development of the national economy.

This circumstance renders possible a specific "united front" which is formed in the colonies against foreign capitalist occupation.[8]

This supports the thesis, accepted by some left-wing African leaders, of "economic neocolonialism": that the so-called Western imperialist powers are attempting to replace political with economic domination in a new conquest of Africa.

Yugoslav economic policy toward Africa, as set forth in 1960 by the Yugoslav diplomat Aleš Bebler, is the same as that of "the progressive and peace-loving forces of the outside world," who must help the African peoples

to achieve economic equality with the non-African countries, and to assure their rapid economic progress . . . [to] keep the neocolonialist tendencies of the developed countries in check, and see to it that the developed part of the world [extends] ample technical and economic assistance to the African countries, without any political conditions (the best guarantee for this would be that this aid should be given through the United Nations).

Bebler places this recommendation under the head of giving moral support to the African peoples in their effort to remain aloof from the conflict which divides the developed countries, and to achieve the maximum degree of mutual cooperation and unity.[9]

Yugoslav Activities in Africa

Because of their geographical propinquity and their earlier attainment of independence, the African states near the Mediterranean were the first with which Yugoslavia established diplomatic and economic relations. Tito visited Egypt at the end of 1955, and Nasser returned the visit in Belgrade in July 1956. Trade, payment, and credit agreements now govern the increasing number of economic relations between Belgrade and Cairo. Yugoslavia provides industrial goods, scientists and technicians, and facilities for the education of Egyptians. Yugoslav and Egyptian organizations frequently exchange visits of delegations, and the exchange of students and professors is growing. Yugoslav trade unions have been particularly active in Yugoslav operations in Egypt and elsewhere in Africa, especially with the All-African Trade Union Federation.[10]

Yugoslav relations with Ethiopia also began early and have become extensive in scope. Tito and Emperor Haile Selassie have exchanged visits, and the Yugoslav export of goods, technicians, and advisers to Addis Ababa has been considerable. In Ethiopia, Belgrade's activities are aimed chiefly at promoting economic and technical ties. There is notably little ideological common ground, but Tito's relations with Haile Selassie are an excellent demonstration of Yugoslav "non-interference in internal affairs."*

Yugoslav relations with the Sudan began in 1955; Tito and Abboud exchanged visits in 1959–60; the Yugoslavs have provided credits, industrial and consumer goods, exports, and military instructors; and, as with Egypt, cultural exchange is increasingly extensive. In British East Africa the Yugoslavs publicly favor such anticolonial African leaders as Jomo Kenyatta of Kenya and Ken-

---

* The extensive relations of Communist Yugoslavia with backward, authoritarian, and conservative Ethiopia are explicable by two facts: Ethiopia was always independent (and thus accessible to Yugoslavia), and the two countries shared a common enemy in Italy.

neth Kaunda of Northern Rhodesia.[11] Yugoslav relations with Morocco, Tunis, and especially Algeria, have been extensive since the mid-fifties, and were given additional (if temporary) strength by the formation of the Casablanca group.

Yugoslav activities in West Africa began seriously at the end of 1959, as states in that area began to gain independence. In January 1960 a Yugoslav "good will mission" visited Liberia, Sierra Leone, Guinea, Ghana, and Nigeria; these contacts were later extended by other Yugoslav delegations to Togo, Mali, the Cameroun, and the Ivory Coast. In December 1960 a Yugoslav preparatory delegation for Tito's visit the next spring toured North and West Africa; it was by then able to benefit from Yugoslavia's support of the Left-wing African position in the Congo crisis.[12]

President Tito's state visit to North and West Africa in March and April of 1961 was a success for Yugoslav policy in that area. He seems to have been received with genuine cordiality, and often with enthusiasm, by many of the new African leaders. During this trip Tito perceptively outlined the Yugoslav appeal in Africa:

> Yugoslavia constitutes an example of how a country that was enslaved and underdeveloped in the past can, with its own forces and in spite of difficulties, raise its level. . . . The people do not know what amount of material aid we can give them, but they are aware that by our presence we can offer them moral and political support.[13]

His visit brought increased political and economic relations, particularly with the Casablanca powers, and he succeeded in lining up general African attendance for his Belgrade Conference.*

The Belgrade Conference itself was not one at which the new African leaders were predominant; the major roles were taken by Tito, Nasser, Sukarno, and (unwillingly) Nehru. However, mere attendance at such a large and well-publicized meeting was for many of them their debut on the international stage—an event for which they could thank Tito. Furthermore, and presumably with Yugo-

---

* In the Sino-Soviet skirmishing at this time, Tito's visit was violently attacked by the Chinese and the Albanians as part of a plot by U.S. imperialists to gain influence in Africa by using Tito as an "agent."

slav assistance, the Belgrade Conference also introduced Adoula and Gizenga to the international set; this gave the Yugoslavs a convenient way to abandon their strong and exclusive support of Gizenga and transfer their relations to the new Adoula regime much more smoothly than the Soviets were able to do.

A Yugoslav Alternative for Africa

A Yugoslav alternative to the Soviet and Chinese interpretations of international Communism had taken shape by the mid-fifties. In his 1954 speech at Oslo, the chief Yugoslav theoretician Edvard Kardelj "relativized" the two fundamental Soviet doctrines of the dictatorship of the proletariat and the "leading" role of Moscow in the "camp of socialism."[14] He declared that a dictatorship of the proletariat (Communist Party rule) was not a necessary condition for the transition to socialism, but rather a function of the degree of economic and social development of a society; it was therefore necessary in Yugoslavia, an underdeveloped country, but it was not in a developed country like Norway. Furthermore, Tito and Kardelj had made it clear almost from the beginning of the Yugoslav break with the Soviet Union that they were unalterably opposed to the Stalinist concept of Moscow's right to serve as the leader of world "socialism." In the Yugoslav view, purely consultative (and therefore genuinely equal) relations among "socialist" states and parties are not only the most effective relationships currently attainable but also the most desirable ones in any case.

This Yugoslav emphasis on the importance of "national peculiarities," as opposed to the Soviet concept of "proletarian internationalism," made Yugoslav (as compared to Soviet or Chinese) ideology less objectionable—even to such moderate, multi-party African states as Nigeria. It clearly got around the Soviet insistence that any socialist state must have an omnipotent Communist Party and a firm alliance with Moscow. Furthermore, the Yugoslav acceptance of "national peculiarities" was extended to include "African socialism," a step that neither Moscow nor Peking has been able to take. In addition, friendly relations with Tito, who was then on relatively good terms with both Washington and Moscow, seemed unlikely to produce either Soviet or American hostility—which the African states were eager to avoid.

The Yugoslav Communists began to analyze African developments, particularly in Guinea, Ghana, and Mali, in terms of their own ideology. They began with the assumption that social and economic transformations in Africa would not "develop in the 'classic' manner."[15] From this, Yugoslav theory on Africa went so far as to recognize the necessity of encouraging foreign private capital investment in order to stimulate rapid economic development. As Vukmanović-Tempo, head of the Yugoslav trade unions, said in 1962:

> It is necessary to attract foreign capital, which would not be invested if demands for higher wages were registered and if by frequent strikes it would be endangered. . . . This, of course, requires an especially developed attitude of the workers toward foreign capital.

In the political sphere he also declared that since there are "no classes" in these countries "it is quite normal that the revolutionary party includes the entire population and that it is organized on a territorial principle."[16]

The Yugoslav regime therefore established, to a much greater extent than the Soviet Union, "party" as well as governmental relations with such leftist, one-party states as Guinea, Ghana, and Mali. The Yugoslav side of these relations was carried on not by the League of Yugoslav Communists but by the Socialist Alliance of the Working People of Yugoslavia, the Titoist mass front organization.[17] Although the leadership of both groups is nearly identical, the supposed difference between them could be of some significance from an African viewpoint. For example, the ruling party in Guinea (the PDG) is a mass organization, open to all inhabitants of the country who wish to join it, and it does not theoretically claim a class-oriented viewpoint; as such, it might have felt uncomfortable dealing with a select, disciplined Communist Party organization. And it should be noted that Yugoslavia has also cooperated with Nkrumah and other leftist African leaders in organizing and supporting such general left-wing agitprop moves as "The World Without the Bomb" conference in Accra in June 1962.[18]

The Yugoslav trade unions, like those of the Soviet Union and the

East European Communist states, have also been active in Africa. Vukmanović-Tempo, their head and one of the chief leaders in Tito's regime, undertook in early 1962 an extensive and allegedly successful tour of the countries of the Casablanca group. On his travels he propounded the Yugoslav interest in one all-embracing world-wide trade union federation and in an active trade-union commitment to the political support of rapid economic development. Yugoslav trade-union policy in Africa has centered on supporting the activities of the leftist All-African Trade Union Federation (AATUF), which is sponsored by the Casablanca group; it has opposed the rival Pan-African Trade Union Organization, and especially the anticommunist International Confederation of Free Trade Unions (ICFTU). It has criticized Chinese Communist operations in the trade-union field but has said nothing about those of the pro-Soviet World Federation of Trade Unions (WFTU).[19]

Yugoslav-African Economic Relations

The primary motive of Yugoslav policy in Africa has been and remains political. It has required, however, an economic base. To understand this, one must first consider Yugoslavia's foreign trade situation, which has been characterized—especially since 1960—by a surplus of imports over exports and a consequently unfavorable balance of payments. Despite the remarkable growth rate of the Yugoslav economy between 1954 and 1960, this pattern seems likely to continue; it has recently grown more serious and is contributing to a renewed economic crisis.

In spite of Yugoslavia's increasingly unfavorable policy toward the United States (which became marked at the Belgrade Conference in 1961), American aid, although reduced, will probably continue at least for a time. Even so, the future of Yugoslav foreign trade is increasingly unfavorable. One reason for this is that Yugoslavia finds itself caught between the rapidly expanding European Economic Community (EEC) to the west and the Council of Mutual Economic Aid (CMEA) to the east. The actual and potential growth of these two discriminatory regional trade groups, even if the United Kingdom and most of the other members of the European Free Trade Association (EFTA) do not join the EEC, seriously threatens the

Yugoslav export market. This danger began to be felt by Yugoslavia in 1960, and awareness of it has increased ever since.

During the 1959–60 period EEC accounted for one-fourth of Yugoslav exports (of which 70 per cent were agricultural or forestry products) and about one-third of her imports. The increasingly integrated and discriminatory agricultural policy of the EEC will make the Yugoslav agricultural export picture even darker. The EFTA now absorbs about 15 per cent of Yugoslav foreign trade; but London will certainly sacrifice Yugoslav foreign trade interests before those of the Commonwealth countries or other EFTA members.[20] To the east, the constantly increasing integration of the CMEA countries also adds to Yugoslav economic difficulties, which the current Soviet-Yugoslav rapprochement may alleviate but can hardly solve. Yugoslavia's foreign policy of nonalignment and her unwillingness to agree in advance to submit to decisions by the EEC Commission in Brussels (should the Commission ever make an offer to Belgrade) will probably prevent her from obtaining permanently adequate aid from the Common Market—one of the reasons, as we shall see, for Belgrade's recent reorientation toward Moscow.

Yugoslavia has therefore been engaged in an active campaign to organize nonaligned nations to combat the EEC (and, to an increasingly lessening degree, the CMEA). In September 1961, at the Belgrade Conference, Tito declared that the establishment of such organizations as the EEC and the CMEA

> constitutes one of the greatest obstacles to closer economic relations and cooperation. . . . For this reason, as well as many others, I feel that economic cooperation among the less developed countries should be established on the broadest possible basis and should include all the nonaligned countries as well as all the other less developed countries which are ready for such cooperation.[21]

Or, as the Yugoslav case was put in an authoritative article at the beginning of 1962 by the Secretary-General of President Tito's office:

> The question is posed, what should the countries which are outside the economic groups of the highly developed countries do? . . . Their activation could fundamentally proceed according to the following lines:
>
> (a) Maximum increase of mutual economic cooperation;

(b) Support of all aspirations for a more universal economic cooperation in the world;

(c) Settlement of relations with integrated groups, protection from unfavorable consequences, coupled with action to develop further economic cooperation with these groups.[22]

Shortly after this statement was made, Tito visited Cairo, where he and Nasser reportedly discussed the calling of an economic conference of nonaligned states to discuss the competition of the European Economic Community—a step that Nehru, who was also present for a short time, apparently opposed.[23] During the visit, the Egyptian government newspaper published an article by Yugoslav Foreign Minister Koča Popović which referred to the Economic Community as an instrument whereby "powers possessing tremendous resources join hands in promoting their own interests at the expense of underdeveloped nations." The article declared that nonaligned states must not be "passive" but must "take such action as may insure effective defense against this economic war waged against them."[24] Tito took the same line in his subsequent visit to the Sudan.

Later in the spring of 1962, and in part in the context of the growing Soviet-Yugoslav rapprochement, Belgrade's anti-Common Market line became even stronger. As one authoritative Yugoslav spokesman wrote in April:

> The European Common Market is not merely an instrument of the interbloc cold war, but also, if not more so, an instrument which gives rise to quite a new and disturbing situation. . . . [It] is a new way of setting up intergovernmental cartels aimed at preserving privileged positions by maintaining unequal cooperation with the outside world and [at] imposing unequal economic cooperation on third countries—of course, primarily on those which are weaker, smaller, and in the process of development. . . . This is really an attempt on the part of a group of industrially developed countries to impose by their economic strength and political power certain relations and conditions of cooperation on countries in the process of development—which can best be designated as "neocolonialism."[25]

Nevertheless, the extent of Yugoslav trade with the Common Market countries, and Tito's continuing desire to avoid total political com-

TABLE 1.—SHARE OF REGIONAL TRADING GROUPS
IN YUGOSLAV FOREIGN TRADE, 1959–62

(*percentages*)

Trade Group	1959 Export	1959 Import	1960 Export	1960 Import	1961 Export	1961 Import	1962 Export	1962 Import
EEC	26.2	28.2	25.6	32.6	26.0	35.7	27.3	28.3
CMEA	30.8	24.7	32.1	25.5	30.9	18.6	24.1	21.2
EFTA	16.0	12.6	15.6	13.9	15.6	12.2	14.7	12.4
Total	73.0	65.5	73.3	72.0	72.5	66.5	66.1	61.9

ECC without Luxembourg in 1962. CMEA without Albania and in 1962 without Mongolia. EFTA without Portugal and in 1962 without Norway.
Sources: For 1959–61: *Statistički Godnišnjak FNRJ*, 1962, p. 188. For 1962: *Indeks*, XII, 2 (Feb. 1963), p. 32.

TABLE 2.—YUGOSLAV LONG-TERM LOANS TO AFRICAN COUNTRIES, 1958–61

Country	Amount (*million dollars*)	Interest (*per cent*)	Date of Credit Agreement
Egypt	10.0	3	1958
Sudan	15.4	—	1958
Ethiopia	10.0	—	1959
Libya	3.0	3	1960
Morocco	5.0	3	1960
Guinea	5.0	3	1960
Tunisia	5.0	3	1960
Guinea	2.0	—	1961

Sources: For Egypt, Sudan, and Ethiopia: Djurić, *op. cit.*, pp. 5–30. For Libya, Morocco, Guinea, and Tunisia: U.N. Economic and Social Council, Statistics of Official Contribution in 1960, Report by the Secretary-General (E/3556), p. 44. For Guinea, 1961: *Politika*, Dec. 15, 1961.

mitment to either East or West, make it likely that Belgrade will try to retain as much as it can of its trade with Western Europe while increasing its trade with the CMEA and nonaligned countries.[26]

The bulk of Yugoslav foreign trade, therefore, is with areas that are rapidly becoming members of discriminatory trading groups. One obvious (but so far largely unsuccessful) Yugoslav countermove has been to attempt to redirect foreign trade toward the developing, nonaligned African and Asian countries. This effort will become more attractive, and perhaps more successful, when more African and Asian countries find themselves in Yugoslavia's situation vis-à-vis the European discriminatory trading blocs. To make it even easier for Yugoslavia, most of these countries are not already associated with EEC or Commonwealth states, precisely because their left-wing political policies make such association as undesirable as it is for Yugoslavia.

Such a realignment of Yugoslav foreign trade with African and Asian countries would also enable Yugoslavia to diversify its exports to include more finished products, as well as to carry out technical assistance activities (such as surveying and construction) whose profits would improve the Yugoslav trade balance. There has already been some progress in this direction. In 1956 the total value of such invisible revenues was $5,100,000, a figure which by 1958 had risen to over $13.3 million.[27]

By the end of 1960 total long-term Yugoslav loan commitments to Africa and Asia amounted to $135 million, but actual expenditures for these loans had reached only $26 million, and almost all of that was spent in 1960. In Africa between 1956 and 1959, Egypt, the Sudan, and Ethiopia got the main share of Yugoslav credits. Yugoslavia was engaged in diversified activity, ranging from the repair of the old Aswan dam in Egypt and the construction of the port of Asab in Ethiopia to the erection of leather, cardboard, and metal processing factories in the Sudan. In the framework of United Nations economic assistance to underdeveloped countries, Yugoslavia provides long-term loans for these activities, most of them at 3 per cent interest. In 1960, parallel with her extended political activity, Yugoslavia concluded credit agreements with Guinea, Libya, Morocco, and Tunisia, thereby extending greatly her export outlets in Africa. (See Table 2.)

The Yugoslav-African trade picture over the last four or five years, in spite of extensive Yugoslav efforts and expectations, still shows relatively slow progress. From 1956 to 1957 total Yugoslav exports to Africa tripled, and imports from Africa more than doubled. If, however, one excludes Egypt from this total, this early progress becomes considerably less impressive. (See Table 3.) In comparison with total Yugoslav export-import figures, the Yugoslav-African trade picture reveals great instability. The 1961 figures indicated

TABLE 3.—DYNAMICS OF YUGOSLAV FOREIGN TRADE WITH AFRICA, 1956–62

(Index: 1957 = 100)

Year	Yugoslavia		Africa (total)		Africa (without Egypt)	
	Export	Import	Export	Import	Export	Import
1956	81.8	71.7	33.1	48.7	57.6	55.0
1957	100.0	100.0	100.0	100.0	100.0	100.0
1958	111.7	103.6	133.0	129.0	145.8	129.0
1959	120.6	104.1	111.3	134.1	134.3	169.0
1960	143.3	125.0	164.8	351.3	200.2	279.9
1961	144.0	137.6	128.0	141.7	129.4	222.9
1962	174.9	134.2	249.9	165.6	407.3	215.5

Source: Computed from Table 6.

TABLE 4.—PROPORTION OF AFRICAN TRADE TO TOTAL YUGOSLAV TRADE, 1956–62

(in per cent)

Year	Africa *(as per cent of total)*		Africa without Egypt *(as per cent of total)*	
	Export	Import	Export	Import
1956	2.11	1.53	1.32	0.68
1957	5.22	2.25	1.88	0.89
1958	6.22	2.81	2.45	1.11
1959	4.82	2.91	2.09	1.45
1960	6.00	6.34	2.63	1.99
1961	4.64	2.32	1.69	1.44
1962	7.46	2.78	4.38	1.43

Source: Computed from Table 6.

TABLE 5.—BALANCE OF TRADE, YUGOSLAVIA AND AFRICA WITHOUT EGYPT, 1956–62

(in millions of dinars)

Year	Volume	Yugoslavia		Yugoslav Trade Balance
		Exports	Imports	
1956	2,259	1,285	974	311
1957	3,999	2,229	1,770	459
1958	5,540	3,249	2,291	958
1959	5,958	2,993	2,992	1
1960	9,418	4,463	4,955	−492
1961	6,829	2,884	3,945	−1,061
1962	12,893	9,078	3,815	5,263

Source: Computed from Table 6.

a drastic decline, particularly in imports from Africa (including Egypt), this being in large part a result of the greatly increased Yugoslav imports from Western Europe in that year. Figures for 1962 show that Yugoslav-African trade rose again to a level almost twice that of 1961 but still lower than the 1960 peak. This latest change arose primarily from an increase in Yugoslav exports (a result of previously granted credits) and improved Yugoslavia's temporarily deteriorating balance of trade with the African countries. (See Table 6.)

The proportion of trade with Africa within total Yugoslav foreign trade is relatively insignificant—roughly 4.5 per cent of exports and an even lower proportion of imports—but may represent the saturation point for some time to come. (See Table 4.) When one adds to this the present Yugoslav internal economic crisis, it becomes clear that the future of Yugoslav-African economic relations is still far from bright. This is all the worse because only with Africa and Asia has Yugoslavia generally had an export surplus.

The small total volume and the scanty statistics available preclude an accurate country-by-country analysis of Yugoslav-African trade. However, certain meaningful groupings of countries in this context can be isolated. The North African countries, the Sudan, and Ethiopia have received the most loans; Algeria and the (former Belgian) Congo fall into the same category, but Yugoslavia has only recently begun to grant them credits. Political considerations have so far inhibited Yugoslav trade with South Africa, the Rhodesias, and the Portuguese African colonies. The third group includes Ghana, Guinea, and Mali—countries politically closely associated with Yugoslavia but at the same time (except for Guinea) active partners in the EEC or the Commonwealth. (See Table 5.) No details by country are yet available for 1962.

In order to reverse this unfavorable trend, Yugoslavia has recently launched an intensive trade promotion campaign in Africa, in combination with its expanding political activities. Yugoslav participation in African trade fairs, organized by the newly established Belgrade Institute of the Federal Foreign Trade Chamber for Economic Propaganda in Foreign Countries, has been increased. Some 120 Yugoslav enterprises participated, for example, in the first Accra trade fair.

TABLE 6.—TOTAL FOREIGN TRADE OF YUGOSLAVIA WITH PRINCIPAL AFRICAN COUNTRIES, 1956–62

(million current dinars; official exchange rate, 1 dollar = 300 dinars)

	1956		1957		1958		1959		1960		1961		1962	
	Export	Import	Export	Import	Export	Import	Export	Import	Export	Import	Export	Import	Export	Import
Total Trade	97,011	142,243	118,533	198,394	132,419	205,504	142,995	206,156	169,848	247,916	170,670	273,087	207,318	266,263
Trade with Africa	2,045	2,179	6,187	4,473	8,230	5,768	6,888	6,000	10,199	15,713	7,922	6,338	15,459	7,409
Africa minus Egypt	1,285	974	2,229	1,770	3,249	2,291	2,993	2,992	4,463	4,955	2,884	3,945	9,078	3,815
Egypt	760	1,205	3,958	2,703	4,981	3,477	3,895	3,008	5,736	10,758	5,038	2,393	6,381	3,594
Algeria	498	277	509	115	795	105	444	0	345	118	164	6	722	101
Ethiopia	83	15	120	532	88	379	146	407	494	695	159	386	302	729
Morocco	221	18	236	121	193	330	184	292	195	917	182	728	624	494
Tunisia	109	39	66	418	162	712	472	683	656	645	434	1,030	...	...
Ghana	14	...	8	...	13	...	61	455	84	319	...	...	...	...
Liberia	7	...	709	...	1,529	2	817	...	1,246	64	...	...	...	...
Belgian Congo	38	...	107	15	37	66	42	124	...	60	...	...	...	...
Rep. of So. Africa	63	128	39	231	41	285	26	557	79	1,318	76	649	...	...
Sudan	42	256	133	21	57	98	364	160	316	68	505	13	1,377	*72
Libya	175	...	169	...	149	5	215	24	176	...	...	...	...	...
Rest of Africa	35	241	133	317	185	309	222	290	872	751	1,364	1,133	6,053	2,419

* Eleven months only. Sources: (1) Total Yugoslav trade and African totals, 1956–61: *Statistički Godišnjak FNRJ*, 1962, p. 188.
(2) Algeria, Egypt, Ethiopia, Morocco, Tunisia, 1956–61: *Ibid.*
(3) Libya, Sudan, Belgian Congo, Republic of South Africa, Ghana, 1956–59: *U.N. Yearbook of International Trade Statistics, 1960*, p. 598; Republic of South Africa, 1960–61: *Statistical Pocketbook of Yugoslavia* (Belgrade, 1962), p. 69.
(4) Ghana, Liberia, 1960: *Yugoslav Survey*, II, 6 (July–September 1961), p. 380.
(5) Libya, Belgian Congo, South Africa, 1960: U.N., International Monetary Fund, and International Bank for Reconstruction and Development, *Direction of International Trade*, Statistical Papers, Series T, XI, 11–12 (November–December 1960).
(6) Sudan, 1960–62: *Commercial News of Yugoslavia* (Belgrade), IX, 3 (Feb. 1, 1963), p. 2
(7) 1962, all countries except Sudan: *Indeks*, XII, 2 (February 1963), p. 32.

In early 1961 Yugoslavia opened a trade exhibition in Khartoum. Tito's 1961 visit to West Africa, as indicated by all the joint communiqués issued, involved trade promotion as well as political activities.

When one considers that Yugoslavia had strong political and even stronger economic motives for its trade drive in Africa, one may well ask why it has had what can only be considered a disappointing degree of success. Primarily, of course, the reason is Yugoslavia's economic weakness in relation to the developed countries of both East and West. The United States, Britain, West Germany, or France on the one hand, and the Soviet Union, Czechoslovakia, or East Germany on the other, are far better able to expand their trade with the developing African countries. They can invest more capital and grant more credits for its promotion. Furthermore, the African countries producing primarily raw materials, naturally at a disadvantage before industrialized countries, can hope to profit more by trade with larger, more prosperous countries—which can absorb diversified exports (including luxury items) and provide a chance to earn hard currencies—than they stand to gain by trading with a relatively poor, soft-currency, importing country like Yugoslavia. Yugoslavia's foreign trade prospects in the whole African area are clearly not too encouraging. The best she can hope for, probably, is an increase in trade with those countries in Africa which, like her, are caught in the bind between the growing EEC and CMEA.

Internal Crisis and Rapprochement with the Soviet Union

Since 1961 Yugoslavia has retreated from domestic liberalization and arranged an extensive rapprochement with the Soviet Union—both developments that are bound to affect Yugoslav policy toward Africa. By early 1962 the Yugoslav economy was again in a major crisis. The high industrial growth rate (15 per cent in 1960) fell to 7 per cent in 1961 and 1962.[28] The liberalization of foreign trade and the further decentralization of industry in 1961 led to an enormous increase in the foreign trade deficit, caused by a rush to import from abroad, particularly consumer goods. (See Table 6.) The loosening of central control over the factories produced a rapid rise in wage fund expenditures, which far exceeded productivity increases.

Bad harvests in 1960, 1961, and 1962 added to the crisis, and political restrictions placed on the private peasantry made agricultural productivity stagnant as well. The regime's increased emphasis on economics rather than politics had demoralized many of the party cadres, and the permanent top-level feud between the Serb Ranković and the Slovene Kardelj reached new heights. Finally, the success of the European Common Market, its implementation in agriculture and the resultant threat to Yugoslav agricultural exports, and the advancing integration of the Soviet camp in CMEA increasingly threatened Yugoslavia with economic isolation.

In 1962 Tito began cracking down internally. His May 1962 speech at Split indicated that he planned a significant increase in political and economic centralization and a major attempt to revitalize the party as the prime directing element in national affairs. Even more strikingly, this and subsequent speeches openly revealed official concern over the problem of national and ethnic hostility within Yugoslavia—an indication that the situation must be serious indeed.

By 1962 the steadily mounting Sino-Soviet dispute made both Khrushchev and Tito more desirous of a mutual rapprochement. Khrushchev's whole policy of a "socialist commonwealth" rather than a totally Moscow-dominated international Communist movement (originally intended to stabilize endangered Soviet influence in China and Eastern Europe) had been greatly intensified by the Sino-Soviet dispute; obviously, he needed allies with which to face China.

The "socialist commonwealth" to which Tito could return was a far cry from Stalin's "socialist camp." For Tito and his associates, particularly the more dogmatic Serb Communists around Ranković, the terms for rejoining the "socialist commonwealth" seemed favorable: it would not seriously impinge on their internal affairs; it would at least partially compensate, through increased Soviet trade and aid, for the damage the EEC threatened to bring to Yugoslavia; it would give the more orthodox Yugoslav Communists a renewed sense of ideological assurance and "fraternal solidarity"; and for Ranković and the Serb Communists it would provide a source of possible support in the event of Tito's death, which would probably trigger increased hostility in Croatia and Slovenia toward Serb Communist hegemony.[29]

Moves toward the rapprochement came in rapid succession. In April 1962 Soviet Foreign Minister Gromyko visited Belgrade, returning Popović's 1961 visit to Moscow; shortly before he arrived, Djilas was rearrested. In May, Khrushchev made a strongly pro-Yugoslav statement, and for the first time since 1948 the Belgrade May Day parade displayed Soviet-made tanks. Yugoslav-Soviet trade agreements were sharply expanded, and exchanges of delegations rose rapidly. Finally, in December Tito visited Moscow and addressed the Supreme Soviet. He indicated that Yugoslav criticism of the Soviet Union and other "socialist states" would cease, that the crackdown on liberal tendencies in Yugoslavia would continue, and that Yugoslav foreign policy, while remaining nonaligned and on friendly terms with the West, would be even more favorable toward Moscow and other socialist states. To be sure, both sides acknowledged that "ideological differences" remained; Tito clearly did not intend to abandon his freedom of action either domestically or among the underdeveloped and nonaligned countries; and he undoubtedly hoped, as in 1956, to acquire more influence within the Communist world. Nevertheless, as of May 1963 Yugoslav foreign policy, in Africa and elsewhere, was substantially in line with Moscow's.

The Sino-Soviet split has produced several alignments within the international Communist movement, notably one alignment on policy issues and another on the organizational issue (*i.e.*, the nature and extent of Soviet control and influence). On policy issues, most left-wing African leaders, like the Yugoslavs, the Poles, and the Italians, will probably be on the Soviet side, although some of them may find the extreme anticolonialism of the Chinese position more attractive. On the organizational issue, however, there is ground for agreement by all small states, even the extremist ones who may favor the Chinese, on the necessity of resisting centralized Soviet control. Such lineups occurred, for example, at the December 1961 meeting of the World Peace Congress in Stockholm and at the Third Afro-Asian Solidarity Conference in Moshi, Tanganyika, in early February 1963. At these meetings the Chinese insistence on giving priority to anticolonialism over general disarmament was shared not only by the

Albanians but also by some African delegates.[30] But on such organizational issues as the degree of relative autonomy to be allowed the various national units within a group like the WFTU, the Chinese could (if only tactically) take the same position as did the Italians and the Yugoslavs at the December 1961 Moscow WFTU meeting.[31] In this complex and slippery field of maneuver, the Yugoslavs and some of the more extremist African states may well find common ground and common possibilities for profit. Tito has a long record of operating successfully on the fringes of the Sino-Soviet complex, and his advice on how to do this has reportedly been accepted with gratitude by Nasser and Sekou Touré.

On the crucial matter of the Common Market, however, Yugoslav policy is likely to diverge further from that of most of the tropical African states. Some sixteen African states, plus the former French colonies (except Guinea) and the Republic of the Congo, are associated with the Common Market, and they are unlikely to give up the trade advantages and increasing economic aid they are receiving from it. The hostility to the Common Market of almost all the ex-British African states, so strikingly demonstrated at the September 1962 London Commonwealth Conference, may not be permanent; even if Britain does not join the EEC, many of these states may well eventually associate themselves with it. There are some recent indications that even Guinea, now engaged in a rapprochement with Senegal and the Ivory Coast, may be reconsidering its hostility to the EEC. The Common Market, however, seems unlikely to make any inviting concessions to Yugoslavia, a Communist country, and one which has had no diplomatic relations with West Germany since 1957 and seems a likely signatory to any Soviet-sponsored peace treaty with the Ulbricht regime. It is not surprising that Yugoslavs have been attacking the Common Market; they would not have gotten much from it in any case.

Yugoslavia's Future in Africa

Tito's undoubted desires to get more influence in the "socialist commonwealth" and to retain if not expand what he already has in Asia and Africa seem at least partially incompatible. For all but the most radical African leaders, his rapprochement with Moscow will hardly increase their trust in his nonalignment, particularly since Soviet and Yugoslav policies in Africa (as elsewhere) are likely to be increasingly coordinated. For the Soviet Union, the Yugoslavs can be most useful in Africa as intermediaries in such countries as Guinea, where Moscow so recently met with humiliation; for Yugoslavia, the small but existing community of interests against Western efforts in Africa (e.g., against the ICFTU and the Common Market) can safely be expanded without decisively imperiling the fruits of its recent African policy.

But it is also true that Soviet-Yugoslav policy alignment toward Africa is unlikely to be either total or permanent. Khrushchev's and Tito's objectives are far from identical, and Tito has too long tasted the joys of independent action to defer completely to Moscow. Nor need rapprochement be lasting: were Khrushchev to die tomorrow, his successors might make a serious attempt at a rapprochement with the Chinese, and for this end they would probably be willing to sacrifice their relations with Yugoslavia. Knowing this, the Yugoslavs are likely to insist on retaining some capacity for independent action. In Africa it appears that they may be adjusting their propaganda line to please Moscow while leaving their activities largely unchanged.[32]

But Yugoslavia must labor under obstacles more formidable even than her rapprochement with Moscow. Not only is Yugoslavia economically weak; despite its attractions for Africans, it is also European. Most African leaders are profoundly isolationist, uninterested in world affairs except when they feel threatened themselves, and suspicious of all outside influence. For an African south of the Sahara, Belgrade, like Washington and Moscow, is very far away; unlike Washington or Moscow, it need not be feared. Where Yugoslav-African interests coincide, Africans will gladly accept Yugoslav help; where they do not, African leaders, unlike Tito (or Nehru or Sukarno), will remain content to cultivate their own gardens in their own way. For these reasons Yugoslavia is unlikely to have any major influence over the thoughts and actions of the new African states.

5

CHINA

Richard Lowenthal

The Communist impact on Africa was greatly strengthened and profoundly modified when a non-white, non-European Communist power finally appeared on the scene as an active political force. Communist China, presenting herself as a former fellow victim of colonial oppression and exploitation, could offer her own experience as a model for the African struggle to throw off the shackles and repair the ravages of imperialist rule. This claim to a special relationship with all colonial and ex-colonial peoples made her not only a uniquely qualified ally but also a potentially dangerous rival for Soviet penetration of the African continent.

The Peking Approach

The claim that the Chinese revolution stands as a paradigm for all anti-imperialist liberation movements was put forth long before the beginnings of Chinese political activity in Africa (which may be dated from the first cultural agreement between Peking and President Nasser's Egypt in May 1955), and indeed, even before the victory of the Communists in China itself: it dates from a textbook for Chinese Communists written by Mao Tse-tung in Yenan in 1939, during the period of their guerrilla warfare against the Japanese occupation.[1]

Mao then argued that his party was fighting imperialism and feu-

The author wishes to express his gratitude to Dr. Franz Ansprenger, the author of *Politik im schwarzen Afrika* and a colleague at Berlin University. Dr. Ansprenger generously placed at the author's disposal his own research material on Chinese activity in Africa, without which this essay could not have been written.

dalism with the support of a grand alliance of classes: the proletariat, the peasantry, the petty bourgeoisie, and the patriotic "national bourgeoisie." It was thus leading a new type of "bourgeois-democratic revolution"—bourgeois-democratic because it was not, at that stage, directed against capitalist private property, but of a new type because it was taking place under the leadership of the "party of the proletariat," i.e., the Communist Party. Mao called it the "new-democratic revolution" and defined it as "a revolution of the broad masses of the people led by the proletariat and directed against imperialism and feudalism."[2]

The advantage of this strategy in Mao's eyes was that it enabled the Communists, with their organization, energy, and flexibility, to take the lead at a time when the proletariat was still weak and the socio-economic conditions for a real "socialist revolution" were missing, and thus to create the conditions for that second stage while still completing, with the support of the "allied" classes, the necessary first stage—the "bourgeois-democratic revolution." Mao was so enthusiastic about his discovery that he proclaimed even then, with a dogmatism that matched his extreme physical isolation, that "this kind of revolution is developing in China as well as in all colonial and semicolonial countries."[3] However, few people outside China heard of it, and even the Communists of other countries apparently took little notice at the time.

Yet ten years later, a few weeks after the conquest of the Chinese mainland had been completed, the same claim was repeated by a Chinese leader before an international Communist forum and was apparently endorsed with only minor reservations by Moscow. Addressing the opening session of a conference of the World Federation of Trade Unions (WFTU) in Peking on November 16, 1949, Liu Shao-chi laid down the rule that "the course followed by the Chinese people in defeating imperialism and its lackeys and in founding the People's Republic of China is the course that should be followed by the peoples of the various colonial and semicolonial countries in their fight for national independence and people's democracy." He defined the essential characteristics of that course as follows: (1) a nationwide alliance of the working class and all other groups and classes willing to fight imperialism; (2) leadership of that alliance in the hands of the working class, which in turn must be led by a highly disciplined Communist Party; and (3) a national liberation army led by the Communist Party "wherever and whenever possible."[4]

The resolution adopted by the Peking trade-union conference, with more reserve, emphasized that each of the colonial and semicolonial countries of Asia should "take into account local conditions and national characteristics and use the appropriate methods to achieve people's unity in the fight for genuine national independence, for democracy and peace, and against the imperialists and their agents"; it did add, however, that "for the correct assessment of these methods, valuable lessons may be drawn from the experience of the Chinese people."[5] Moreover, Liu's speech was reprinted in full not only in the Cominform weekly, but also in *Pravda*—a significant sign of endorsement.[6] Finally, Liu's claim of China's exemplary role was soon requoted editorially in the Cominform weekly, with emphasis on the need for broad, nationwide united fronts against imperialism under Communist leadership, in an article designed to urge that policy on the Indian Communist Party.[7]

Since 1949 the importance of colonial "liberation movements" of various types has grown steadily and has gained increasing recognition from strategists of the Soviet bloc and the international Communist movement. The "Chinese model," however, has proved as difficult to imitate in the colonial and ex-colonial countries as the "Soviet model" of 1917 proved in Europe. To this day, North Vietnam remains the only country besides China where an anti-imperialist national front under Communist leadership has conquered power. (In Cuba, the Communists never led the Castro movement before it was victorious, and indeed allied themselves with it only at a late stage of its development.) Elsewhere, the map of the world has been transformed, in part by the emergence of new sovereign nations without revolutionary conflict with the "imperialists," and in part by anti-imperialist national and social revolutions led by intellectuals and officers whom the Communists regard as representatives of the "national bourgeoisie." As a result of these events, endorsements of the Chinese claim to serve as a more or less typical, if not universal, model for revolutions in colonial and ex-colonial countries have long disappeared from the Soviet and international Communist press. In the 1960 Moscow declaration of 81 Communist parties, there is only the bland assertion that the Chinese revolution, "by giving a further powerful impetus to the national liberation movement, exerted tremendous influence on the peoples, especially those of Asia, Africa and Latin America."[8]

The Chinese Communist leaders themselves, as we shall see, have often been as ready as their Soviet allies to seek practical relations of "peaceful coexistence" with the new "bourgeois nationalist" governments, and even to join in active cooperation with revolutionary nationalist movements under non-Communist leadership. But they have not abandoned their ideological claim. "The Chinese revolution," wrote Liu Shao-chi in October 1959, on the tenth anniversary of the founding of the Chinese People's Republic, "has a great attraction for peoples in all the backward countries that have suffered, or are suffering, from imperialist oppression. They feel that they should also be able to do what the Chinese have done." And he went on to repeat Mao's strategic discovery of how to combine the advantages of "revolution by stages" with those of "uninterrupted revolution": "The firm grasping of the hegemony in the democratic revolution by the proletariat through the Communist Party is the key to ensuring the thorough victory of the democratic revolution and the successful switchover from the democratic revolution to the socialist revolution."[9] It is true that no other method of achieving Communist power in those countries has so far succeeded at all: if the Chinese prescription has been found difficult to apply, its authors may well feel that it is still the only one that has proved its worth.

In Chinese eyes, then, the countries of Asia, Africa, and Latin America remain the potential field for revolutions of the Chinese type, the area in which they have a special contribution of ideological leadership to offer. But the Chinese Communists know from their own experience that the formation, maturing, and victory of a Communist Party may well take several decades; and these same vast regions of the world in which they hope for revolutions are also of more immediate and short-range concern to China as a state. Like its Russian counterpart, Chinese foreign policy springs from two roots: considerations of "normal" power politics—of the "national interest"

—and concern for the ideological vision of the road to world communism. These two motivations continuously mingle, interpenetrate, and modify each other. If the peculiarities of their revolutionary experience have turned the Chinese Communists' ideological vision toward "Afro-Asianism," their power politics have been turned in the same direction by the peculiarities of their international situation—notably, their unsolved territorial conflict with the United States over Taiwan, their concern with American alliances and bases in Asia, and their separation from Western Europe, made doubly strong by the weakness of diplomatic links and the existence of a Soviet geographical shield (or barrier) between them.

The foreign policy of Communist China naturally took shape first in Asia. Policies toward Africa and later Latin America developed by extension from those first conceived for Asia, while policies toward Europe remained for a long time a mere echo of Soviet policies. Again, the central formative experience for Peking's Asian policy was conflict with "United States Imperialism"—not merely with the U.S. as the leading power of the postwar "imperialist camp" and the principal obstacle to Communist expansion, as it appeared to the Soviets, but as a specific and deadly enemy of the Chinese People's Republic, a direct physical threat to its birth and survival. As the Chinese Communists saw it, the United States had supported Chiang Kai-shek in the civil war, and had continued to use him as a puppet to justify their own occupation of the Chinese island of Taiwan. United States troops under the U.N. flag had approached the Chinese border during the Korean war, and had clashed with the Chinese "volunteers" in the first bitter and bloody external war fought by the new state. United States diplomacy had got the majority of the United Nations both to condemn Communist China's intervention in Korea as aggression and to refuse her the place in the world organization that she considered rightfully hers; it was also the direct cause of the reluctance of many other countries to take up diplomatic relations with Peking or to sell her vital goods. A single archvillain thus filled the roles of past counterrevolutionary interventionist, recent wartime foe, and present-day leader of the forces of world reaction; the U.S. became at once the chief class enemy and chief national enemy of China.

The overriding objective of Peking's Asian policy has therefore always been to keep United States bases and alliances as far away as possible from China's borders. According to the situation, this objective could be furthered by a variety of means—from direct military action by supporting anti-imperialist revolutionary movements (Communist or non-Communist) to the wooing of "bourgeois nationalist" governments to keep them out of the South East Asia Treaty Organization (SEATO). The one means that never seems to have been seriously considered is a direct effort to normalize relations with the United States; that is viewed as hopeless so long as no responsible Americans, critics of the policy of non-recognition included, are prepared to accept Peking's title to Taiwan and to abandon its protection.

The difference between Russian and Chinese hostility toward the United States thus promotes different tactics. In trying to consolidate and extend the territory under their control and to reduce the cohesion and influence of the Western bloc, the Soviets are free to alternate between two methods: they can direct their military, diplomatic, and revolutionary pressure and their political and economic offers toward individual exposed pro-Western states or they can propose an over-all accommodation with the West and even suggest a Russo-American dialogue on the division of the world. The Chinese Communists, unable to use the second method, and viewing every hint of its use by the Soviets with intense suspicion, take little interest in any efforts to influence American and over-all Western policy by the impact of diplomatic proposals on public opinion.

This, in turn, leads to a difference between Russian and Chinese attitudes toward the "uncommitted" governments of the "third world." For the Chinese even more than for the Russians, all such governments have the essential negative merit of keeping out American bases. But short of coming under Communist leadership, there is only one way in which they can acquire positive merit in Chinese eyes: by engaging in armed conflict with one of the imperialist powers, or by actively supporting liberation movements involved in such a conflict, and thus weakening the "imperialist camp" by compelling a dispersal of its forces. The Soviets, on the other hand, can also see positive merit in the support of such uncommitted countries for some of their own proposals in the United Nations, and they are generally

conscious of the indirect influence they may exert on Western policy-
formation by influencing the policy of "third" countries for which
the West is forced to compete; conversely, they see in the spreading
of colonial wars of liberation not only a chance of weakening the
enemy but also a risk of provoking him to undesirable lengths which
has to be carefully controlled. Accordingly, the Soviets, while naturally preferring those uncommitteed countries whose neutrality is
more "positive" in their rejection of "imperialism," will constantly
endeavor to influence all of them by economic aid and political argument. The Chinese, on the other hand, do not hesitate on occasion
to bully and offend major uncommitted countries, stopping short only
of measures that might drive them into military alliance with the
West; they will consistently befriend only those who are committed
to an active anti-imperialist struggle.

Chinese policy toward new states and nationalist movements thus
began with the negative objective of preventing them from concluding alliances with the West, and then added the positive objective of
involving them whenever possible in armed conflict with the West.*
To some extent, this policy is clearly in harmony with the ideological
preference for "liberation by armed struggle" derived from the Chinese Communists' own revolutionary experience; but it is not determined solely by doctrinaire considerations. Ideologically, both the
Chinese and the Russians regard the "national bourgeoisie" as an
unreliable force, and a fortiori an undesirable leader, in the anti-
imperialist struggle. Practically, both are prepared to cooperate with
governments and movements led by "bourgeois" nationalists, even if
the latter persecute their native Communists, so long as these governments and movements can in fact be useful in the overriding conflict
between the Communist powers and the West. The difference is that
the Russians judge this usefulness by willingness to give support to
Russia's general policies on peace, disarmament, European security,
and decolonization; the Chinese, however, measure it much more

* In China's relations with her immediate Asian neighbors, other objectives do
play a role; among them are deterring support for opposition groups in Chinese-
controlled territory, extending China's strategic frontiers, establishing Peking's influence over the overseas Chinese population, and creating Communist satellite
regimes. But at present these are of no importance for the broad line of Chinese
foreign policy that is extended to Africa.

specifically by readiness either to engage in direct armed conflict with the "imperialists" or to give active support to associated movements that are so engaged.

As we shall see, Chinese support for nationalist governments and movements under non-Communist leadership may actually be far less inhibited, either by tactical caution or ideological reservations, than Russian support—provided only that the nationalist leaders concerned meet the exacting Chinese standard of anti-imperialist militance. On one side, they are less concerned than the Soviets about the possible risks of all-out support for local "wars of liberation"; on the other hand, they are more willing to avoid all ideological criticism of certain "bourgeois-nationalist" leaders from a class point of view, so long as they are satisfied about the role of these leaders in the anti-imperialist struggle. In recent years, the Russian and the Soviet-controlled international Communist press has frequently criticized the domestic policies of Afro-Asian nationalist statesmen who were at the time receiving Soviet economic aid; the current needs of Soviet diplomacy and the long-term needs of the development of Communist parties in the new countries were met by the simultaneous use of different channels. The Chinese Communists, while equally aware of the two needs, have generally avoided speaking with two different voices in public: they have officially adopted ideological criticism when the anti-imperialist attitude of a "bourgeois nationalist" government has ceased to satisfy them, but they have silenced all public criticism when they have considered it a valuable fighting ally.*

The Chinese Entrance into Africa

When the Chinese Communists in 1949 announced their claim to ideological leadership of revolutionary movements in "colonial and semicolonial countries," they were only just emerging from a prolonged geographical isolation. The Peking conference of Communist-controlled trade unions from Asia and Australasia addressed by Liu Shao-chi was one of the first occasions on which they could reach an

* The first attitude can be seen in the Chinese attacks on Nasser in 1959, and the second in Peking's silence on the nonrecognition of the Algerian Communist Party and the banning of the Moroccan Communist Party by the nationalist leaders of those two countries.

international forum of fellow Asians; as for Africans, it is doubtful whether any contacts with them existed at all, apart from occasional meetings between Chinese and African expatriates in Moscow.

In most of Asia, however, neither governments nor Communists could henceforth afford to ignore the new revolutionary power that had arisen in China. Within a year, Peking had established itself as a major factor in the Asian balance of power with an influence on Asian Communist policy second only to Moscow's; the creation of an Asian liaison office of the WFTU with its seat in Peking was at least an outward, technical recognition of that influence.

It was different at first in Africa. The physical impact of the new Communist empire was hardly felt to the west of Pakistan, and certainly not beyond the Indian Ocean. As for the sparse Communist cadres and the more important front organizations in colonial Africa, they owed their existence to the Communist parties and Communist-controlled trade unions in the "imperialist" mother countries, and their connections with the Communist world movement continued to depend exclusively on those West European mentors at least until late 1955.[10]

It is noteworthy, moreover, that while the subordination of the West African pro-Communist unions to the French Confédération Générale du Travail (CGT) was gradually ended after 1955 in favor of the creation of independent Pan-African unions assisted and influenced directly by the WFTU, this important sector of WFTU activity continued to be handled largely by its French personnel.[11] The current intensified drive for the training of Communist cadres and the preparation of orthodox Communist parties in tropical Africa is again conducted under the guidance of British and French Communists. At no stage has there been evidence of major Chinese influence on the African operations of the WFTU or of the other worldwide front organizations—with the exception, perhaps, of the World Federation of Democratic Youth and the International Union of Students; it seems safe to say that before 1956 their influence in this field was nil.

In fact, the Chinese breakthrough into Africa was first achieved on the diplomatic plane and only later extended to the plane of organized political influence. Diplomatically, it was prepared at the Bandung Conference of Asian-African states in April 1955, where

Premier Chou En-lai met President Nasser; it was consummated with the opening of full diplomatic relations between Egypt and China just over a year later. Organizationally, the Chinese got their first real bridgehead for political activity in Africa when the Afro-Asian People's Solidarity Conference met in Cairo in December 1957 and established a permanent international secretariat there.

The Bandung Conference was the first broadly inclusive assembly of sovereign governments from Asia and Africa. Its initiators, the "Colombo group" of newly independent Asian nations, were animated by a common concern to speed the end of colonial rule throughout both continents and to ensure conditions of peaceful development for the emerging new countries. Being in part neutralist, in part pro-Western in outlook, they also invited governments of both types. In addition, Prime Minister Nehru, who had signed the famous "five principles of peaceful coexistence" with Chou En-lai in 1954, had secured invitations for Communist China and North Vietnam; Russia, not regarded as an Asian country, was left out.

The organizers of the Bandung Conference thus had no intention of staging an "anti-imperialist" propaganda rally. But the tactical skill of Chou En-lai in championing both peaceful coexistence and anti-imperialism succeeded in creating an impression that there existed a united front of Communists and neutralists, based on the common conviction that Western colonialism and Western military pacts were the only real dangers threatening the independence of the new nations of Asia and Africa. The formal decisions of the conference fell considerably short of meeting the wishes of either Peking or Moscow, but this general impression remained as a major gain for Communist propaganda.

Since Chou had been, along with Nehru and Nasser, one of the dominating figures of the conference, it was also a major gain for the prestige of his regime and the beginning of its impact on the African imagination. Nasser was then the only modern nationalist heading a sovereign African state, and his first meeting with the Chinese premier occurred at a moment when the recent conclusion of the Baghdad Pact had made him particularly susceptible to anti-Western arguments: his Pan-Arab goal required the strict independence of the Arab states from outside power blocs, and the new tie between Iraq and the West was an affront to this concept. It has been claimed that Nasser's Bandung contact with Chou was an important factor in his decision to approach the Soviets for arms deliveries soon after his return; it is certain that this contact prepared the ground for Egypt's becoming the first African state to establish official relations with Communist China. A cultural agreement was concluded on May 31, 1955, and a trade agreement in August. Nasser's full diplomatic recognition of Peking finally took place in May 1956, when tension between Egypt and the West had much increased following the disclosure of the Soviet-Egyptian arms deal, and it contributed in turn to that further deterioration of Egypt's relations with the West that was to lead, after the United States' refusal of credits for the Aswan dam project, to the Suez crisis.

The Cairo Embassy thus became the first basis for Chinese activity in Africa—a basis that Peking owed not to its participation in any Soviet-controlled organization, but primarily to the contacts and influence it had gained by its own skill. It got busy at once in establishing further contacts throughout the continent; but for many months, only cultural and economic activities emerged on the surface.[12] In the meantime, joint Soviet-Chinese efforts proceeded first to create an organized machinery for the propagation of their version of the "Bandung spirit" in Asia, and then to extend its activity to Africa.

Even before the Bandung Conference met, the Communist-directed World Peace Council had attempted to influence its outcome and to make up for the absence of Soviet representatives at Bandung: it persuaded certain Asian politicians to convene an unofficial "Asian Conference for the Relaxation of International Tension" in New Delhi on the eve of the Bandung meeting. Here, Soviet delegates from the Central Asian republics took part along with the Chinese, but the spokesmen from the non-Communist countries did not represent their governments. Reaching agreement on a platform combining peaceful coexistence with militant anti-imperialism was therefore easier, if less significant than at Bandung; what was significant was the decision to set up an "Asian Solidarity Committee" and to call for the formation of affiliated national committees in various Asian countries, including the Soviet Union—in short, to try to create a permanent organizational link between Asian nationalist movements and the Soviet bloc.

Overshadowed by the incomparably more important assembly of government leaders at Bandung, the New Delhi meeting apparently made little impact on Asian opinion; and more than a year passed before even the Soviet branch of the Committee was set up. But in December 1956, the Committee managed to arrange an Asian Writers' Conference in New Delhi; and when some Egyptian writers attended, radiant in the glory of their country's recent triumph over imperialist aggression in the Suez crisis, it eagerly seized the opportunity to propose an expansion of its activity from Asia, where the struggle for national independence was already beginning to recede into history, to Africa, where it was only just approaching its decisive phase. The Committee decided then and there to rename itself the "Afro-Asian Solidarity Committee" and to send a delegation to President Nasser, asking for permission to hold a big "Afro-Asian People's Solidarity Conference" in Cairo.

The delegation—which included the Chinese writer Yang Shuo, the Indian secretary of the Committee, the secretary of the Soviet national committee, and a Japanese—arrived in February 1957. Nasser, although still the celebrated hero of anti-imperialists everywhere, was doubtless also conscious that Egypt, with her trade links to some Western countries broken and with others severely strained, was drifting into economic dependence on the Soviet bloc to an undesirable degree. He seems to have accepted the honor of being host to the conference with some reluctance, and took precautions against allowing a Communist propaganda machine to annex Egypt's newly won prestige in Africa: negotiations with the delegation were entrusted to his close associate and specialist for anti-imperialist propaganda in Africa, Anwar as-Sadat, who agreed to the holding of the conference in Cairo on condition that the permanent secretariat of the Committee be transferred there and the key positions staffed accordingly. In fact, the conference, meeting in Cairo in the last days of 1957, chose Cairo as the seat of the "Afro-Asian Solidarity Council" as it was now called, elected Anwar as-Sadat its president (with one Russian and one Indian vice-president), and made another Egyptian, Yussef as-Sibai, its general secretary; ten more secretaries were to be nominated by the national committees of the Soviet Union, China, five other Asian, and three other African countries.[13]

The organization that emerged from the conference was thus not a Communist front organization of the pure type, but a kind of joint enterprise of the Communist powers and the Egyptian government, with the Communists bringing in their Asian and Nasser his Arab followers, and both sides pooling their contacts to build up African sections, while competing for influence over the independent neutralists. But inside reports suggest that Yussef as-Sibai (who had been acceptable to the Communists because of past cooperation in the "peace movement") proved a weak figure, and that as the activity of the new secretariat unfolded, it came to be increasingly dominated by the representatives of the two Communist powers, the Russian (G. M. Abdurashidov) and the Chinese (at first Yang Shuo, later Chu Tsu-chi).

The Cairo conference, in which Communists and Nasserites competed for the palm in anti-imperialist zeal, had a far greater effect in Africa than the whole of the Committee's previous activity had had in Asia. Riding the tide of such recent events as the winning of independence by Morocco, Tunisia, and Ghana, the Suez war, and the Algerian rising, it became the first great continent-wide rally of awakening anti-Western nationalism and Pan-Africanism of various types. It was thus natural that the subsequent work of the organization created in Cairo was almost entirely devoted to African problems. As one of the strongest states in Africa, with traditional links both to Arabic-speaking North Africa and to the Islamic element in sub-Saharan Africa, Egypt could have exerted considerable influence on this nationalist movement even without the cooperation of the Communists. It was the Communist powers, coming in from outside Africa on the "Afro-Asian ticket," who profited greatly from their association with Egypt and the opportunity afforded by the Cairo conference for getting closer to the new movements.

Moreover, though the Soviet Union and China closely cooperated in establishing this new link with African nationalism, the benefits they got from it were quite unequal. As mentioned earlier, the Soviets had long controlled a network of African contacts through the West European Communist parties and the African branches of their world-wide front organizations; and while some of these old contacts were so encrusted by long isolation that they could not adjust to the new situation of quickly rising mass movements, others ably seized the opportunity to prove their capacity for leadership.

The Chinese Communists had no such old contacts of their own, and their access to the contacts of the world-wide front organizations had been only by leave of the Soviets and as their junior partners. But in the new contacts created under the flag of Afro-Asian solidarity, the Chinese not only came in from the start on an equal footing with the Soviets—they actually had an advantage in being an authentic Asian power, while the Soviets were only admitted as Asians *honoris causa.* The Chinese advantage of being non-European and non-white, of being former victims of imperialism turned victors, and of being a poor and underdeveloped country still visibly in the process of modernization was bound to register with Africans in any case; but it was certain to be far more important in a body specifically devoted to anticolonial struggle than in organizations whose work centered on propaganda about peace, international working class solidarity, or long-range Marxist programs.

Thus the first African organization in which the Chinese could from the start cooperate with the Soviets on a footing of equality became also the one that offered the best chances for eventual competition with the leading power of the "socialist camp." It was noted soon enough that the Chinese delegations at conferences organized by the new Council tended to outnumber both their Soviet and Egyptian counterparts; and before the Cairo secretariat had completed its first year of operation, it was announced that Peking had pledged a bigger contribution for its next annual budget than had Moscow—28,000 to 25,200 dollars.[14] But at the time, this still appeared as competition within a firm framework of cooperation; there was no recognizable difference of policy toward Africa.

A Sino-Soviet Division of Labor?

There was, however, an obvious difference of emphasis. The Soviet Union and China had different strengths and weaknesses in their ability to influence the new states and political movements of Africa, and since each concentrated on its strong points there appeared to be at least a natural division of labor between them. At the Cairo conference, both the Soviet and Chinese delegation leaders—Sharaf R. Rashidov, then President of the Supreme Soviet of Uzbekistan, and Kuo Mo-jo, Vice-President of the Standing Committee of the Chinese People's Congress and head of the Chinese section of the World Peace Council—made programmatic political speeches. But in addition, the Soviet delegation presented a report on Afro-Asian economic cooperation (by the Armenian economist G. A. Arzumanian), and the Chinese delegation presented one on the strengthening of Afro-Asian cultural ties (by Chu Tu-nan).[15]

On one side, this corresponded to the vastly greater ability of the Soviets to offer development credits, and to the proportionately greater importance attached by them to the use of economic strength as a political weapon. Rashidov's political speech had already promised a large amount of disinterested Soviet aid for the economic development of the peoples of Africa as well as of Asia, and had quoted Mao Tse-tung as a classic witness to Soviet altruism. Arzumanian supplemented this promise with an elaborate doctrine of "economic independence," which he defined as a cutting of the old economic ties based on the one-sided division of labor between advanced and backward countries inherited from imperialism and the establishment of a new division of labor based on the industrialization of the former colonies with Soviet help and the imitation of some crucial features of the Soviet economy.

In the language of Soviet theory, what Arzumanian proposed is known as the "non-capitalist road of development." Without using those words, he made the essential points that political independence was desirable only as a precondition for "economic independence" (i.e., for a thoroughgoing reorientation of trade ending in dependence on the Soviet bloc) and that the solution of the crucial internal economic problems of investment and all-round development in a "socialist" sense could be largely determined by the impact of Soviet aid and Soviet influence.

By comparison, the economic contribution China could offer was marginal. Combined with Soviet efforts, it might become important in special strategic cases, such as China's participation in large-scale cotton purchases from Egypt to help finance Egypt's purchase of arms from Russia; but in general, it was designed more to impress people's minds than to influence the economic structure of whole countries. The possible amount of trade was limited from the start by the non-complementary character of the Chinese and most of the African economies; but although the figures involved were modest, the style in which economic contributions were made was often spectacular, as in the case of the gift of 4.7 million dollars to Egypt shortly after Suez, or the two shiploads of rice given to Guinea after her break with the French community.

Chinese participation in the fairs of Casablanca (since 1957) and Tunis (since 1958) has also been much admired, both for the variety of the exhibits and the care taken to show products and techniques that might be of special interest to poor countries in the process of development: it was the example of ingenious self-help rather than the promise of powerful outside aid that the Chinese wanted to stress. In fact, the attractive Chinese exhibitions proved effective pacemakers first for trade agreements and later for full diplomatic relations. The Chinese also successfully offered the aid of specialized advisers —rice-growing experts for Guinea, tea-planting and soil experts as well as some textile and metallurgical technicians for Morocco, and aluminum technicians for the Sudan.

If even in the economic field the Chinese in Africa have had to rely on communicating an attitude rather than on using the pull of economic power, their position as an ancient but poor and struggling nation becomes a positive asset in the field of "cultural exchanges." In reading Chu Tu-nan's Cairo report, one is struck by the deliberate identification with the audience: it is claimed that Chinese, Indians, Arabs, and African Negroes are all equally the heirs of great ancient civilizations that have been ruined by Western imperialism, and whose heritage can be rescued and revived only in a common effort to create a new civilization for all mankind comprising the best traditions of each. There is in this approach a heady mixture of pride and flattery; there is also, on a more practical level, a most plausible argument for promoting cultural exchanges of all kinds—by making agreements between governments, inviting visits of "delegations" from various movements, sending lecturers and receiving students, offering art exhibitions and translating African writers into Chinese, exchanging Moslem pilgrims and football teams, mounting continental tours of Chinese acrobats, making gifts of printing presses. In the vast field of cultural exchange, the Chinese are the pioneers; they seem far ahead of the Russians, who, being so much more similar to Westerners in their contented possession of the techniques of material power, may excite more envious admiration but less hopeful curiosity.

In the field of more directly political propaganda by controlled news services, broadcasts, and the printed word, the Chinese also have made a unique effort. A daily English news service, relayed in Morse code at dictation speed, was started by Peking Radio for the benefit of African editors at the end of 1956. The New China News Agency opened its first African office early in 1958 in Cairo, at the seat of the Solidarity Council, and followed with branch offices in all the key capitals of militant nationalism—Rabat, Conakry, Accra—as soon as Chinese diplomats were accredited there. These offices report in full detail the activities of the anti-imperialist movements that Peking wishes to support, besides distributing NCNA's service of Chinese and world news—which is, incidentally, picked up by many papers in countries where the Chinese cannot operate so freely. For the benefit of the small but important African audience that can tune in to short-wave broadcasts, Peking Radio began in September 1959 to transmit a one-hour English program twice daily; since then, the number has been increased to four, then five daily transmissions (for different regions), and programs in French, Portuguese, and Swahili have been added, apart from a Cantonese program for overseas Chinese in the area.

Monitoring experts of the Western governments seem unable to agree on whether the total number of radio hours beamed by China exclusively to Africa exceeds the Soviet effort in this field; but there can be no doubt that it is at least of the same order, that the extent, variety, and strength of the Chinese transmissions are being steadily increased, and that their influence is far from negligible. Finally, wherever Peking's missions are admitted, Chinese magazines, pamphlets, and books appear in abundance and arouse considerable interest; and this is in addition to the underground circulation of some of this literature—like Mao's famous writings on guerrilla tactics—in countries where they are banned but highly topical.

In addition to "cultural exchanges," and press and radio propaganda, one highly developed technique of Chinese political influence is to invite visits from all kinds of African "delegations"—politicians and trade unionists, journalists and youth leaders, women's and Chinese-African friendship groups. They may be formally invited by a host of organizations: the Chinese Foreign Policy Institute, the Society for Cultural Relations with Foreign Countries, the Chinese Committee of the Afro-Asian People's Solidarity Organization (headed by Liao Cheng-chih), the Chinese-African Friendship Society (founded in April 1960 and headed by the trade-union leader Liu Chang-sheng); or they may be invited simply by the Chinese counterparts, if any, of their own organizations. In practice, it appears that all those organizations are largely interlocking and that the effective selection of visitors depends on the Chinese representative at Afro-Asian headquarters or at the local embassy.

The standard tour for visitors includes, besides some industrial, agricultural, and educational showplaces, an interview with one or more of the top Chinese leaders, and at least one solemn Peking meeting with some 1500 selected representatives of the Communist Party and all possible "mass organizations," at which assurances of solidarity are exchanged and frantically applauded. The value of these interviews and meetings, often arranged even for comparatively minor figures, is not only that they flatter the vanity of the visitors; the constant flow of these meetings on African affairs and the publicity given to them, particularly in news services and magazines intended for foreign circulation, serve as public proof of the importance attached by the Peking leaders to the struggle for African freedom, and hence as an earnest of their willingness to take risks and make sacrifices in support of that struggle. Of course, African delegations of this kind are often invited to Russia and other Communist countries; but nowhere are they given such unfailing and concentrated attention, and nowhere do they follow each other with such frequency and regularity. (The lowest estimates suggest that since 1959 there have never been less than 60 in any one year.)

The impact of a visit to China, however impressively arranged, may prove to be of limited duration. More lasting indoctrination can be imparted to Africans who come to China as students, even if they intend to prepare for a profession other than revolutionary politics. The Chinese Communists are making systematic efforts to influence the future leaders of Africa by this particular method: as early as January 1958, the International Union of Students is known to have maintained a sanatorium for African and Asian students in the neighborhood of Peking.[16] Reliable figures are lacking, but we know that bulk invitations were issued for students from countries that were just gaining independence—for example, in 1960 from the formerly Belgian Congo and from Somalia.[17] In April 1961 an association of African students in China was formed.[18] Reports speak of many hundreds of Asian, African, and Latin American students controlled by the "Institute of Foreign Students" in Peking and of frequent complaints about their strict isolation from the Chinese population.[19]

When all the evidence is sifted, however, the impression remains that the total number of African students in China must still be considerably below that in Russia, quite apart from other centers in Eastern and Western Europe. In this field, so vital for the training of future Communist cadres, Chinese keenness may not be able to compensate fully for the disadvantages of distance, the language barrier, the prestige of Soviet science and technique, and the comparative weakness of Chinese influence on international organizations like the WFTU, which play an especially active role in the selection of potential cadres and their distribution for future training.

So far we have observed a division of roles within Soviet-Chinese cooperation in Africa since the beginning of 1958. The points of relative Soviet strength have been economic aid programs, the organizational contacts of the old international front organizations and particularly of the WFTU, and the training of African students and future cadres. Against this, the points of relative Chinese strength have been cultural exchanges, the use of information media, the new machinery of the Afro-Asian People's Solidarity Organization, and the "delegation" technique of influencing African political movements.

But beyond these different roles, we can also discern a tendency of the two Communist powers to concentrate on different African countries; and this fact, being more directly connected with the difference in the international situations of Russia and China, and hence with the specific objectives of their respective African policies, has proved of far greater consequence for the later development of their policies than the emphasis on different fields of activity noted so far.

Areas of Chinese Concentration

We have seen that the Soviet approach to Africa, just as to other parts of the world, has been two-pronged: on the one hand, Moscow has tried to establish good relations with as many independent African governments as possible; on the other, it has sought to control the trade unions and to foster the training of future Communist cadres. The Soviet government has developed diplomatic contacts and economic ties for the present on the lines of "peaceful coexistence"; the Soviet Communist Party has meanwhile sought to build up ideological influence and class solidarity for the future on the lines of "proletarian internationalism."

Taken together, these two types of Soviet activity here practically covered the whole of Africa. Even a despotic, semi-feudal state like Ethiopia has received substantial Soviet economic aid and a huge diplomatic mission, to say nothing of fulsome flattery on the occasion of the Emperor's 1959 visit to the Soviet Union. Even an obvious preserve of "American capitalism" like Liberia was honored in 1960 by a visit from N. A. Mukhitdinov, a member of the Soviet Presidium. Where no such diplomatic approach is possible, there is still a chance for underground activity: a banned Communist Party continues its work in South Africa, and one of the Angolan liberation movements, the Movimento Popular de Liberatacão de Angola (MPLA), is run by Moscow-controlled Communists and quite openly supported by the Soviets.[20] But with most of the neutralist African states, both Soviet policies are operated simultaneously through different channels, even at the risk of occasionally coming into conflict. Aid for the United Arab Republic has been accompanied by protests against Nasser's treatment of Egyptian and Syrian Communists; a Soviet state visit to King Hassan of Morocco does not exclude support for his left-wing opposition and for the banned Communist Party of Morocco; and even in Guinea the cordial relations with Sekou Touré's government and his ruling party, the Parti Démocratique de Guinée (PDG), have suffered from the consequences of Communist cadre-building activity.

By contrast, the Chinese approach is more nearly single-minded: for the reasons outlined above, it is almost wholly concentrated on militant anti-imperialist movements. If a government is identified with such a movement or effectively committed to its support, Peking will back it to the hilt. If the government is "subservient to the imperialists" or suspected of seeking a deal with them, Peking will as resolutely back the opposition. It follows that where governments are pro-Western or truly neutral and opposition is weak, Chinese activity finds little scope; far more than that of the Soviets, it is concentrated on a comparatively small number of strategic African countries which may be described as either the "battlefields" or the "staging areas" of anti-imperialist wars of liberation. Such battlefields were Algeria, the Cameroun, and later the Congo; and when Egypt, a former battlefield, proved unsatisfactory as a staging area, Morocco and Guinea took its place.

Active support of the Algerian Front de Libération Nationale (FLN) has been the core and center of Chinese policy in Africa from the beginning; together with the fact that Egypt gave Peking its first chance of entry, the crucial role attributed by the Chinese to Algeria makes it impossible to draw a line between Chinese policies for Arab and Negro Africa—and this, in fact, is a distinction never made in any Chinese pronouncements. The FLN was, of course, represented at the Cairo Afro-Asian conference; because it was conducting the only major anticolonial war then in progress, it was offered a vice-presidency of the Afro-Asian Solidarity Council, although it does not seem to have filled the post. When its leaders formed a Provisional Government (G.P.R.A.) in the fall of 1958, the Chinese People's Republic was the only Communist government to recognize it at once. After that, official delegations of the G.P.R.A. visited Peking five times, and detailed arrangements both for the financing of Algerian arms purchases in the Middle East and Europe by an interest-free loan ("to be repaid after independence") and for the training of selected Algerian officers in China are believed to have been made as early as the spring of 1959.[21]

The fact that China was alone among the Communist states in making such public and official commitments to the Algerian Nationalists should not be taken as proof of a Soviet-Chinese policy disagreement on Algeria prior to October 1959. The FLN enjoyed the full support of the Soviet bloc and the world Communist movement, and this included financial aid.[22] European Soviet bloc states are known to have taken an active, if concealed, part in supplying arms to the FLN; particularly involved were Czechoslovakia, which has long specialized in arms exports, and Albania, which served as a transit country.[23] (The importance of a Communist-controlled Mediterranean port for North African operations may indeed have contributed to the growth of Chinese interest in Albania.) But China enjoyed greater freedom of maneuver than the Soviet Union and its European satellites because of her lack of diplomatic relations with France; she was thus able to recognize the G.P.R.A. without risking any harmful repercussions. Her leading public role in this matter was thus at first fully compatible with a planned division of labor within the bloc.

What was distinctive about the Chinese commitment, however, and what went beyond the requirements of such a division of labor, was Peking's insistence on the importance of the Algerian struggle as a model for the whole of colonial Africa. On innumerable occasions, Chinese orators and leader writers repeated the formula that the Algerian struggle had set a brilliant example for the liberation of all African people. Their other favorite stereotype was that imperialists never abandon their colonial possessions voluntarily but have to be forced out by "struggle"; while in itself susceptible of interpretation as advocating both violent and nonviolent action—and used in this broad way by the Soviets—this became, when coupled with the Chinese stress on the Algerian example, an argument for the inevitability of violence.

In fact, the only other armed anticolonial struggle in progress in Africa at the time was the guerrilla war conducted by the Union des Populations du Cameroun (UPC) in the southern part of the French Cameroun; and while this had the disadvantage of a regionally and tribally limited basis in the population, it had the advantage that its leaders had received a Marxist training and become Communists or near-Communists during long association with the French CGT and the West African Rassemblement Démocratique Africain (RDA), of which the UPC had once formed a part. Its president and representative in exile, Dr. Felix-Roland Moumié, took an active part in the first Afro-Asian conference in Cairo and in the Solidarity Council set up by it, and the Chinese at once established close cooperation with this group. Until the outbreak of the Congo troubles of 1960, all Chinese statements on Africa regularly mentioned the struggle in the Cameroun immediately after that in Algeria, and in October and November of 1959, Dr. Moumié became one of the first major African leaders to visit China.

The original basis for Chinese contacts with these revolutionary movements, as for all Chinese activity in Africa, had been Egypt. But relations between Nasser and the Communist powers—the Soviets as well as China—had deteriorated by 1959. The initial cause for this was not, as has sometimes been asserted, the persecution of Egyptian and Syrian Communists in the United Arab Republic, but the backing given by the Communist powers to Kassem's new Iraqi regime in its opposition to Nasser's Pan-Arab plans.[24]

Moscow and Peking then had great hopes of gaining a control over the young Iraqi revolution which they had been unable to secure over Nasser's established dictatorial regime; the consequent Communist opposition to Pan-Arabism, expressed both in support for Kassem and in a demand for greater Syrian autonomy, was the major motive for Nasser's internal anti-Communist measures. Khrushchev allowed the Syrian Communist leader Khalid Bakdash to call for federalist and democratic reforms in the United Arab Republic from the rostrum of the 21st Congress of the Soviet Communist Party in February 1959, and he personally took issue with Nasser's anti-Communism and his pressure on Iraq both at the Congress and at a Moscow diplomatic party in mid-March. Peking, which had shared in the benefits of Iraq's new orientation and concluded a treaty with Kassem in January, also shared in the subsequent press polemics with the U.A.R. Finding the usefulness of Cairo as a basis for continent-wide activity correspondingly reduced, and even fearing a possible reconciliation between Nasser and the "imperialists," Peking naturally looked for new bases elsewhere.

The most urgent need, of course, was for a base adjoining Algeria. Of Algeria's two independent neighbors, Tunisia hesitated to establish full diplomatic relations with Peking, but Morocco was willing, not only because of the comparatively substantial economic effort which had made Peking one of its major trading partners,[25] but also because of its own curiously complicated internal and external situation. For Morocco, although a semi-autocratic Islamic monarchy, also had a strong left-wing nationalist movement based on the trade unions, and one of the leaders of this left wing, Abdallah Ibrahim, had been entrusted with the government in December 1958. Moreover, nationalism was kept militant by unsatisfied territorial claims.

In these conditions, the struggle for prestige and power between the king and the democratic political forces became largely a competition in nationalist zeal, of which practical solidarity with fighting Algerian nationalism was one of the most convincing proofs. Diplomatic relations with China were thus established in the spring of 1959 in order to facilitate Chinese aid for the FLN, and one of the most important consequences of this was the opening of a Chinese consulate at Ouida on the Algerian frontier, which was also the principal base of exiled FLN forces in Morocco.[26] Since then, Peking's relations with Morocco have been consistently maintained on the basis of a common anti-imperialist front with Moroccan nationalism, whatever its social and ideological complexion; when the Ibrahim government banned the Moroccan Communist Party in September 1959, and when the ban was upheld by an appeals court the following February, the Chinese mission broke off all contact with its Moroccan comrades and the Chinese press refrained from any criticism of the ban.[27]

The other important new base opened up for Chinese activity in Africa after the spring of 1959 was Guinea. This center of the militant wing of the political and trade-union movements of French West Africa had for some reason played no role in the Cairo conference and the original creation of the Afro-Asian Solidarity Council. Yet by late 1956 its Marxist-educated leaders had already taken the initiative in creating the first independent Pan-African trade-union organization, the Union Générale des Travailleurs d'Afrique Noire (UGTAN), formally founded in Conakry in January 1959; and in September 1958 they had led their country in voting for the first breakaway from the newly formed French Community.

The economic cost of this decision was heavy, but the gain in political authority for the Guinean leaders among militant African nationalists everywhere was at least equally great; a few months later, at the first All-African People's Conference in Accra, the Guinean representative in Ghana, Abdoulaye Diallo, made General Secretary of this first large-scale Pan-African organization. From then on, Guinea and Ghana were both cooperating and competing as centers of support for struggling nationalist movements throughout sub-Saharan Africa. While Dr. Nkrumah had been the first to gain independence and to proclaim the Pan-African idea as the guiding star of a sovereign government, Sekou Touré had achieved independence in more dramatic conditions and had older ties with Communist parties and front organizations outside Africa and with the Soviet bloc; moreover, the main areas of acute conflict in Africa at that time happened to be French-speaking, and the Camerounian UPC leaders in particular had old links with the leaders of the ruling Parti Démocratique de Guinée (PDG) from their common past in the RDA. All these facts—together, perhaps, with the suspicious circumstance of Dr. Nkrumah's American studies—may have played their role in making Peking opt for early relations with Guinea.

At any rate, the first visit to Conakry of the new Chinese ambassador to Morocco took place immediately on his arrival in Africa in April 1959, and he brought a gift of 5,000 tons of rice. Formal diplomatic relations were agreed upon when a member of the Guinean government visited Peking in October and signed a cultural agreement. In the meantime, the Soviet Union had granted Guinea a loan of 140 million rubles, and high-ranking representatives of both the Soviet Union and China, as well as of other Soviet bloc states, had attended the Fifth Congress of the PDG in September, along with a representative of the French Communist Party.[28]

But what was probably most important for the Chinese was that Guinea was rapidly becoming a refuge for the exiled leaders of opposition groups from various French colonies, as well as a training ground for cadres at the UGTAN school at Dalaba, which was supported with money and materials by the WFTU.[29] Here, then, the Chinese Communists might find a chance to do what could no longer be done in Egypt, and what seemed very difficult for them at the WFTU schools in Eastern Europe: to gain direct influence on the training of future African leaders. By May 1959, Dr. Moumié had transferred his headquarters from Cairo to Conakry and had been given an office right in the National Assembly building there.[30] Contacts with the more militant wing among the leaders of the Mali federation—those who came from the Union Sudanaise branch of the RDA, and were later to run the new Mali state after the breakaway of Senegal—were intimate. There was also in residence an exile group from the Ivory Coast. With all of them, Peking could now keep in touch through its mission in Guinea.

Among the African politicians who came to Guinea in 1959 for a period of study was Antoine Gizenga from the Congo, who had already founded his Parti Solidaire Africain (PSA) in April of that year.[31] The Leopoldville riots in January, which occured shortly after the return of Congolese delegates (including Patrice Lumumba) from the All-African People's Conference in Accra, were followed by a rush of demands for independence, steps toward self-government, and party foundings. As a result, the Chinese Communists came to list the Congo among the areas due for early militant liberation movements.[32] However, they seem to have had hardly any contact with Lumumba's Mouvement National Congolais until he visited Conakry in April 1960, on the eve of the pre-independence elections, for the Second Afro-Asian People's Conference. Pre-independence invitations to Peking suggest that the Chinese had pinned their hopes partly on the "Parti du Peuple," a small Marxist sect whose leader, Makwambala, was later to become president of the Congolese Society for Friendship with China, and party on the PSA, which combined the local popular following of Cleophas Kamitatu in parts of Leopoldville province with the presence among the party leaders of a Marxist group around Gizenga.[33] At any rate, Peking does not seem to have exerted any influence on events in the Congo before the proclamation of independence on June 30, 1960; nor did it, apparently, in any of the other African colonies—such as Nyasaland, Kenya, and Uganda —from which it hopefully reported troubles at that time.

While concentrating its efforts in the above African countries and regions, Peking also attempted to win recognition from and establish routine diplomatic relations with newly independent, uncommitted countries that were not militantly anti-imperialist. It succeeded in establishing such relations with the Sudan in November 1958; but here, as with the later development of similar relations with Ethiopia, Nigeria, Tunisia, Tanganyika, etc., the event was of no importance for the general policy of the African countries or for Peking's policy toward them. And in particular, it did not prevent the Chinese Communists from giving political support to extremist opposition groups in those countries (as in the Sudan or Nigeria) or from bolstering criticism of their governments by more militant rivals from outside.

It must be said at this point that our account of Chinese strategy toward the different African countries has not drawn on any explicit discussion of the subject in the Chinese press—because no such discussion has taken place. There is, in the published materials accessible outside China, no sign of a Chinese Potekhin, let alone of a school of Chinese Africanists that could discuss such matters as the differences in historical background, the variations in economic and social structure, and the different prospects of political development between Arab Africa and Negro Africa, between different regions of sub-Saharan Africa, or between countries that have lived under a French and a British regime. Even general statements of Chinese policy toward Africa refer only in the most cursory way to the peculiarities of African class structure—barely enough to support the assertion that Mao's "classical" four-class alliance against imperialism and feudalism is applicable in principle. The Western analyst is thus forced to extrapolate a general strategy only from the known facts of Communist activity, and his conclusions must therefore be advanced with a special caution.

The Policies Diverge

In the autumn of 1959 a major conflict developed between the general foreign policies of Moscow and Peking, and this had immediate effects on their respective African policies. The differences in the international situation of both countries, and hence in their conceptions of their interests and priority objectives, had existed long before, and it has been suggested above that they gave rise to somewhat different approaches to African affairs. But no tangible disagreements on practical decisions of foreign policy had emerged between the two Communist powers before 1958; and even then, they remained confined to some specific issues—the handling of the Yugoslav heresy, the Middle Eastern crisis produced by the Iraqi revolution, and the bombardment of Quemoy—none of which touched Africa directly, and none of which generated a public dispute on the over-all direction of the foreign policy of the Communist bloc.

By contrast, the issues raised in 1959 by Khrushchev's visit to the United States and by his preparations for a summit conference were both acute and all-embracing; they were at once reflected in a sharp Russo-Chinese clash on policy toward Algeria, in disagreements concerning policy toward the Cameroun, and in a prolonged struggle for influence in the Afro-Asian solidarity movement. Further disagreements arose in some phases of the Congo crisis, though here they did not destroy the framework of general militant Soviet-Chinese cooperation. At the same time, the increasing awareness of the Soviet and Chinese Communist leaders that they were now involved in a world-wide rivalry for the control of revolutionary movements also began to affect the long-term planning of their African policies.

The basic dispute between the Soviet and Chinese concepts of Communist strategy concerns the relation between coexistence diplomacy and revolutionary pressure in the present world situation. While both Moscow and Peking admit both methods in principle, Moscow insists on controlling the risks of violent revolutionary conflict and advancing whenever possible by negotiation, including negotiation with the main enemy, the United States; it expresses this preference by describing "peaceful coexistence" as the "general line" of its policy, to which local conflicts, including revolutionary movements for colonial liberation, must be subordinated whenever necessary. Peking distrusts direct negotiation between the Soviets and the United States, denies the risk that local "wars of liberation" may escalate into world war, and seeks to weaken the main enemy by multiplying the areas of violent conflict and thus compelling a dispersal of his forces; it expresses this preference by saying that the

"general line" of world Communism must be "struggle against imperialism," to which the struggle for peace by diplomatic means must
be subordinated as one of its aspects.

One of Peking's major weapons in this dispute is the charge that
Moscow's coexistence diplomacy leads to a betrayal of the colonial
revolutionary movements for the sake of peace. Although this charge
was not made before the conflict became acute, the argument that
"peaceful coexistence" must not be applied to colonial struggles had
been advanced by Peking for some years past and lay behind its concentration on violent anticolonial movements. As early as the end of
1957, Kuo Mo-jo, leader of the Chinese section of the World Peace
Council, had stated this position in his report to the Cairo Afro-Asian
Conference: "in the Afro-Asian countries," he said, "the struggle for
national independence and against imperialism and colonialism
forms an integral part of our movement for safeguarding peace. We
must first obtain independence and equality, then we can live in
peace."[34]

In January 1959 the same theme was introduced, still in a non-
polemical tone, by a Chinese participant in the Moscow symposium
entitled "The Decay of the Colonial System of Imperialism after the
Second World War," sponsored by the editorial boards of the Soviet
periodical "International Affairs" and the Chinese "Shih-chieh Chih-
shih." Choosing as his topic "the interrelation between the movements for national liberation and for the defense of peace," Hsun Fo
argued that no contradiction could arise between the two, because
both were aspects of the struggle against imperialism and were thus
mutually reinforcing. This applied even more when the anticolonial
movement took the "higher form" of armed struggle, he claimed.
For, he argued, the anticolonial armed struggles in Asia, Africa,
and Latin America, by mobilizing against imperialism the concentrated forces of the peoples in these vast regions, had substantially
diminished the capacity of imperialism to unleash world war and
thus greatly strengthened the forces defending world peace! If the
peoples refrained from armed struggles for liberation because of the
risk of imperialist intervention, such appeasement of the imperialist
aggressors would only increase the risk of their aggression leading to
world war. The right course was for the national movements of Asia,

Africa, and Latin America to direct their blows against this aggression "with the all-sided support of the socialist camp with the Soviet Union at its head."

The paradoxical theory that the cause of peace can best be advanced by armed struggle—based on the simple trick of equating the "cause of peace" with the cause of the anti-imperialist "camp"—was thus fully developed before the issue became acute. When that happened, the argument was simply turned into an accusation of appeasement against Khrushchev and incorporated into the general case against the "revisionist" betrayal of Leninism.

In Africa, that issue first became acute over Algeria, as a result of President de Gaulle's first offer of Algerian self-determination on September 16, 1959, and of the coincidence between this turning point of French Algerian policy and Khrushchev's visit to the United States.

The first Algerian response came from the small Algerian Communist Party; in two doctrinaire statements it rejected de Gaulle's plan as "unacceptable."[35] It was supported in this stand by the French Communists. The second reaction, from the G.P.R.A., was far more cautious, a fact reflecting that body's responsibility for the actual fighting movement in Algeria: before the end of September, it had proposed to negotiate about guarantees for self-determination and offered to stop fighting if the guarantees were satisfactory.

Within a few days of these events, both Larbi Bouhali, the general secretary of the Algerian Communist Party, and a G.P.R.A. delegation headed by Ben Khedda arrived in Peking for the tenth birthday of the People's Republic,[36] and so did Khrushchev on his return journey from the United States. We may assume that both Algerian views were explained to the Chinese leaders on that occasion; the Chinese made no immediate public comment, but it seems remarkable that this was the least publicized of all the Peking visits by representatives of the G.P.R.A. It was also the least publicized of all Khrushchev's visits; his talk with Mao about the consequences of his American journey for Soviet policy plans did not even result in a joint communiqué—only in a bitter warning against "Trotskyite adventurism" uttered by Khrushchev after his return to Moscow.[37]

The Chinese leaders, then, must have decided their Algerian policy in the light of their broader disagreement with Khrushchev on the desirability of a *détente* with the West. On October 17, 1959, the New China News Agency denounced the de Gaulle proposals as "nothing but a sugar-coated poison pill."[38] A fortnight later, in the same speech to the Supreme Soviet which contained the warning against "adventurism," Khrushchev welcomed the same proposals, saying they "could play an important part in the settlement of the Algerian question." The French Communists immediately made the necessary *volte face* and began to campaign for negotiations on the basis of the proposals of the G.P.R.A. In this, they were followed by the whole international Communist movement—except for the Chinese, who repeated that the de Gaulle offer was "nothing but a trick from A to Z" and that the Algerian people would continue their struggle until they had won "true independence."[39] By the end of the year, Peking had begun to suggest to the G.P.R.A. that it might send volunteers and planes.[40]

For the first time, the two Communist powers were thus on record as giving sharply opposite advice to the major anticolonial fighting movement on the African continent; and as the months passed without any new move by de Gaulle (who had difficulties in keeping his army in line against the rebellious settlers), events seemed to justify Peking's advice rather than Moscow's. Of course, Moscow was not advising the FLN to stop fighting in the hope of a negotiated settlement; on the contrary, the Soviets were doing their best to organize pressure on France through the United Nations. Yet the mere fact that Khrushchev was planning to pay a state visit to France in late March in preparation for the "summit" meeting imposed limits on the criticism of French policies by Soviet spokesmen and forced them to take a mildly optimistic view of the prospects for a negotiated settlement in Algeria. This was enough to enable the Chinese opponents of negotiations to make the Soviets appear to many African nationalists as the defenders of dangerous illusions about the nature of imperialism, if nothing worse.

In May 1960 the G.P.R.A. sent a new delegation under Belkacem Krim to China to negotiate for increased aid; it was careful not to accept the offer of Chinese volunteers but to allow France and the Western powers to think it might do so unless negotiations began in earnest. This time, the G.P.R.A. visit was eagerly grasped as an opportunity to publicize China's unwavering solidarity with the struggling colonial peoples of Africa; and the communiqué signed by the visitors accepted the Chinese formula that "so long as the colonialist oppressors and imperialist aggressors are not eliminated and the national independence of all the peoples not recognized, genuine and permanent peace will be impossible" because "the securing of world peace depends on the resolute struggles of the peoples of the world against imperialism and colonialism."[41] Even the Algerian Communists now raised their voices again and claimed credit for having seen through de Gaulle's "insincerity" at once.

By this time, however, with the "summit" meeting exploded and the Berlin issue postponed, Moscow had less need of de Gaulle's good will and also could more easily compete for the applause of militant African nationalists. Soviet spokesmen now stressed that the choice of either violent or peaceful means of liberation was not a matter of principle but depended solely on the actions of the enemy, and that violence was a legitimate weapon when peaceful means had been exhausted.[42] When the first Franco-Algerian contacts took place at Melun in the summer, it was the Chinese turn to explain that it was a success for the FLN that the French "could not avoid asking for negotiations" and that China, having supported the FLN's struggle, "also supports negotiations as a means to win independence."[43] For the time being, the conflict had been reduced to a difference of emphasis; nor did it resume its former intensity when the Melun talks failed and the G.P.R.A. sent its Prime Minister, Ferhat Abbas, to Peking and Moscow. For by then, Khrushchev was engaged, by way of preparing for the showdown with the Chinese at the Moscow world conference of Communist parties, in proving his anticolonialist zeal by a bravura performance at the United Nations, and *de facto* recognition of the G.P.R.A. fitted well into that design.

During most of 1960, the development of the Cameroun issue constituted a kind of minor parallel to the Algerian quarrel: here, too, the Chinese favored continuation of armed struggle, the Soviets an attempt to end it by negotiation. The difference was that the French Cameroun was granted independence on January 1, 1960, and that the UPC rising was regionally limited; if French troops had been authorized to stay in the country by the agreements preceding independence, it could be argued that it was precisely the rising, allegedly directed against them, that caused the new government to keep them there. On the other hand, the Communists in the Cameroun did not (as in Algeria) exist as an organization separate from the national insurgents: there was no recognized Communist party, but the leaders of the rising were themselves Communists who regarded their own conquest of power as the only satisfactory outcome of the anti-imperialist struggle.

In August 1959, with preparations for independence already in progress, the UPC had declared that it would not lay down its arms unless all foreign troops were withdrawn and unless it could participate in a new national coalition government that would supervise the elections.[44] These demands were refused and fighting continued; nevertheless, the Soviets made diplomatic contact with the Ahidjo government as soon as independence was granted, and they seem to have promised to urge the UPC to negotiate terms for becoming a legal opposition party.[45] In fact, while Dr. Moumié warned of the dangers of "fictitious independence" at the Second All-African People's Conference held in Tunis in January 1960, one of his vice-presidents, Abel Kingué, put forward new conditions for a cease-fire and participation in the elections scheduled for April: he still demanded the withdrawal of foreign troops and the restoration of full democratic freedoms, but he no longer insisted on participating in the government.[46] But these demands were not granted either. Meanwhile Peking continued to back the UPC rising as a continuing struggle for "true independence," and Dr. Moumié hurried off for a second, unpublicized visit to Peking. When he returned to his Conakry headquarters in April, he was firmly committed to support of the Chinese line.[47]

The concrete divergence between Soviet and Chinese policies toward Algeria and the Cameroun, as well as their now deliberate use of different formulas for the priorities to be accorded to "peaceful coexistence" and "anti-imperialist struggle," must have been reflected in the organs of the Afro-Asian solidarity movement from the start. The African neutralists and nationalists found themselves increasingly called upon to decide between the arguments put forward by the rival Communist powers. Moreover, the issue was complicated for them by the aftermath of the quarrel that had arisen in 1959 between both Communist regimes and Nasser's U.A.R.

As we have seen, that quarrel had been caused chiefly by the conflicting hopes placed by Nasser and the Communists on the future course of the Iraqi revolution—in the direction of Pan-Arab unity under Egyptian leadership on the one side, and of growing Communist influence on the other. By the late summer of 1959, however, both hopes had faded: Kassem had consolidated his rule after successively defeating Nasserites and Communists, and the quarrel had accordingly lost its point. However, this change in the situation was recognized more quickly by Moscow, keen as it was on mobilizing all possible neutralist sympathies in the pre-summit period, than by Peking, which was not interested in wooing neutralist opinion for diplomatic purposes but only in support for militant anti-imperialist actions. The incident of Khalid Bakdash's renewed attack on Nasser at the birthday celebrations of the Chinese People's Republic in October 1959, which led to a walkout of the U.A.R. ambassador and a diplomatic protest, was a hangover from the tensions of the previous spring rather than a major cause of new policy differences between Peking and Moscow. But by making Moscow's return to friendliness more conspicuous, it weakened Peking's otherwise not unfavorable position in the competition for influence on the Africans in the Afro-Asian movement, and this at the same time that China's chances with the Asians were being impaired by her national conflicts with India and Indonesia.

Most Africans naturally refused to tie themselves firmly to either the Soviet or the Chinese side in the new dispute; they tended to follow the Chinese lead when the question concerned support for militant anticolonial movements, but to take the side of Soviet caution when the choice between neutralism and direct bloc intervention in Africa seemed to be the issue. One of the first disputed votes in the Afro-Asian secretariat (reports of which leaked out in December 1959) concerned a message of greeting to the Second All-African People's Conference, due to convene in Tunis in January 1960. As proposed, this message welcomed the imminent emergence of a number of new sovereign African states that would be free of military ties, and proclaimed the "historic responsibility" of Asians and Africans "to bridge the gulf between the two armed camps."[48]

The Chinese opposed this text as spreading neutralist illusions, and found themselves in a small minority—reports agree that they were supported only by Guinea.[49] Again, at the Second Afro-Asian Conference held at Conakry in April, where Chinese influence was generally strong (the Chinese had sent the largest delegation and had even arranged for a troupe of Chinese acrobats to perform there at the time), the Chinese delegation caused a general shock when it opposed the statement in a Soviet-drafted resolution that economic development of the new countries could be greatly speeded up if the cold war and the arms race were ended: the Chinese objection was that they would not be a party to the spreading of illusions about the nature of imperialism.[50]

On other issues, however, the Chinese were by no means isolated. The Tunis All-African conference called for increased aid to the Algerian struggle, appealing to the independent governments of Africa to recognize the G.P.R.A. and to form an African volunteer corps.[51] The report of the Cairo secretariat to the Conakry Afro-Asian conference went further and spoke of an "Afro-Asian volunteer army" for Algeria—a formula that would have sanctioned Chinese volunteers.[52] This was anathema not only to the Soviets, as First Deputy Premier Mikoyan publicly pointed out in Baghdad even while the conference was in progress.[53] It was not desired by the FLN either, which liked the threat of Chinese intervention well enough, but shrewdly suspected that it might not like the reality. In the end, the Conakry resolution upheld the idea but postponed its application: it suggested that a new "Afro-Asian summit" should be called, this time uniting governments and "mass organizations," to set up an effective Afro-Asian alliance for the support of all struggling liberation movements, including a permanent "Afro-Asian volunteer corps" for use wherever needed. This proposal had come from Dr. Moumié, who had just returned from China, and the only thing about it that could have pleased the Soviets was that it had no prospects of being carried out. The Conakry resolution on coexistence and disarmament, while endorsing these Soviet slogans, also embodied the Chinese formula that the elimination of colonial exploitation was a precondition for their realization.[54]

By maneuvering between the Chinese and Nasser's men, the Soviets did rather better on the organizational questions discussed at Conakry. With Chinese support, they got the Solidarity Council transformed into an "Afro-Asian People's Solidarity Organization," with an Executive Council of 14 African and 13 Asian states (including North Korea, North Vietnam, and Outer Mongolia) and with a rotating chairmanship; but they helped the U.A.R. defeat a Chinese move for transferring the seat of the secretariat to Conakry—only an office for liaison with the All-African People's Conference was installed there.[55] Another decision was to set up a special "Solidarity Fund" for the support of liberation movements, but this was not implemented for several months. The Soviets, already controlling the corresponding fund of the WFTU, presumably showed little interest in it.

In November 1960, however, the Fund was formally created at the Beirut meeting of the Executive Council; and when its composition and the statute adopted in February 1961 were published, they contained some surprises. Its seat was to be Conakry, its chairman Ismail Touré, and its two deputy chairmen Mehdi Ben Barka, external representative of the Moroccan Union Nationale des Forces Populaires (UNFP), and Chu Tzu-chi, the Chinese member of the Cairo secretariat. Of the four other members of its board, one came from the U.A.R., two from Indonesia, and one was the leading Soviet orientalist Gafurov; but the statute provided explicitly that in urgent cases, the disbursing of aid to movements resisting armed imperialist aggression could be decided by the chairman and his two deputies alone, provided only that the other members were informed afterwards.[56]

Thus an international organ had been created through which the Chinese Communists could support revolutionary liberation movements in Africa free from any effective Soviet veto; and the timing suggests that this important concession may have formed part of the temporary Soviet-Chinese compromise reached in Moscow at the end of 1960. But while Chinese influence in the Afro-Asian Solidarity Organization can hardly have been strong enough to achieve this last result without Soviet consent, the concession would not have been

made if the Chinese had not already proved themselves a more effective independent partner and rival of the Soviets in Africa than in
most other parts of the world.

The Congo crisis, which began in July 1960—only two weeks
after the grant of Congolese independence—has on the whole promoted unity rather than divergence within the Sino-Soviet alliance.
It broke out at a time when the Soviets were already bent on repairing
their reputation for militant anticolonialism in Africa, and it gave
them an opportunity to draw some of the new African states closer to
their side. Nevertheless, there have been signs of Soviet-Chinese
disagreement in at least two phases of the crisis, reflecting the differences in the attitude of the Communist powers to the United Nation and to the uses of constitutional legality.

There was, of course, no Communist Party in the Congo. The
Soviets and the Chinese seem to have agreed at the Conakry Afro-
Asian conference to give some financial and political backing to the
only effective nationalist party, Patrice Lumumba's Mouvement
National Congolais (MNC), and also to Antoine Gizenga's left-wing
Parti Solidaire Africain (PSA), with its local following in Leopoldville province.[57] The two men had emerged as Premier and Deputy Premier of the new government, and had been furnished with
some French Communist advisers who had moved over from Guinea;
Dr. Moumié had moved over, too. But all this was far from amounting
to Communist control, nor could it appear as such to experienced
Communists; at best, it was an opportunity to exert some influence
on what promised at any rate to be a chaotic development. It seems
likely that from the beginning both the Soviets and the Chinese Communists saw the importance of the Congo not as a possible base for
establishing a stronghold of their power but as a field for continent-
wide propagandist exploitation of the conflicts that were bound to
arise in this vast territory, with its singular combination of wealth in
raw materials and poverty in trained African cadres.

Thus when the crisis broke with the mutiny of the "Force Pu-
blique" and the Belgian intervention, the Soviets were ready with a
fully prepared charge that this was a plot by all the NATO powers
against the independence of all the new African states, and Peking
gladly echoed this line. But the Soviets also welcomed the news that

the Congo government had appealed to the United Nations Security Council, not because they expected this to have any effect, but precisely because they did not. As Khrushchev said on July 12, an appeal to the Council was "the right thing to do," but "The Security Council can hardly be expected to give sympathetic consideration to the justified demand of the people of the Congo. This body should be shown for what it is, so that the peoples can see that the Security Council has been turned by the U.S.A. into an instrument for suppressing the freedom-loving peoples and keeping the peoples in colonial bondage."[58]

In other words, Khrushchev welcomed a debate in the United Nations as the best chance to "unmask" the policy of the Western powers, particularly the United States, in the eyes of the colonial and ex-colonial nations; and he expected them to unmask themselves by justifying Belgian intervention, or at any rate refusing to authorize action against it. When the Security Council decided instead to call on Belgium to withdraw her troops and to offer the Congo government the aid of U.N. forces, the Soviets first had to welcome this as "a useful step."[59] Their next move was to build up a case that the U.N. force was not acting in accordance with its mandate—a charge that now had to be made out primarily against the Secretary-General, Dag Hammarskjöld.

The Chinese, caring less about world opinion and more about direct anti-imperialist action than the Soviets, refused to bother much about little Belgium and concentrated on denouncing the United States. But the first Chinese government statement, issued five days after the first Security Council resolution, made no mention of the U.N. at all; instead, it talked of "the sacred right of the Congolese people to safeguard and consolidate their independence by their own strength" and of the need to defeat the imperialist intervention "by the unity of the African peoples with the peoples of Asia, Latin America, and the rest of the world."[60] Clearly Peking heartily disapproved of U.N. intervention from the start, but it could not say so publicly because Moscow had blundered into initiating it!

A few days later, Liao Cheng-shih charged at a Peking rally that U.N. intervention was the very form chosen by the U.S. "to cover up its large-scale infiltration into the Congo."[61] This charge was repeated endlessly from then on, while the Deputy General Secretary of Gizenga's party, Theodore Bengila, advised his government from the Peking rostrum "to appeal to those whom it deems fit . . . to safeguard the territorial integrity of our country."[62] After another month the Chinese *People's Daily* disclosed that at the time of the first Security Council resolution, "a solid body of decent opinion" had pointed out "that this U.N. resolution would open the door wide to U.S. imperialist intervention in the Congo and constitute an odious precedent for infringements, in the name of the U.N., on the sovereignty of newly independent countries." It went on to cite "apologists of U.S. imperialism" who had tried to justify their actions "by contending that U.N. intervention was requested by the Congolese government," and replied that "the position of the Congolese government can in no way serve to absolve U.S. imperialism of its crimes."[63] The Soviet vote in the Security Council was never mentioned.

During this time the Soviet press was equally critical of the actions of U.N. personnel in the Congo, but it still had to demand that they act in accordance with the Soviet interpretation of their mandate. Only in September, when the U.N. had in fact swung the struggle in favor of Kasavubu, by temporarily depriving Lumumba of control over the radio station and airfields, did the Soviets launch their all-out attack on Hammarskjöld and call on the African states to withdraw their troops from the U.N. force. Even in those critical days, Vice-Premier Gizenga appealed to China for volunteers and material aid "to defend the territorial integrity of the Republic of the Congo," but asked the Soviet Union merely to use its veto against the U.N. attempt to put the Congo under tutelage.[64] But Peking did not actually attempt to send volunteers to the Congo to fight the U.N. forces; and Moscow now tried hard to end U.N. intervention by protests in the U.N. and by direct appeals to the participating African states. From that moment on, agreement between Moscow and Peking was complete; the Peking line was accepted. As the *People's Daily* sneeringly put it at the very time of the Moscow world conference of Communist parties: "Some naive people originally were inclined to believe that the U.N. could help the Congolese people. . . . They did not realize that the U.S. has always used the U.N. as an instrument for aggression, and that inviting in the U.N. means letting in U.S. imperialism."[65]

From then on—through the murder of Lumumba and the recognition of Gizenga's Stanleyville government as the "legitimate central government of the Congo Republic" by both Communist powers— full agreement between Russia and China seems to have persisted; the diplomatic missions of both reached Stanleyville in July 1961, with the Soviets arriving first.[66] By then, however, the U.N. had worked out proposals for recalling the elected parliament—largely on the initiative of African states. Gizenga seems to have hesitated for some time whether to demand only that parliament be convened under U.N. protection with the U.N. guaranteeing his personal safety, or whether to insist on political conditions, such as the removal of the "traitor" Kasavubu from the presidency and his own confirmation in office, before agreeing to go before parliament; in the end, he made no political conditions, and after more hesitation agreed to serve in the new government of Cyril Adoula.

The paucity of available comment does not permit us to assert that during this period of hesitation the Soviets advised for, and the Chinese against, acceptance of the U.N. scheme for the restoration of parliamentary legality in the Congo, but the record makes it seem likely. It is certain that the formation of the new Adoula-Gizenga government was accepted by Moscow without reserve. Not only did it promptly move its diplomatic mission back to Leopoldville, but by its propaganda endeavored to commit the new government to the heritage of Lumumba, calling on it for action against the Katanga "separatists," and backing its demand for United Nations support for such action.[67] It is equally certain that the Chinese reaction was different: the Stanleyville mission was called home with the ill-humored explanation that the legal government of Gizenga had "terminated its existence" and the Leopoldville government was maintaining diplomatic relations with "the Chiang Kai-shek clique."[68] The U.N. action against Katanga was analyzed by Peking as simply another American competitive move against the Belgian capitalists, carried out, like all American moves in the Congo, through the U.N.[69]

By the late months of 1961, the old Moscow-Peking disagreement over the tactical advantages of using the U.N. machinery and the relative importance of staying in tune with neutral African opinion was thus fully restored—although it was now expressed more quietly, because of the obviously weakened position of both powers in the Congo.

Gizenga's inability to accept fully his role in the new legal framework and his return to Stanleyville, which resulted in his removal from office and ultimate arrest, may well have been due in part to the impact of this renewal of conflicting advice from his powerful friends. After the arrest, Moscow and Peking once again found themselves united in a campaign of protests and warnings that Gizenga was to suffer Lumumba's fate, but the tone remained significantly different: Peking continued to treat Gizenga as the Congo's only true patriotic leader and heaped insults on Adoula as a stooge of the imperialists; Moscow, while criticizing Adoula, avoided personal insults and did not withdraw its invitation to him to visit the Soviet Union.

In the first two years after the African policies of Moscow and Peking began to diverge openly, the effects on their total influence were remarkably small. Where the two powers continued to cooperate, as in the main part of the Congo crisis, they made a considerable impact: the sharp differentiation between the militant anticolonialism of the so-called "Casablanca group" and the more cautious neutralism of other African states was to some extent the fruit of Russo-Chinese exploitation of such events as the Katanga secession and the killing of Lumumba, as well as the prolonged horrors of the Algerian war. Where they quarrelled, their differences appeared to most African onlookers as comparatively minor and liable to be resolved by the course of events—as indeed they were in a number of cases. In some ways, the Communist powers may even have derived positive benefits from being able to offer a choice of alternative policies to African nationalists; to the extent that they have, the effects of a genuine dispute may have been similar to those of a mutually agreed-upon division of labor.

Of course, many activities of the Communist powers were hardly affected by the dispute at all. The establishment of diplomatic relations between Communist China and Mali in 1960, or the conclusion of China's Treaty of Friendship with Ghana during Dr. Nkrumah's visit to Peking in 1961 (a treaty explicitly based on the principle of peaceful coexistence between states with different social systems), could have taken place in just the same way within a framework of harmonious Sino-Soviet cooperation.[70]

That was not the case, however, with the earlier Treaty of Friendship with Guinea, which was concluded during Sekou Touré's Peking visit in September 1960. Both the text of that treaty and the circumstances surrounding its conclusion clearly reflected a Chinese desire to establish a special relationship with this small African country that should be independent of, and indeed sharply different from, its relations with Russia. From the start, Touré's visit was celebrated with a warm cordiality and a wealth of publicity unusual even in Communist propaganda, and the "first treaty of friendship with an African country" was described as a momentous stage in China's relations with the African continent. The intention to establish between the two countries a type of bond differing from the normal sort of "coexistence" between Communist and uncommitted states was underlined by the nature of the Chinese loan to Guinea: in conspicuous contrast to the slightly larger Soviet loan of 140 million rubles, the Chinese loan of 100 million rubles was to be free of interest—and it was also stipulated that Chinese experts working in Guinea should have a standard of living not exceeding that of their local opposite numbers. (Following this example, the smaller loan granted to Ghana a year later was also given free of interest.) Clearly, these terms were intended to suggest that the Soviets were moved by material self-interest in their aid agreements whereas the Chinese were motivated only by the spirit of fraternal solidarity.

The whole proceedings suggested the hope that Guinea and its ruling party, the Parti Démocratique de Guinée (PDG), could become an ideological bridgehead for China on the continent. The joint communiqué signed by Liu Shao-chi and Sekou Touré endorsed the Chinese thesis that "so long as colonialism continues to exist and the colonial and semicolonial peoples continue to be oppressed, it will be impossible for the world to have a genuine peace"; in return, it contained the unusual tribute that "the Chinese side considers that the Guinean government and people have made outstanding contributions in supporting the other African peoples . . . and promoting African solidarity."[71]

The special nature of the treaty bears witness to the Chinese recognition of Guinea's importance as a center for contact with opposition movements from other African countries, and to the ideological affinities revealed in the voting of Guinean representatives in the Afro-Asian Solidarity Organization, in the Chinese efforts to get the Organization's seat transferred to Conakry, and in the choice of Ismail Touré as chairman of its Solidarity Fund. In seeking to give lasting expression to those affinities, the treaty became one of the steps marking the transition from short-term policy divergence to long-term Russo-Chinese rivalry in Africa.

The Impact of Long-Term Rivalry

In retrospect, it appears that the fall of 1959 marked not a passing phase of acute disagreement but a true watershed in Soviet-Chinese relations—the moment at which the leaders in Moscow and Peking finally became aware that they had to prepare for a prolonged period of rivalry for control of the world Communist movement. The conflict might know its compromises as well as its crises; it might or might not be ultimately contained within a framework of formal unity and alliance; but it could no longer be permanently bridged. For that, the differences of interest and outlook had proved too serious and persistent.

In its origin, this new awareness of inevitable long-term rivalry had very little to do with Africa in particular; the vital difference turned on the risks to be taken by Russia and China in pursuing their common antagonism to the Western alliance, and above all to the United States. But it must have forced both of them to re-examine their long-term views on the formation and control of Communist parties and their road to power in all parts of the world. Such rethinking was particularly likely to affect their activities in tropical Africa, where few Communist parties existed as yet, and where both the Soviet and Chinese interpretations of Lenin's famous concept of a two-stage revolution in colonial and semicolonial countries had proved equally difficult to apply.

Traditionally, both Soviet and Chinese Communists had followed Lenin in distinguishing a first, national and "democratic" phase of that revolution, directed against imperialism and feudalism, from a second, "proletarian" or "socialist" phase. Both also had agreed on them forward, overcoming their hesitations, creating their own organizations for the working class and seeking to win influence on the peasantry, but not actually contesting the leadership of the bourgeois nationalists before the latter had completed their "historical task."

The Chinese Communists, on the other hand, had tried this policy in the 1920's, on Stalin's advice, with disastrous results. Later, under the need for assuring the victory of the first phase by forming a broad national front comprising the patriotic elements of the bourgeoisie as well as the working class, the peasantry, and the petty-bourgeois strata; in the second phase it was thought sufficient for the workers to keep the bulk of the working peasants on their side. But under Stalin the Soviets had always believed that during the first phase of the revolution the leading role was bound to be played by the "national bourgeoisie" (which in Soviet language generally includes nationalist intellectuals and officers); the task of the Communists during this phase was to act as independent but loyal partners of the political organizations of that "national bourgeoisie"—urging Mao's leadership, they worked out a new recipe: the Communist Party must seek to achieve leadership of all the patriotic classes even during the first phase of the revolution. Mao's "New Democracy," as it was developed in the struggle against the Japanese occupation, claimed to be based on a broad alliance of social classes, but it was *not* a coalition of independent political forces representing those classes—it was already a Communist one-party regime. Thus the transition to the second, or "socialist" phase, meant a change in the policy of the regime and in the "class basis" claimed for it—but not a transfer of power, not a change in the *political* nature of the regime itself.

In the actual course of later colonial revolutions, and in Africa in particular, the Soviet idea of the necessary leadership of "bourgeois" nationalists in the first phase had proved generally realistic, inasmuch as the numerical weakness of the working class and the organizational and political weakness of the Communists allowed no other choice.

But while the Chinese recipe was thus made inapplicable by the lack of Communist parties that could have played a "leading role" from the beginning, the Chinese misgivings about the Soviet alternative nevertheless were largely confirmed, for the "bourgeois nationalist" leaders, once in power, showed a remarkable capacity for entrenching themselves, and often they effectively suppressed the Communists to avoid being overthown, as planned, in the "second phase" of the revolution. Moreover, as the process of decolonization advanced, more and more former African colonies achieved national independence without any kind of revolutionary conflict, and nationalist regimes were established which could hardly be described as revolutionary in any sense.

The likelihood of a speedy increase in the number of African states that would emerge without serious conflict with the "imperialists" became obvious in the course of 1959; and the recognition of this, together with the experience of the widely differing developments of various nationalist regimes of ex-colonial states—from Egypt and Iraq to Indonesia and Cuba—seems to have been a major stimulus toward a Soviet revision of the Stalinist version of the two-stage revolution. The new strategic concept of the "independent state of national democracy" as the form in which the ex-colonial countries would make their transition to the "non-capitalist road of development," which was finally worked out by the Soviet ideologists in preparing the draft of their new party program between 1959 and 1961, reflects a double shift of interest: away from the original struggle for "national liberation" toward a struggle to influence the domestic and international orientation of the new states, and away from a predominant reliance on diplomatic and economic means of influence toward a reactivation of the local Communist Parties.[72]

In this revised strategy, the winning of "formal" national independence is considered a mere precondition for the true anti-imperialist and democratic revolution, which is to achieve real independence from the imperialist economic system and to open the non-capitalist road. Furthermore, the vital role of the working class and its organizations for the victory of this anti-imperialist and democratic revolution is emphasized far more than previously; the national bourgeoisie is still supposed to "lead" at first in the sense of heading the government, but only the friendly pressure from the local Communist Party and Communist-controlled trade unions from within and the attraction and aid of the "socialist camp" from without can ensure that the government moves in the right direction. Finally, neither the creation of the "national democratic" regime nor its transformation into a "socialist" one must necessarily take the form of violent revolution: under favorable conditions the Communist Party, by a skillful combination of loyalty to the nationalist leaders and organized pressure from within and without, may first push the government onto the right road while ensuring its own full freedom of organization, and then profit from this situation to increase its share of power until the time is ripe for a peaceful takeover of leadership.

The new Soviet strategy for ex-colonial countries in general, and for the new African states in particular, thus combines a reduced emphasis on revolutionary violence with increased attention to independent Communist organization and working class action. Its elaboration was accordingly accompanied by a new drive to step up the ideological training of Communist cadres and encourage the formation of Communist Parties in tropical Africa. But as it coincided in time with the new expectation of lasting Soviet-Chinese rivalry, the working out of both the new strategy and the organizational measures for its implementation seem to have proceeded without any Chinese participation. Instead, we find a marked increase in the contribution made by the West European Communist Parties—the parties of the old colonial powers—both to the concrete study of African problems[73] and to the new cadre-training and party-building effort; and this effort, it should be noted, is being carried forward with the fullest use of their old channels of contact, which are outside the Chinese-infiltrated machinery of the Afro-Asian Solidarity movement.

One of the first indications of the intensified drive to train ideologically reliable African cadres occurred at the WFTU's new all-African training school opened at Budapest in September 1959. In a farewell speech to the participants in the first course, WFTU general secretary Louis Saillant reminded them that the working class had a historical task beyond the struggle for national independence, and warned against the rise of a "neo-reformism based on nationalism" in the African trade unions if the workers of Africa wished to gain more than a change of masters, the unions must lead the struggle for democratic liberties in the new states.[74]

In October 1959 a new periodical entitled *The African Communist* made its appearance. Officially published by the (illegal) South African Communist Party from a London address, it was explicitly described as "a forum for Marxist-Leninist thought throughout our continent"; an introductory statement in its first four issues called on readers all over Africa to use the magazine as a basis for forming discussion groups, which, it said, "may became the foundation-stones of great and important Communist Parties in many lands that will bring salvation to your country." In short, the magazine is intended as an international policy-making organ and a "collective organizer" for the whole of tropical Africa, and articles from it have been reprinted as authoritative by organs of the Communist press elsewhere.[75]

While featuring articles from South and West European Communists and following the Soviet line in world affairs, *The African Communist* has emphasized the existence of class problems in African society. It has argued the need for independent working-class organization and action and has launched polemics against the "petty-bourgeois socialism" of left-wing African nationalists who deny the importance of the class struggle and the need for Communist Parties; this criticism has even been applied to Sekou Touré and the other leaders of the PDG, and to the "un-Marxist" cult of Dr. Nkrumah as a savior.[76]

Naturally, preparations for the formation of orthodox Communist Parties in tropical Africa are not confined to such public propaganda. *The African Communist* soon listed a number of "socialist groups" in different parts of Nigeria, along with a clear implication that practical efforts toward unification were in progress.[77] In January 1962 the formation of a recognized Communist Party was announced from Basutoland.[78] Nor is the drive confined to English-speaking areas: in the autumn of 1960, the role of Communist groups in the Somali nationalist movement was given public recognition, and a few months later the initiative of "Marxists" in starting the Angolan MPLA was disclosed by its leader, Mario de Andrade, in the columns of *Pravda*.[79]

While these efforts must have given the Soviets a head start over their Chinese rivals in the creation of African Communist Parties, however embryonic, they have also brought new complications for Soviet diplomacy. Soviet spokesmen have repeatedly hailed Guinea, Ghana, and Mali as the African models of a "national democratic" development, and delegates of the ruling parties of these three states were even invited to address the Twenty-Second Congress of the CPSU in October 1961. But none of these parties is willing to tolerate a rival Communist Party or an organized Communist faction within its ranks; and in the case of Guinea, Communist factional activities carried on in the official teachers' union and youth organization, allegedly with the help of Soviet, French, and Senegalese Communists, played a major role in provoking a crisis in Soviet-Guinean relations late in 1961, from which they have not fully recovered since.[80]

The first Chinese Communist response to the new Soviet strategy for Africa was apparently one of cautious reserve rather than of agreement or active criticism. On one side, the idea that more and more African states would achieve independence without violent conflict with the imperialists did not fit into the Chinese picture of the world; yet it was a fact that at least "formal" independence was being granted in that way in a number of cases, and the Soviets seemed justified in concerning themselves with the distinction between "formal" and "real" independence. On the other hand, the increased Soviet emphasis on the role of the working class in the struggle for "real" independence seemed to move closer, in however halfhearted a manner, to the traditional Chinese view that the Communists, as the party of the working class, must take the lead from the beginning of the colonial revolution. On this point, the Chinese thus simply maintained their own position without making it the subject of renewed polemics.

For instance, at the Peking session of the General Council of the WFTU in June 1960—the session that saw a major Chinese assault on Soviet disarmament proposals and coexistence policies—the WFTU's secretary for Africa, I. Zakharia, delivered a report on the struggle against colonialism. In accordance with the new Soviet line, he stressed the need for the trade unions to avoid subordination to the "national bourgeoisie" and develop an autonomous working class program for the future even before the achievement of national independence.[81] The resolution that was voted on the subject called on the workers to "assume a *leading* role in forming and consolidating a united national front, based on the alliance of workers and peasants and rallying all other anticolonial forces."[82] There have been no reports of serious debates with the Chinese on this point. Clearly, they had no reason to be dissatisfied with this formula, even though to the Soviets it meant no more than Communist leadership in forming a coalition with "bourgeois-nationalist" partners.

But when this Soviet view was made explicit in the new strategy of "national democracy" as defined at the 1960 Moscow conference of Communist parties and subsequently interpreted in Soviet journals, the Chinese refused to make any use of the new concept. Although they did not attack it directly, they implicitly rejected it in an authoritative article published in mid-1961 on the corresponding phase of their own revolutionary experience.[83] This article speaks throughout of a "people's democratic united front" where Soviet and international Communist documents now speak of a "national democratic front," and of a "people's democratic dictatorship" where the Soviets refer to an "independent state of national democracy" as the organs for completing the "democratic" phase of the revolution.

The difference here is not purely verbal: the Soviet concept implies a real, if transitional, sharing of power between the Communists and their "bourgeois nationalist" partners; the Chinese concept requires the assumption of full power by the Communists as a condition for completing even the "democratic" revolution. Accordingly, the Chinese can speak of a peaceful transition from the "democratic" to the "socialist" phase of the revolution—i.e., from one phase of Communist rule to the next—but never of a peaceful victory of the "democratic" revolution, in which the Communists must first win power. The Soviets, in contrast, admit the possibility that both phases —the original entry of the Communists into a ruling coalition and the later ousting of their nationalist partners—may be accomplished peacefully in favorable circumstances.

Chinese insistence on the "leading role" of the Communist parties in the "democratic revolution" has remained, however, somewhat perfunctory—the repetition of a traditional shibboleth rather than the expression of a serious concern with the present problems of the ex-colonial countries. In practice, Chinese discussion of the concrete developments on the African scene has been concerned neither with the leading role of the African Communist parties (which are as yet barely in process of formation, nor even with the analysis of class conflicts, but almost exclusively with the potential for militant anti-imperialist struggle.

As late as July 1960, when Soviet analysts were already busy discussing the "unreliability" of the African "national bourgeoisie" and the need for independent working-class action, the first systematic Chinese treatment of "The Awakening of Africa" (the article by Feng Chih-tan mentioned earlier) still stressed that bourgeois and intellectual groups in many African countries had one after another joined the national liberation movement, owing to their conflict of interest with imperialism. In fact, the article mentioned the different classes only in order to enumerate their contributions to the common anti-imperialist struggle, with special emphasis on the role of the peasants —the bulk of the population—in making possible, by their massive participation, the "liberation wars" in Algeria and the Cameroun.

The main concern of Feng's presentation of the Chinese "general line" on Africa was with the alleged growth of *armed* anti-imperialist struggle in Africa—a growth which, in contrast both to the facts and to the Soviet analysis, he claimed to be characteristic for the new phase of the movement. As he put it: "In the past year and more, in the wake of Algeria and the Cameroun, anticolonial armed revolts of varying scale broke out in the Congo, Nyasaland, Ruanda-Urundi, Uganda, and other places." It was true, he explained, that as armed suppression was failing the imperialists were also trying, as an alternative tactic, to bribe the "right wing of the African bourgeoisie" by compromise offers of "peaceful transition to self-rule," in order to paralyze the fighting will of the African people. But even when they granted formal independence, they were seeking to retain the reality of political, economic, and military control. To accept such compromises in the name of "peaceful coexistence," as advocated by "modern revisionists," meant to accept "freedom for the imperialists to exercise a rule of violence over the African people, while the colonial peoples are deprived of all freedom to terminate this unjust colonialist rule of violence with just violence."[84]

The evident lack of Chinese interest in a closer analysis of the African class situation indicates that the Chinese Communists do not intend to compete against Soviet influence among African revolutionaries with arguments based on the class struggle. But it does not follow that they have not perceived the obvious long-range challenge of the Soviet effort to exclude them from the training of African Communist cadres and the formation of new parties; rather they have responded to the Soviet claim to a "monopoly of class-consciousness" by insisting on their own monopoly of anti-imperialist militancy and by charging the Soviets with opportunistic appeasement of the imperialists. Judging the revolutionary promise of African movements and groups not in terms of their class character but exclusively in terms of the actual or expected violence of their clash with the colonial powers or other white oppressors, the Chinese have continued to concentrate their energies on those movements where the national situation seemed to favor violence. At the same time, they have reacted to the growing Soviet use of such world-wide front organizations as the WFTU and the World Peace Council (WPC) on the African scene by pursuing increasingly ruthless exploitation of their more favorable position in the Afro-Asian People's Solidarity Organization (AAPSO) and its branches.

Thus the Chinese have made special efforts to maintain close and friendly relations with the Algerian FLN after the achievement of Algerian independence; even after the Algerian Communist Party was banned by the new government towards the end of 1962, and the Soviet Communists published an official protest, the Chinese kept silent and continued both to supply aid and to invite a steady stream of FLN officials to Peking.[85] Chinese support of the armed rising of the UPC in Cameroun continued unchanged after the mysterious death of Dr. Moumié (poisoned in Switzerland in November 1960); in July 1961, a group of Camerounians arrested on their return from China were found to have been trained there in the tactics and techniques of guerilla warfare as well as in the Chinese version of Communist doctrine.[86] More recently, however, the insurrectionary movement appears to have become increasingly isolated in its struggle against an independent government, and this has enabled Moscow, with the help of the French Communists, to split the exiled leadership of the UPC and to regain control of one group.[87]

Chinese contacts with the leaders of the Guinean PDG have not fulfilled the high hopes originally placed by Peking on this small country, whose importance on the African scene has been somewhat reduced with the shifting of the main drama of decolonization from West to East, Central, and South Africa; but they have remained friendly and have not been affected by the rapid cooling off in Soviet-Guinean relations that has occurred since the end of 1961. Relations with Ghana have become increasingly cordial as Dr. Nkrumah has felt frustrated in his Pan-African ambitions, and while Nkrumah has carefully refrained from taking sides between Moscow and Peking, he has not hesitated to give public support to China against neutral India.

In the Congo, Chinese moral support has continued to go exclusively to Gizenga, but Peking does not disguise its bitterness about developments there, which it regards as a severe setback to the "true" liberation movement.[88] In Angola and the other Portuguese colonies, it competes with Moscow in demonstrative support for the Communist-directed MPLA, whose leaders have so far avoided a choice between the two rival centers of world Communism. Peking also gives maximum publicity to the struggle of the non-Communist Zimbabwe African National Union in Southern Rhodesia.[89] No effective contacts seem to exist with the long-established Communist Party of South Africa, any more than with the young parties in Basutoland and Nigeria; but there may be some with the Communists in the Malagasy Republic (Madagascar).[90]

In East Africa, official Chinese relations are closest with Somalia, whose nationalists have irredentist claims on neighboring Ethiopia and Kenya as well as on French Somaliland. Although both Moscow and Peking were early supporters of the Greater Somali League— which the Communist circles originally built up by the Italian CP as well as more students in Soviet bloc countries have recently been told to join—the Soviet Union has so far hesitated, in view of its friendly relations with the Ethiopian autocracy, to commit itself to support Somali's territorial demands; China, however, has no such inhibitions and is known to have financed arms purchases for an irredentist movement in French Somaliland.[91] Another pro-Chinese stronghold is the Arab-controlled Zanzibar Nationalist Party (ZNP) and the Zanzibar Federation of Progressive Trade Unions in the same

British island colony off the East African coast; to the dominant Arab elements in Zanzibar, which fear being swamped once the island joins a federation of the new East African states, Chinese opposition to such a federation has appeared more definite than that of the Soviets. But this may prove a vanishing asset once federation comes about.[92]

Independent of the search for close political friends and revolutionary allies, Peking has also, of course, continued the effort to develop diplomatic, economic, and cultural relations with as many as possible of the new African states. Thus a cultural delegation toured East Africa at the end of 1962, and diplomatic relations have been established and trade agreements concluded with Tanganyika and Uganda.

The "Fronts" Organize the Schism. The Twenty-Second Congress of the CPSU, by producing the public breakdown of the Sino-Soviet compromise that had been negotiated after prolonged debate at the 1960 Moscow conference of 81 Communist parties, also marked the beginning of a much more open struggle for control of the revolutionary movement in Africa. For the two preceding years, from the fall of 1959 to the fall of 1961, the leaders in Moscow and Peking had given the impression of preparing for a protracted but carefully controlled rivalry within a common world movement. After the clash at the 1960 congress, they rushed to organize their separate worldwide factions as quickly as possible, as if in anticipation of an inevitable early schism: the dispute was openly extended from the ideological to the organizational plane.

Of the crucial ideological issues, the one that touched Africa most directly concerned the relative priorities of the diplomatic "struggle for peaceful coexistence" and the revolutionary "struggle against imperialism." In organizational terms, this naturally raised the question of the relationship between the World Peace Movement and the Afro-Asian People's Solidarity Organization, with the Soviets proclaiming primary importance for the former and the Chinese championing the independence of the latter. In Africa, the factional schism between the followers of Moscow and Peking has thus largely assumed the organizational form of a struggle between these two "fronts."

The Chinese opened the attack at the Stockholm session of the World Peace Council (December 16–19, 1961). In speeches that were subsequently published, Liao Cheng-chih and Liu Ning-yi declared that the peace movement "should not be required to follow every step in the diplomatic moves of this or that country," that disarmament slogans were inapplicable to nations struggling for liberation or to newly independent countries, and that "fighters for peace" must give full support to the national liberation movement and not seek to tone it down for the sake of "peaceful coexistence."[93] The pro-Soviet majority recognized, in the words of Velio Spano, the Italian Communist and member of the WPC presidium, "that there was a fundamental contrast between the two political lines and that any attempt at reconciliation would be quite useless."[94] The matter was brought to a vote over the name to be given to the next World Peace Congress; the Soviets had proposed to make it a congress "for general disarmament and peace," but the Chinese supported an amendment, proposed by the Guinean delegate Diallo Seydou, to label it a congress "for peace, national independence, and disarmament." The amendment was defeated by 166 votes to 24, but Spano's pro-Soviet account admits that the minority included "some African and Asian delegations," and the speech by Seydou in particular, as published by the Chinese, was outspoken in its opposition to treating disarmament as the core of the peace movement.[95]

The Stockholm vote settled the victory of the Soviet line in the WPC, and the Chinese did not renew their public opposition when the World Peace Congress met in Moscow as planned in the summer of 1962, for they had decided to concentrate on the more favorable ground of Afro-Asianism. At the conference of Afro-Asian writers, held in Cairo in February 1962, the fight was conducted only in committee, but there Peking seems to have won all along the line: Chinese opposition prevented a resolution for "general and complete disarmament," moved by the Turkish writer Nazim Hikmet (a member of the WPC bureau living in Moscow) from reaching the floor, and it also defeated a Soviet proposal to hold the next conference in Mongolia. The familiar Chinese charges that the Soviets were putting disarmament and coexistence ahead of national liberation were stated by Mao Tun, the chairman of the Chinese writers' union, with such vehemence that his Soviet opponent, Mirzo Tursun-zade, complained of "distortion," and neutral participants described the Chinese per-

formance as "Russian-baiting." It was in the lobbies of this conference that Chinese representatives were first reported to have talked
of the need for the "colored nations" to band together against "the
whites."[96]

After this experience the Soviets evidently concluded that they
could no longer rely on controlling the AAPSO and that it was time
to develop the propaganda of the WPC—the parent body from which
the AAPSO had once sprung—on African soil. As early as the Gaza
session of the AAPSO executive, held in December 1961, and during
the immediately following Stockholm meeting of the WPC, the Soviets had accepted a proposal for a three-continent conference of
Asian, African, and Latin American movements for national liberation.[97] But they had suggested that the conference should be prepared
by the Asian and Latin American regional organizations affiliated to
the WPC together with the All-African People's Conference; this attempt to prevent an extension of the AAPSO to Latin America was
at once opposed by the Asians.[98] After the Moscow Peace Congress
of the summer of 1962, to which a number of African leaders were
invited, the WPC started to found National Peace Committees in one
African country after another; by October no less than nine new
African committees were claimed.[99] Other Soviet-controlled international "fronts" followed the same line: in August 1962 the Lenin-
grad congress of the International Union of Students added some
African students to its executive,[100] and in February 1963, the World
Federation of Democratic Youth (WFDY) decided at its Budapest
session to send delegations to tour both West and East Africa in the
course of the year.[101]

The third Afro-Asian Solidarity conference met at Moshi, Tanganyika (February 4–11, 1963) in this atmosphere of highly organized
factional struggle, with the Cuban and Sino-Indian crises of the preceding autumn still reverberating. Tanganyika had been chosen as
its site because it had in the meantime become the most important
legal center for the African leaders from the Rhodesias and the Portuguese colonies; but both President Nyerere and the most broadly
representative African regional organization, the Pan-African Freedom Movement of East, Central, and South Africa (PAFMECSA),
welcomed the conference with some misgivings, as clearly shown by

their warnings to Africans against being dragged into other people's quarrels. The Soviets, who had just proposed a truce in public inter-Communist polemics, also pressed the Chinese delegates at Moshi to avoid an open clash, and an appeal of the WPC not to debate divisive issues was distributed to the delegates.[102] But the Chinese showed from the start that they were bent on a ruthless, if not a public, struggle: they succeeded in making the conference refuse official status to the seven-man delegation of the WPC and to the delegations of other world-wide "fronts," permitting only those members of such delegations who had also national mandates from African or Asian countries to address the conference;[103] they specifically arranged rejection of the mandate of Nazim Hikmet, the "Moscow Turk" who had moved the disarmament resolution at Cairo the year before; they even suggested, unsuccessfully, that the PAFMECSA representatives might object to the participation of a "white" Soviet delegation![104]

In a message of greeting to the conference, Mr. Khrushchev had cited his own policy during the Cuban crisis as an example of how to save the national independence of a country threatened by the imperialists while preserving world peace;[105] and Tursun-zade, who again led the Soviet delegation, stressed the same point as well as the need for disarmament.[106] By contrast, Liu Ning-yi, who led the Chinese delegation, cited the victory of the Algerian people as proof of the superiority of the revolutionary will over modern weapons, warned against trusting the "so-called assurances" of allegedly "sensible" imperialists, and called for support for the five-point demands of the Castro government; the idea that the underdeveloped nations might benefit from disarmament agreements by receiving increased economic aid he called "deceitful nonsense" calculated to weaken the fighting spirit of oppressed peoples.[107]

Throughout the conference, the volume of Chinese publicity for its proceedings was far greater than that of Soviet publicity, though daily reports appeared in both countries. The reports showed that only the Indian delegate, Chaman Lall, had explicitly supported Khrushchev's Cuban policy;[108] and he was alone in demanding a resolution favoring the "unconditional acceptance" of the proposal by the Colombo powers for settling the Sino-Indian border conflict, and after walking out of the conference because its political committee rejected the proposal, he returned and had to content himself with a vague recommendation acceptable to the Chinese.[109]

Generally, while the Chinese did not succeed in getting all their slogans incorporated in the conference resolutions, they were strong enough to prevent anything that was not acceptable to them and to achieve much that was disagreeable to the Soviet Union. In particular, both the general declaration of the conference and its political resolution described the struggle for national liberation as "a mighty force in achieving peace and disarmament" and not, as the Soviets would have had it, peaceful coexistence and disarmament as creating the best conditions for national liberation.[110] Finally, the resolution calling for a "conference of the three continents" in Havana and the establishment of a preparatory committee of six Asians, six Africans, and six Latin Americans did not confine participation to organizations affiliated to the WPC, even for Latin America, but called for maximum participation of "all organizations opposing imperialism, colonialism, and neo-colonialism."[111]

Soviet comment did not at once indicate the dissatisfaction Moscow must have felt at this. Perhaps the first hint that the Soviets believed the AAPSO had outlived its usefulness appeared toward the end of March, when Tursun-zade wrote in *Pravda* that the Soviet Union would always render comprehensive effective assistance to freedom-loving peoples "regardless of the form the liberation struggle will take."[112] About the same time the Indian Communist leader (and vice-president of the WFTU) S. A. Dange rejected an Indonesian proposal for an "Afro-Asian workers' conference" because the Chinese would only use it to introduce "ideological differences"; the AAPSO, he argued, had not proved immune to these tactics.[113] By April 1963, a World Federation of Democratic Youth seminar in Algiers on the anticolonial struggle led to open and bitter quarrels, with the Chinese complaining about discrimination by the chairman; it resolved to form an African Youth Committee and a committee for aiding colonial peoples, without even mentioning the AAPSO.[114] Conversely, an Afro-Asian journalists' conference held at Jakarta, run by the AAPSO under strong Chinese influence and outside the control of the International Organization of Journalists, decided to set up an "Afro-Asian Journalists Association."[115] Clearly, both sides were entrenching themselves in rival organizations in every field.

In May of 1963 a comprehensive though still cautious statement of the Soviet case against the AAPSO finally appeared.[116] The author of this statement, who had attended all the major Afro-Asian and Pan-African conferences as a Soviet correspondent, suggested that the form of the movement no longer corresponded to the content of African political developments. He said that the rise of a large number of African states with differing political orientations required, on the one hand, intergovernmental conferences of a diplomatic nature, on the other hand, international movements with common ideological principles; he claimed that the AAPSO was too unrepresentative for the first purpose and too disunited for the second. The Moshi conference had not dared to attack African governments that were being run by neo-colonial "stooges" for fear of offending against Pan-African solidarity; yet it had shown dangerous chauvinistic tendencies in refusing the right to speak to white representatives of progressive world organizations—a fact admitted in this article for the first time. But the colonial liberation movement, the article said, could achieve its aims only if it strengthened its solidarity with progressive forces everywhere, and added that perhaps *ad hoc* conferences called on important specific issues would serve this purpose better than the AAPSO.

The role played by China was nowhere explicitly mentioned in this article. Yet beyond the organizational issue, it set forth the essence of the Soviet response to the latest development of the Chinese ideological position. In the most exhaustive statement of that position so far, published at the beginning of March,[117] the Chinese Communists had for the first time put forward the thesis that the colonial, semicolonial, and ex-colonial countries of Asia, Africa, and Latin America constitute "the focus of world contradictions," and that the revolutionary struggles of the oppressed nations of these areas "are decisive for the cause of the international proletariat as a whole." To this thesis, which was repeated in the letter addressed by the Chinese to the Soviet Communists in June 1963, on the eve of the abortive Moscow talks between the delegations of both parties,[117] the Soviets replied by insisting on their own decisive role as the advanced power center of the "socialist world system," and by giving stern warnings against playing up to the chauvinistic and racial prejudices of the underdeveloped peoples and isolating them from the main force of the "socialist" countries and the working class of the industrial nations, without whose help, in the Soviet view, no successful struggle for liberation from colonial rule would ever have been possible.[119]

Conclusions

As the Sino-Soviet conflict has become more open and bitter, the division of African activities between the two Communist powers, which had developed naturally from their different capacities and opportunities, has hardened into a factional schism, with each side seeking to promote its policy through different organizations. Among a few militant nationalist groups, and particularly in the machinery of the Afro-Asian People's Solidarity Organization, Chinese influence has grown stronger at Soviet expense. The Soviet Union, on the other hand, has not only consolidated its initial advantage in the field of so-called trade-union organization and of the formation of cadres for Communist Parties, but has endeavored with some success to extend the influence of its other international front organizations on African soil and to get African leaders to join their directing bodies. Yet it is becoming increasingly doubtful how much real impact Communist power is making on the thinking and actions of the most representative movements and personalities of present-day African nationalism, or how far it is really succeeding in building a foundation for the growth of effective Communist movements in Africa.

In fact, the total influence of the Communist powers on Africa seems to have declined since the end of 1961, and the recrudescence of the Sino-Soviet conflict since the Twenty-Second Congress of the CPSU has played a major part in this development. So long as the policy divergences between Moscow and Peking appeared to African eyes as comparatively minor and transient, as they did until 1961, they did very little harm to the attraction exercised by the "socialist camp" as a whole. But the mounting evidence that the conflict was serious and might be lasting was bound to raise many doubts about whether Communist power politics were really different in principle from "imperialist" power politics—especially since it coincided with increasing impact of American support for African nationalism and increasing distrust of any policy that tended to set Africans against Africans. Chinese whisperings about Soviet affinity with the "white" imperialists was probably confirmed by the disappointing amount of Soviet aid, combined with overbearing manners and political interference, as in Guinea; Soviet warnings against Chinese "adventurism" fell on a soil prepared by weariness with bloodshed and disorder in the Congo and the Cameroun, by the negotiated end of the Algerian war and its bitter economic aftermath, and by the spreading knowledge of Peking's severe economic setbacks. The absence of many representative African personalities from the Moshi conference and the warnings of President Nyerere have shown that seven years after the beginning of decolonization in tropical Africa many African leaders are taking a more detached view of Communist propaganda; and the efforts of Moscow and Peking to discredit each other's policies naturally tend to increase that detachment.

Nor can the growth of Communist Parties with real prospects be effectively assured merely by such efforts as the Soviet and West European Communists have lately been making in this field. That kind of growth can be initiated only by leaders with true political ability and ambition who can genuinely identify themselves with the cause of international Communism without losing a sure grasp of their own strategy and tactics that is needed to win popular confidence. Such successful and impressive identification is possible with a truly worldwide idea; it is also possible with a unique world power in which all hopes are vested. But it becomes extremely difficult when the idea is represented by two rival alien powers. Elsewhere established Communist Parties under experienced and popular leaders may push the new doubts aside and live on by a kind of pseudo-revolutionary inertia, or they may even seek to exploit the new situation to win increased independence. But where no established Communist Party and leadership exists—as in most of Africa—the obstacles to building up the necessary authority for an ideology that has appeared only in rival interpretations will be formidable.

To the more gifted and ambitious of Africa's nationalist intellectuals, Communism's greatest attraction is probably its value as an

engine for uniting the national will behind an effort toward modernization; its greatest drawback in their eyes is that its ideology is
not founded on African premises. The Soviet-Chinese rivalry for the
correct interpretation of this ideology not only focuses attention on
its foreign origin but also destroys the attraction of unity. In the long
run, that rivalry is therefore likely to confirm the African intelligentsia's determination to find their own independent "road to socialism" without following any ready-made Communist model.

But the question today is no longer only what the Communist
powers are doing to Africa, but also what their rivalry for influence
in Africa is doing to them and to their ideology, particularly in the
case of China. Step by step Peking has come to count on the colonial
revolutions first for weakening the imperialist enemy by an ubiqui-
tous war of attrition, then for disturbing any attempt at a Russo-
American dialogue by a succession of crises, and finally for proving
its superior revolutionary zeal in the factional struggle for control of
the world Communist movement. The further the conflict with Moscow has developed, the larger the importance of the colonial struggles
for liberation has loomed in the consciousness of the Chinese Communists, until they have finally come to see these struggles as "the *focus*
of world contradictions" and as *decisive* for the victory of world
Communism—a view that is closely bound up with their vision of
themselves as the champions of a world-wide front of the colored
masses that is to achieve that victory. In that vision, the working
classes of the advanced industrial nations are reduced to the role of
mere auxiliaries of the liberation struggle of the colored races; the
historic mission that Marx assigned to what Arnold Toynbee has
called the "internal proletariat" of Western civilization has been transferred by Mao to Toynbee's "external proletariat."

Such a transfer goes far beyond Lenin; in fact, it reverses the
roles envisaged by Lenin when he first conceived the alliance between
the industrial workers and the colonial peoples—for Lenin never
doubted that the colonial peoples would be the auxiliaries of the
workers. But the persistent failure of the industrial proletariat of the
advanced nations to seize power under the Communist banner on one
side, and the Communist victory in underdeveloped China and the revolutionary ferment among colonial peoples on the other, have brought

about a situation in which the would-be followers of Lenin have to choose between his belief in the Marxian proletariat and his unconditional devotion to revolutionary struggle: Leninism is disintegrating into its Marxist and non-Marxist elements, with the industrialized Soviet Union of today increasingly stressing the Marxist side, and poor, backward China championing a belief in revolution at any price —even if it be a racial revolution.

It was in the African activities of both countries that this tendency first manifested itself, years before it was consciously formulated into its present alternative principles: the Soviet preoccupation with the embryonic class aspects of African politics, and the Chinese concentration on anticolonial violence. Rivalry on this unfamiliar continent has been a catalytic factor in bringing out the latent contradictions of an ideology unsuited to African conditions. In the long run, this may prove to be the most lasting effect of the Communist attempt to shape the destiny of Africa.

6

CONCLUSION:

THE AFRICAN CHALLENGE

Zbigniew Brzezinski

It is sometimes forgotten that the Communist states began their efforts to penetrate Africa while under a great many handicaps. They undertook to compete for influence and prestige with the two most advanced and highly developed areas of the world, the United States and Western Europe. In purely material terms the competition is thus between a rich, highly skilled, and capital-exporting complex of states and a Communist world still struggling to overcome its backwardness, comparatively short of capital even for domestic investment, and composed in the main of countries only now moving from the phase of predominantly agrarian economy to an agrarian-industrial one.

To be sure, East Germany, Czechoslovakia, and the Soviet Union —the most industrially advanced Communist states—carry most of the economic burden of Communist efforts in Africa; but in recent years there have been major stresses in their domestic economies, and competition from the Common Market has increased the demands, particularly for investment, made on them by the other Communist members of the Council for Economic Mutual Assistance. Competing with the West is thus not an easy task for them. The challenge is even more difficult for China and Yugoslavia, the two other Communist states active in Africa. The Chinese domestic failures are now a matter of public record, and the Yugoslav economy, sustained in part by American aid, has been badly threatened by the Common Market. Furthermore, none of the Communist countries (with the limited exception of Czechoslovakia) had any significant prior contact with Africa; they began their effort without established trading patterns, few personnel skilled in the byways of African business and with personal contacts among the Africans, and no tradition of producing goods suitable for the African market.

In many ways the situation was not much better in the political field. Independence had not come to the African states in the fashion prescribed by the Communists. To be sure, there was conflict and occasional violence, but by and large the Western powers (except the Portuguese) departed before exhausting all their opportunities for coercion and relinquished power to the African elites that they had trained. That these elites were often (but not always) bitterly hostile to the departing colonialists does not alter the fact that they had been conditioned, influenced, and inspired by their former sovereigns. A highly symbolic and politically important aspect of this is the fact that English and French have become the languages of the new elite, thereby making them susceptible to continuing European cultural influence and even imperceptibly shaping their thought patterns. Indeed, the success of the new African elites in getting their former colonial masters to leave was due in large part to their acceptceptance of the colonialists' way. This is a general political phenomenon, and many of the smaller Soviet-dominated countries (like Poland and Hungary) have applied such pressure against the Soviet Union.[1]

Although the new states were born in peace and not in revolution, the new rulers often quickly adopted revolutionary slogans and even revolutionary methods; but they used these rather pragmatically to stimulate a sense of nationalism, to overcome forces inimical to social-economic progress, and not least of all to gain a firm and exclusive hold on the spoils of power. The nonrevolutionary rise to power of the African elites thus created for the Communist states problems of ideological adjustment. In short, the Communist states were not only economically weaker than the West; they were politically and ideologically inexperienced in African ways, linguistically and culturally alien, and often even unable to grasp the importance of tribal loyalties (instead of class conflicts) in Africa.

There have been, however, some compensating advantages. Certain basic Marxist assumptions, particularly the alleged causal relationship between capitalism and imperialism, have become deeply ingrained in the thinking of many of the new elites, who were often trained by left-wing Europeans.[2] In general, there is also an inherent inclination among the first-generation political intelligentsia to seek "big answers" and universalist creeds. This was once true in Europe and Russia, and to the extent that it is true in Africa today, Communism has a special attraction, especially since it is linked to a technical revolution that the Africans ardently desire for themselves. This susceptibility often produces the sort of "ecstatic emancipation" that initially exaggerates existing hostility toward former rulers and leads to intense and pointed acts of self-assertion. There could be no more pointed way of expressing this self-assertion than by showing special amiability and consideration for the enemies of the former colonial powers. This explains, in part, the double standard by which some Africans in international affairs favor the Communist camp and make excessive criticisms of the West, even though the African rulers proclaim themselves, with sincerity, to be otherwise neutral and uncommitted.

Furthermore, the Communist idea of "neocolonialism" has gained wide acceptance among the African elites, sensitive as they are about their new independence and suspicious that the old masters wish to return under new auspices. Indeed, the concept of neocolonialism seems to be displacing Lenin's notions about imperialism as the most popular conceptual stereotype by which Africans can explain their view of the West's relationship to them.

An even more powerful advantage is that no Communist state has ever been a colonial power on the African continent. Their appearance in Africa is thus not viewed with the same suspicion as is a Western, or even an American initiative. The concept of neocolonialism, widespread among the African elites, is thus psychologically rooted in their past colonial relationship with the West. To many Africans, Hungary, or the Asian parts of the Soviet Union colonized by the Russians, are simply not cases of colonialism.

Thirdly, there is a certain feeling among some of the new elites, including the growing strata of the intelligentsia, that what is now happening in the Communist states has greater historical relevance to them than what has happened in the West.* The Communist states, precisely because they are relatively backward (in comparison with the West), are undergoing rapid development under conditions that have at least a superficial similarity to those in which the new African states must work. The ambitious and impatient rulers of the new states cannot fail to notice that the Communist states are characterized by the centralization of political power in the hands of a disciplined elite committed to effecting rapid social reconstruction; that this elite mobilizes the masses, thereby breaking down all the intermediary groups that restrain the exercise of political power; that they subject the citizen to intense politization, and thereby create in him a sense of political commitment; and finally, that they use political control to effect rapid development.

It is not surprising that most African statesmen visiting the Soviet Union, even if they consciously attempt to avoid identifying themselves with the U.S.S.R. in international affairs (and particularly against the West), do express admiration for the way the Soviet Union is carrying out its modernization. Neither the huge price paid by the Soviets in human life nor their continued failures, especially in agriculture (which ought to be seen as a real economic lesson for Africa), have been enough to inhibit this admiration. Finally, Soviet, Chinese, Czechoslovak, or Yugoslav leaders never tire of pointing out to African visitors that their country is a "multi-national" state—a useful reminder that the Communist system also offers models for building nations out of diverse nationalities and tribes.

* In this connection, it is interesting to note the symptomatic public opinion poll conducted early in 1962 among 300 African students from the French-speaking African states by the Senegalese sociologist Jean Pierre N'Diaye in collaboration with *Jeune Afrique* (published in Tunis). He divided his respondents into three groups, in relation to population: Group 1 from Guinea and Mali (the Left); Group 2 from the Ivory Coast, Dahomey, Senegal, Togo, and the Upper Volta (the neutrals); and Group 3 from the Cameroun, Congo-Brazzaville, and Gabon (pro-West). The tabulation below (based on *Jeune Afrique*, No. 7, June 4–10, 1962, pp. 16–17) shows the responses to his question, "What economic order do you desire for your country?":

	Total	Group 1	Group 2	Group 3
Integral socialism (Soviet model)	38%	57%	30%	38%
Communal socialism (Yugoslav model)	30%	21%	30%	38%
Liberal socialism (Scandinavian model)	20%	12%	29%	12%
Liberal economy	7%	5%	7%	6%
Don't know	5%	5%	4%	6%

The Communist and Western Strategies

It is in this setting of inherent disadvantages and certain special opportunities that the Communists' strategy for Africa is shaped and applied. The content of the strategy gives evidence of Communist awareness of these conflicting factors, even though Communist spokesmen, as noted earlier, have complained about the general level of ignorance in the Communist camp about things African. The strategy is geared to extract the maximum advantage from the available opportunities, and all the Communist states—from the Chinese "extremists" through the Soviet and East European "centrists" to the Yugoslav "revisionists"—stress their anticolonial outlook as the point of departure for their approach to Africa. As a Soviet theoretician put it: "The chief and most substantial thing that unites the socialist states and the non-socialist national states is their general anti-imperialist position—a common interest in the most rapid possible liquidation of the colonial system, in the all-round economic and cultural advancement of peoples temporarily lacking in their development, and in the establishment of genuine national equality and lasting peace on earth."[3]

With anticolonialism serving as the bridge establishing empathetic access, economic and political penetration is meant to create an initial beachhead. Judging from the available evidence, economic aid and trade is not considered by the Communist leaders to be of decisive importance, and there are good reasons to suspect that it is given on the basis of assumptions quite different from those that guide corresponding Western economic programs. Western programs, to be sure, also have African good will in mind, but by and large Western aid is channeled in the firm conviction that it makes little difference how the African leaders act *now*, whether they are friendly or hostile to the West; that what is considered decisive is that their societies reach the stage of "take-off" in the processes of modernization, with the expectation that subsequently many of the tensions and hostilities to the West will inevitably subside. In a curious paradox, the West's economic aid tends to be based on a historicism that discounts the importance of subjective African attitudes and stresses the shaping of objective social-economic conditions.

The Communists, perhaps making the most of economic necessity, stress the opposite. They cannot commit as many resources as the West, but it appears from the earlier analyses in this book that they do not commit perhaps even as much as they could (although any judgment of this sort involves a fairly arbitrary conclusion as to what is feasible). Their economic policies are designed to influence the subjective attitudes of the African elites and eventually the masses. This is even true of the Yugoslavs, who are much less militant than the others and who reject Soviet and Chinese orthodoxy and the need for a disciplined Communist camp. Economic penetration is thus much more politically oriented, and is, in fact, only part of the political penetration designed, in the first stage, to establish a community of outlook in international affairs, hopefully with subsequent domestic consequences in the African states. It is interesting in this connection to recall that Moscow did not initially object to Chinese emphasis on the special relevance of their experience for the underdeveloped countries, since that clearly furthered Communist goals. It was only when the Sino-Soviet dispute began to have consequences for the Soviet position of primacy within international Communism that the Soviet leaders became more concerned with the implications of any universalization of the Chinese experience.

The Communist calculation is that the initial beachhead will expand once the political impact has been made and consolidated. At that stage, the expectation is that the *subjective* attitudes of the ruling elites will begin to affect the shape and content of economic development. With the political "commanding heights" firmly in hand, the rulers would be in a position to determine the character, the form, and the pace of modernization. At this point, the Communist hope is that their socio-economic "model" will come into play. The politically sympathetic rulers, growing more hostile to the West and perhaps also experiencing pressure from various sub-elites (students, young intellectuals, impatient planners, etc.) that have come under Communist influence will then move step by step toward emulating Soviet domestic experience, adopting its organizational forms, then justifying this doctrinally by Marxist argumentation. In fostering this pattern of development the East Europeans, in some ways more skilled and less branded with past Stalinist brutality, can be of the greatest assistance. With the gradual adoption of Communist experience, the subjective African political predisposition would be supplemented by the mounting pressure of objective economic necessity, and the Marxist-Leninist balance will be restored. The sequence is almost the perfect reverse of Western projections.

In spite of the professed Communist support for African unity, Communist leaders probably welcome the Balkanization of sub-Saharan Africa, with the attendant economic complications and bitter political rivalries. The emergence of a Pan-African formation could impede the Communist takeover in individual states, on the Cuban model, and in its foreign policy a united Africa might well be less friendly to the Communist world than Ghana or Mali. In a setting of disunity, orderly economic growth and the development of political maturity are bound to be inhibited by all sorts of conflicts, which in themselves create openings for external intrusion, intrigue, manipulation, and intervention. Gradually the internal political and economic radicalization of the "subjective and objective situation" is to push the new states of "national democracy" into the first stages of proletarian dictatorship. At the same time, conflicts with white settlers in East and South Africa will help to inflame passions and thereby create new opportunities for Communist activity. As the preceding chapters have indicated, Soviet writers have discussed this prospect fully and without restraint.

Shortcomings of the Communist Strategy

It should be noted, however, that the successful implementation of this strategy is inhibited by several complications inherent in the present condition of the Communist world. First of all, a continuing Communist problem is the universal Communist failure in the agricultural sector, a failure that becomes especially embarrassing in dealing with a continent that is primarily agrarian.[4] Not only do these failures expose an inherent economic inadequacy; they also have embarrassing political overtones: they undermine the Communist argument that their method of industrialization can be carried out without Stalinist violence, which the Soviet leaders now try to interpret as merely a personal aberration. Poland's Gomulka came much closer to the truth when he pointed to Soviet collectivization as the evil that set in motion a chain reaction ending in Stalinist terror. Although Gomulka did not himself make the connection between Soviet collectivization and industrialization, their interdependence is familiar to anyone who has studied the Soviet model.

It is true that two Communist countries may point to modest successes in their agricultural sector and to simultaneous industrialization. A Polish or a Yugoslav Communist may argue that his country's experience permitted relative independence for the peasantry and effective, state-controlled industrialization—an assertion, however, that weakens the universal validity of a general Communist "model," since it implies greater efficiency for two deviant types. Secondly, neither country has achieved self-sufficiency in development; both are heavily dependent on foreign aid, and in the Yugoslav case much of this has come from the West. Thirdly, for reasons of bloc unity and ideological orthodoxy, the Poles are inhibited from stressing their "deviant" way as a superior alternative to the orthodox Soviet method; and the Yugoslav claims to such superiority seem a bit hollow when viewed in the perspective of the more than one billion dollars of foreign aid obtained from the "capitalist" United States.

Another complication in translating the Communist model into African reality arises because there is no Communist revolutionary experience that is applicable and appealing in the African context. The Soviet revolution took place in a far more highly developed country, in the wake of a disastrous war. The Chinese revolution involved the extension of a protracted war against a foreign invader into a civil war, in which the Communist leadership succeeded in mobilizing the peasantry. The Cuban revolution overthrew a dictatorship that was portrayed as an agency of American imperialism. These roads to power are simply not available to African states.

Moreover, in trying to establish contact and penetrate the new states effectively, it would be impolitic to advance a strategy that points to the eventual destruction of the present elites. The concept of "national democracy" therefore implies that the present elites themselves will lead the new states, step by step, into the socialist phase, and that although some "antagonistic contradictions" may develop along the way, the basic progress will be without violent conflict. But this poses another problem: the only Communist state that claims to have achieved a "peaceful revolution" is Czechoslovakia, which was a highly developed state with a parliamentary tradition and a strong Communist Party—which makes the relevance of its experience doubtful.[5] Furthermore, the understandable vagueness of Communist calculations concerning the turning point in the transformation of a "national democracy" into a proletarian dictatorship inevitably stimulates legitimate suspicion among the African elites about the sincerity of the Communist professions of friendship. Late in 1960, Sekou Touré gave a vivid demonstration of this suspicion to the startled Soviet ambassador.

The economic failure of the Chinese has also been a blow to Communist prestige and appeal. For reasons specific to internal Communist bloc policies as well as to the capabilities of the Soviet economy, the Soviet Union has not exerted much effort to prevent the economic calamities that China has experienced. True, Chinese international prestige was the first to suffer, but the external image of Communism as the best and most dynamic method of overcoming backwardness has suffered as well.

Lastly, Yugoslavia has also helped to undermine the effectiveness of the Communist "model." As we have seen, Yugoslavia (much like Israel) is not feared and is hence more able to reach the Africans who are conscious of the fact that the Soviets are engaged in a global conflict. To some extent, this is also true of the East Europeans, who profit somewhat from it. But the Yugoslavs are much more pragmatic and less doctrinaire in their approach than the East Europeans, and their neutralism makes them automatically more acceptable to the Africans. The Yugoslavs, especially Marshal Tito himself, have no inhibitions about presenting themselves as the standard-bearers of a "third way," even though it is one basically characterized by methods normally associated with extreme left-wing Socialism or Communism, and in that they challenge the claim of the other Communist states that Communism is a universal and tried solution to be adopted in all its ramifications. The relative decentralization of the Yugoslav economy and its retention of the market mechanism is especially attractive to countries in which even the basic statistical data and skills required for a highly centralized economy are sorely lacking.

Effective coordination of Communist activity and policy is thus limited primarily to the Soviets and their East European satellites. The East Germans, the Czechs, the Poles, and the others help to "civilize" Communism, to make it less of a big-power phenomenon, and the more advanced economies and more sophisticated trading methods of the Czechs and East Germans serve the Communist cause in good stead. But even here, the evidence seems to suggest that there is as yet no systematic pooling of resources and effort, that the Council of Economic Mutual Assistance has not yet created effective organs for coordinating external Communist economic activity. Coordination seems much more advanced in the political sphere, in which mass front organizations like the WFTU or the Peace Congresses permit a more effective orchestration of the political-ideological approach.

The Implications of Communist Diversity

The Communist diversity that has become apparent in recent years—especially as seen in the Sino-Soviet-Albanian triangle and the independent Yugoslav role—has made any further coordination difficult. Although factionalism as a consequence of the Sino-Soviet dispute has not yet reached the intensity that it has in Asian Communist parties, it doubtless has made itself felt among the extreme left-wing African circles. There has been evidence of open Sino-Soviet conflict at international gatherings to which Africans have been invited, and the confusion resulting from the propagation of two alternative Communist "general lines" cannot but destroy the myth of Communist unity. This is of some importance because one of the attractions of Communism to intellectuals has been its claim to universality and its boast that the Communist world would be free of international discord. The exchanges between the Soviets and the Albanians—such as the charge that Albanians have mistreated Soviet technicians and the countercharge that the Soviet Union has attempted to use economic aid to exact political concessions from Albania—have dispelled this myth.

In this connection, Sino-Soviet differences have helped to reveal certain calculations that the Communists might have preferred to leave unsaid for a while. The Soviet interest in the class content of the "national democracy" and their open differentiation between the national bourgeoisie and the more revolutionary and class-conscious elements of society are an integral part of the phased Soviet approach. That has also been the case with their emphasis on peaceful coexistence as complementary to the struggle for liberation. The Chinese lack of concern with this issue, coupled with great interest in galvanizing anti-imperialist leaders into open conflict with the West, shows the degree to which their approach is colored by their own experience. The competition between the two, and their inescapable dialogue, may in turn educate the African elites to follow with greater perception the often elusive arcana of Communist politics and initiatives. Warnings to that effect have been sounded by interested Communist commentators:

> The dogmatists . . . including the representatives of the Albanian Workers Party, advocate the thesis that peaceful coexistence as the general line of the socialist countries' foreign policy allegedly conflicts with the demand for the earliest possible liquidation of colonialism. According to them, the principles of peaceful coexistence hamper the development of the national liberation struggle, divert it to a "secondary track," and force it to stagnate. They put the question as follows: What is the main thing for Africa at the moment—peaceful coexistence or the anti-imperialist struggle? If the peoples of Africa and other subjugated countries are to fight the imperialists, can they at the same time advocate universal and complete disarmament, which is an integral part of the principles of peaceful coexistence? Thus, they say, the peoples would deprive themselves of their main weapon! . . . The barren standpoint of the dogmatists causes them—without their wishing to do so subjectively—to objectively hamper the establishment of the united anti-colonial front and thus weaken the struggle against the chief enemy, imperialism. In contrast to this, the consistent application of the principles of peaceful coexistence is the life-giving water also for the African deserts and virgin forests and "the last nail in the coffin of colonialism."[6]

The disintegration of Communist universalism may in turn further encourage and legitimize the already strong inclination of African leaders to formulate their own African versions of socialism, borrowing liberally from Communist and non-Communist experience, and sometimes personalizing it—as in the case with Nkrumaism. As long as Communism presented a homogeneous front, its claim to possess the key to the future and to have solved the problem of social development had a certain ring of authenticity. Internal discord and the appearance of Yugoslav, Soviet, Chinese, and Albanian ways to Communism increasingly means that there is no single way. The desperate Soviet efforts to formulate new general principles, and to tolerate some measure of national diversity, are even likely to strengthen the conviction of Africans of the correctness of their own particular methods.[7] The Soviet position is also likely to be threatened by the increasing Chinese inclination to combine their greater revolutionary fervor with a racial appeal. To the extent that the Chinese succeed in stamping the Soviets as white, and therefore not really different from the English or the French, they automatically decrease the appeal of the other East European Communist states and also undermine the significance of the Communist ideology. If only a colored Communist state is Africa's *true* friend, then it is color and not Communism that is the decisive force in world affairs.*

But while Communist diversity has in many regards prevented the formation and application of a coherent and coordinated strategy, there are certain positive aspects to it. The diversity also undermines the African image of a monolithic Communist camp and thus dimin-

---

* The efforts of the Soviets and the Chinese to discredit each other in African eyes continue to grow more strenuous. At the Ninth International Conference for the Banning of Nuclear and Hydrogen Weapons, held in Hiroshima in August 1963, Miraji M. Ali, a speaker described as a "Zanzibar leader," charged the Soviet Union with complicity in the murder of Lumumba. He was backed by the Chinese delegate, Chu Tzu-chi, who said that Russia had "helped U.S. imperialism in the murder of Patrice Lumumba."

Radio Moscow replied on August 14, in a Swahili language broadcast beamed to Africa, by describing the Chinese charge as "a lie, or madness, or wicked slander." On August 17 *Izvestia* carried an item "unmasking" Miraji M. Ali as a mere "ex-hospital attendant in Zanzibar," and as "a poorly educated person" who now lives "in grand style" in Peking.

Meanwhile, the Chinese leaders, in welcoming the Somali Prime Minister to Peking on August 6, warned that Africans must discriminate between the U.S.S.R., which is in "collusion" with the United States and pursues a "capitulationist policy," and China, which is internationalist and is pursuing a "people's revolutionary policy." The over-all impact on Communism of such reciprocal abuse is destructive organizationally and ideologically, and serves to discredit both the U.S.S.R. and China.

ishes African fears of excessive identification with a particular bloc. The sight of "independent" Chinese or perhaps occasionally Albanian Communists, not to speak of the Yugoslavs, reassures Africans that even becoming Communist does not necessarily entail the loss of state independence. This is a very important consideration, given the strong nationalist feelings of the new elites and the Western efforts to present the Soviets as the authoritarian leaders of the other Communist-ruled states. Furthermore, the diversity within the bloc allows greater differentiation among local Communist sympathizers, some of whom otherwise might have been repelled. Thus the moderates are attracted by the Polish or even the Soviet Communists and their policies; the local technical personnel may be more impressed by the East Germans or the Czechs, who compete with Western specialists more effectively than the other Communists, Soviet included; the militants, eager to undertake violence, find their inspiration among the Chinese. In effect, this results in a certain "objective" division of labor between the Communist powers, irrespective of their inability to accomplish this on the "subjective" plane because of the discord among them.

There is even a sense in which the Soviet and Chinese strategies are automatically complementary. The Soviets appeal to those who are more preoccupied with "neocolonialism" and who see in Soviet economic aid and in the Soviet model a shortcut to modernization through a "respectable revolution." The Chinese way appeals to those who are still struggling against colonialism and who feel that an armed struggle—"the revolution militant"—is the only means. Subjectively uncoordinated and often conflicting, the Soviet and Chinese methods objectively reinforce each other. For example, in West Africa the indiscriminate application of the Chinese strategy could result in a violent rejection of the Communist camp by the ruling elites. At the same time, in Zanzibar, close to the centers of direct conflict in Mozambique, Southern Rhodesia, and even South Africa, the Chinese seem more influential.

The diversity also weakens the anti-Communist impact of errors committed by any one Communist group. In the past, an error in Soviet or Chinese action would almost inevitably be generalized to apply to Communism as a whole. Now, whenever that happens, a

Communist ambassador can tactfully explain that the specific incident was caused merely by the ignorance, etc., of a given Communist state, which would make it less likely that far-reaching implications concerning Communism in general would be drawn from such a specific incident. The episode involving the Soviet ambassador in Conakry is a case in point; it did not rebound against the Poles or the Czechs. Similarly, the Soviets need not shoulder the blame for any excesses committed by the Chinese.

The usefulness of diversity is particularly great for the Yugoslavs. There is no doubt that they have helped to strengthen the appeal of neutralism on the continent and that their less dichotomic views of historical development have been important in weakening the Soviet appeal by providing a critique of Marxism-Leninism that is immanent, and hence more effective in persuading some of the Marxist-influenced African elites. At the same time, however, the Yugoslav Communists have made Communism much more palatable to many Africans and have given it a veneer of respectability that even the Soviets (with their embarrassing Stalinist past) or the East Europeans (whose independence may sometimes be open to doubt even among the Africans) do not provide. Thus in a broad perspective, the Yugoslavs might be performing the function of acclimatizing Africans to an ideology that would otherwise appear alien and too antinationalist to them.

In fact, for reasons entirely unrelated to Africa as such, there is now the danger that the Yugoslavs may be forced to tone down their efforts to proselytize Africans to their "socialist neutralism," which they had been doing primarily at Soviet expense, and actually align themselves more closely with the Soviets. As we have seen, the impact of the Common Market on Yugoslavia caused the Yugoslavs to seek Soviet economic assistance.* The Soviet approach to international politics is much more politically motivated than that of the West, and the Soviet leaders most likely demanded a shift in the political line of the Yugoslavs in return for any aid. The Yugoslav agitation against the Common Market and the more radical shifts in economic

* The Yugoslavs were also very active in organizing the special conference of nonaligned nations that met in July 1962 in Cairo to discuss some common responses to the challenge posed by the Common Market.

and political organization adopted by Tito in the summer of 1962 are hence to be viewed with apprehension insofar as Yugoslav activity in Africa is concerned.

The Yugoslav case illustrates the complexity of motives behind the involvement of the Communist states in Africa. The Yugoslavs have sought additional international stature and the breakdown of their isolation between the two major world blocs. The direction of their efforts, however, is also very much affected by European economic changes, and by the domestic political situation in Yugoslavia. There is little doubt that future Yugoslav policies will be much affected by the problem of succession to Tito and by the orientation of the eventual successor. Chinese policy is shaped as much, if not more, by the Chinese attitude toward the United States as by any inherent Chinese interest in Africa, and by the Chinese desire to provoke the Soviets into adopting a more militant posture. Even the East European Communist states have their own national motives and interests; good economic reasons for closer relations with Africa have already been indicated, and there is also the quest for legitimacy involved in the efforts of the Communist elites to establish good relations with the new states. It is thus not merely a matter of following in the Soviet footsteps.

Similarly, the stimulation of anti-Westernism also has certain desirable by-products outside the Communist interest in Africa as such. It can be used to obstruct Western efforts to develop or improve its nuclear forces by anti-nuclear campaigns especially directed against the French tests in Africa; it can be used to advantage to weaken the Western position on Berlin. Since mid-1962 it has been used with great intensity to focus African hostility against the Common Market, a development dreaded by the Soviets but one which also poses real economic dangers to some of the African states as well.

Thus even limited economic compatibility between Africa and the Communist world is used as a weapon against developments in the West that the Soviets fear, irrespective of their actual impact on Africa. Likewise, some East European economists see in economic cooperation between the underdeveloped regions, including Africa, and the Communist world a way by which the paramount position of the United States in world markets may be gradually undermined.[8]

The foregoing motives supplement and bolster the ideologically rooted Communist interest in the merging nations of Africa. While ideology is an important source of inspiration in Communist conduct, its influence is much more potent when it corresponds to what appears to be in the general "national interest" of a given Communist state.

The Soviet Quest for Revolutionary Relevance

In many ways the Communist ideology has given the Communists a more acute insight into the dynamics of African affairs than has the superior but often static experiential knowledge of the Western nations. Thus the Communists were concerned much earlier than Western sociologists or political scientists, not to speak of statesmen, with the basic social-political forces at work in the underdeveloped nations, and particularly with the relations among the radical intelligentsia, the urban masses, and the peasantry. This preoccupation, although often highly dogmatic in its outward expression, has nevertheless given the Communists a sense of political dynamics that has only recently become widespread in the West.

Of the Communist states it would appear that the Soviet Union is ideologically the most productive, developing elaborate ideological structures both to explain the thrust of African development and to justify its own policies, which are much less activist in actual practice. On the other hand, the Chinese approach, which relies on a few simple revolutionary formulas, is marked by greater preoccupation with revolutionary action and is concerned with doctrinal elaborations. One is tempted to speculate that the elaborate Soviet efforts to formulate special phrases and to invent new formulas like "national democracy," belabored in painful detail by the Soviet ideologues, may be a reflection of increasing Soviet technological and economic maturity and, therefore, also of the Soviet sense of growing irrelevance to the impatient masses of the underdeveloped lands.

In the self-consciously "revolutionary" assertions of the Soviets and in their elaborate effort to show that Africa can be understood within the categories advanced by the Soviet ideologues, there is something faintly reminiscent of American efforts to prove that the American Revolution is still the motivating and nurturing force of social change in the world, particularly in the new states. Indeed, the stronger that sense of irrelevance, the more intense the efforts to establish through programmatic statements, declarations and affirmations, and ideological writings, a sense of pertinence which in real life is somehow lacking and is felt by those involved to be lacking. Many reflective Americans have pointed to the danger that America is seen by the new nations as not pertinent to their concerns, and they have emphasized the need to rediscover the American Revolution and to make it relevant to the new nations.

Thus what is striking about much of the Soviet "literature" on the subject of the new nations, produced in the increasingly developed and smug Soviet Union, is the tortured dialectics, the efforts to prove that the October Revolution is still relevant and that so is the Soviet Union of today, in spite of the unwillingness of that Soviet Union either to undertake major economic sacrifices on behalf of the new nations or to run political and military risks to promote their revolutions. The turgid Soviet elaborations stand in sharp contrast to the old simple revolutionary prescriptions. Perhaps, as Peking once put it, "that is why the Chinese pamphlets on guerrilla war are so much in demand in Asia, Africa, and Latin America, and are considered as something precious even when they are no more than tattered rags, becoming illegible as they are passed from hand to hand."[9]

This self-conscious quest for relevance may also stem in part from the fact that Communists of the Soviet and East European variety are for the first time dealing on a large scale with much less developed nations than their own. The revolutionary intensity of Communism has been fed by the impact of industrialization, with all its dislocations and tensions, and also by national feelings of frustration, inferiority, and ambition—especially among the Russians (and lately the Chinese), who saw in Communism a vehicle of both rapid modernization and national power *in relation* to the more advanced part of the world. The Russian involvement in the new nations, on the contrary, puts them almost for the first time in the position of the more advanced partner, to whom the less-developed people turn for guidance and inspiration. This reduces the important and often neglected component of psychological inferiority, which played such an important role in the Russian revolutionary orientation. At the same time, the rather rapid creation of the new states meant that the

Soviet involvement had to follow the conventional diplomatic state-to-state forms, and the Soviets did not have the opportunities inherent in a prolonged condition of revolutionary ferment among colonially oppressed nations. This, too, channeled Soviet revolutionary propensities, in spite of continued efforts at subversion (e.g., in Guinea in 1961), into the more established patterns of international politics, with certain revolutionary-inhibiting tendencies. It is noteworthy that on both scores the Chinese situation differs, and so does their political line and conduct.

The Soviet participation in the international game has had some further consequences. The political complexion of Africa varies a great deal and to promote its ends the Soviet Union has had to discriminate in its tactics. It has thus cultivated those states that have set off on a more radical path—Guinea, Ghana, and Mali, the "national democracies" of the Soviet perspective—but it has also courted the other African states, including those closely associated with France. For example, within the short space of two weeks in June 1962 Khrushchev hosted first the head of the Mali Republic, Mobido Keita, and then the head of the Senegal government, M. Dia. The first identified himself closely with the Soviet Union, praised it as "the hope of the freedom-loving and peace-loving peoples," and in the final communiqué endorsed the Soviet proposal of "a general and complete disarmament."[10] The communiqué then condemned "the new form of colonialism which, under the guise of economic aid, seeks to preserve old colonial privileges," adding that "the Soviet and Mali governments have agreed to do everything possible to contribute to the elimination of this threat"; called for "the restoration of the legitimate right of the Chinese People's Republic in the United Nations"; and asserted the Soviet government's "high evaluation" of Mali's role in Africa.

Two weeks later, Dia was feted by Moscow. The final communiqué issued on this occasion differed in significant respects. It called for "general and complete disarmament under strict international control," had no reference to the new forms of colonialism or to Communist China, and the Senegalese Prime Minister went out of his way to tell his hosts that "he did not become Communist while here" and that "our methods and temperament were not always in harmony." Nonetheless, he, too, was hailed by Khrushchev as a "dear guest" and Senegal was assured of Soviet friendship. In both cases, limited aid agreements were concluded and exchanges were arranged.

The Soviet conduct was motivated by the calculation, quite rational under the circumstances, that a single-minded approach to the diverse front of African states would be self-defeating and that a multifaceted policy was preferable.[11] This is precisely the same dilemma that the United States had faced in dealing with more and less friendly neutralist states, and it has also adopted an elastic, "non-moralistic" approach as more suitable. However, unlike the United States, the Soviet Union sees itself also as the standard-bearer of a uniform world outlook, and its ambivalent actions do have the effect of blurring the Communist general line, confusing some Communist supporters and weakening the revolutionary morale of others. Also, this elasticity implies acceptance of the full independence of countries, which, like Senegal, are associated with France and have been condemned as French vassals by the other more radical African states. Last but not least, the progressive alienation of the Brazzaville-Lagos grouping from the Soviet (not to speak of the Chinese) position shows that an indefinite straddling of inter-African conflicts is not likely to be possible. But taking sides will mean making enemies as well as friends.

This example highlights also a broader and older problem that has plagued the Communists for a long time, and still has not been satisfactorily resolved: What should be the relationship between Communists and nationalists? The radical Chinese solution runs the risk not only of alienating the ruling national bourgeoisie but of creating conditions that could prompt the West to intervene more actively—a dilemma sure to involve demands to the Communist states for larger aid and including major risks in case of local wars. On the other hand, the Soviet formula runs the distinct risk of actually promoting a measure of social stability and of unwittingly assisting the West in guiding the new states through the difficult transitional stage. What makes the situation even worse is that the Soviet Union, having become engaged in some economic aid and assistance, can no longer disengage itself from it without producing a violently hostile reaction among the recipients, with the West again benefiting.

Signs of Communist impatience with the new nationalist elites and fears that they may be now becoming "objective" impediments to the further evolution of the new states in the direction of Communism have recently become much more evident. The *World Marxist Review*, for example, in an article entitled "The Working Class of Africa and the National-Liberation Movement," stressed that no fundamental changes are possible without an initial *political* takeover from "the imperialists" by the African nations followed by growing self-assertion of the African proletariat as a class. Noting that nowhere in Africa does this class yet wield power, the journal observed that its acquisition is not a matter of mere agreement with the bourgeoisie but of prolonged labor, which involves also increased class-consciousness on the basis of "Marxism-Leninism, the science of the leading role of the working class." The article concludes: "If the African working class has not yet become the leading class in the young African states, it is because politically it is not as yet organized as a class, it does not have as yet its own clearly expressed ideology."[12] Although in the late spring of 1962 Khrushchev still stressed that "under contemporary conditions the national bourgeoisie has not yet exhausted its progressive role," he also felt compelled to warn that "more and more it reveals an inclination for agreement with reaction."[13] In other words, if it follows the Communist line, the national bourgeoisie automatically becomes progressive.[14] Increasingly in 1962, Communist endorsements of neutralism were coupled with a much more overt insistence on domestic reforms carried out in closer cooperation with the Communist world.* Although still unwilling to adopt the Chinese prescriptions, the "centrists" were thus showing signs of uncertainty about the efficacy of their policies.

The African Challenge to Communism

Underlying these doubts was the increasing realization that the nationalist leaders of the new nations were beginning to forge primi-

---

* This statement from the organ of the Czech Communist Party is typical: "[Economic] independence presupposes realization of fundamental economic and social transformations. . . . Accordingly, the struggle for economic independence is not merely an economic assignment, but . . . the paramount political task that can be met only in a determined fight against imperialism and domestic reaction, in cooperation with the countries of the global socialist system, and in conditions of the policy of peaceful cooperation and coexistence of two global social-economic systems." (E. Paloncy, "Build-up of the Anti-Imperialist Front," *Rude Právo*, March 21, 1962.)

tive but more and more socially conscious "ideologies" designed to give a sense of national direction and individual dignity to their peoples. In doing so, they were in effect not only gradually crystallizing an alternative to Communism but often negating many of the basic philosophical and social assumptions that guide the Marxist-Leninists. The notion, widespread among the "nation-builders" that a national community is above classes, is viewed by Communist theorists as a direct challenge, designed by the national bourgeoisie to obscure class contradictions in their societies, thus inhibiting the "democratic" development of class conflict as the basic force affecting the economic and social transformation of the societies.[15] Similarly troubling to the Communists are such concepts as "the African personality," as expounded by Nkrumah, and the idea of "Negritude" ("the whole complex of civilized values—cultural, economic, social, and political—which characterize the black peoples, or, more precisely, the Negro African world") put forth by Leopold Senghor.[16] Both conceptions run counter to the basic Marxist-Leninist assumptions about the nature of individual and collective behavior and could thus obstruct the Communist effort to infuse the new African sense of self-identity with a predominantly anti-Western, anticolonial content.*

What makes this even worse from the Communist standpoint is that many of the African leaders claim that their programs are "socialist." This claim is often made not only by those African leaders who are sympathetic to the Communist world but also by those who are not. Thus in addressing Khrushchev, Prime Minister Dia of Senegal categorically asserted that his country was being developed "on the basis of socialism" (which drew applause from the Soviet audience), but he quickly informed his hosts "that we do not pretend to be Marxist-Leninists" and then, almost adding insult to injury, ambiguously observed that "we are only people of good will."[17] Similarly, the President of the Central African Republic announced in July 1962 that his country had chosen "the way to socialism," and

---

* Thus the *World Marxist Review* (No. 7, 1962), while ostensibly defending Nkrumah against his domestic critics, condemned the views of some Africans that Marxism is a "European ideology" and that Africa needs an "African ideology." The journal observed that such views were supported by "financial circles of London and Wall Street."

then cited Israel as a good example of it.[18] Claims to be "building socialism" have been voiced by other African leaders, ranging from Sekou Touré to Nasser (especially in his statement on "Arab socialism" in *The Charter* of May 1962). This phenomenon has been attacked by Communist theorists, who see intentional deception behind it:

> Once independence is won, a struggle for the subsequent character of a state sets in. Discrepancies between the national bourgeoisie and the working class tend to become increasingly sharper. It becomes evident that the exploitative nature of the bourgeoisie as well as its class limitations make it impossible for this sector to conduct a fight for a conclusive liquidation of the imperialist influence and for the effectuation of maxims of the national liberatory revolution all the way—until victory is won. As an example, in one salient question, namely that of the future trend in these countries, the stance of the national bourgeoisie is unstable. Since the masses oppose the capitalistic method and since the national bourgeoisie as such begins to realize that rapid economic advance cannot be ensured by capitalistic methods, *this bourgeoisie speaks of non-capitalist ways and sometimes even of building "socialism."* Yet the measures it proposes to ensure economic progress in effect support a strengthening of capitalism.[19]

Similarly, the new program of the CPSU, adopted in 1961 by the Twenty-Second Party Congress, explicitly attacks those who "advance theories of 'socialism of the national type,' propagate socio-philosophical doctrines that are, as a rule, variations of the petty-bourgeois illusion of socialism, an illusion which rules out the class struggle. These theories mislead the popular masses, hamper the development of the national-liberation movement, and imperil its gains."[20]

The choice that the "centrist" Communists would prefer to avoid, but may not be able to, especially if pressure from the more militant Communist Parties forces the issue, is this: either provoking an outright clash with the new nationalist leadership and reasserting the alleged Communist patent on how to build socialism, which would probably weaken some state-to-state ties; or continuing to cultivate nationalist leaders, which carries the political danger of actually undermining Communist ideological purity. The Soviet expectation, however, is that this dilemma may be avoided since the African elites may not be able to solve their internal "contradictions," while conflicts with European powers (whether in Angola, Rhodesia, or, more probably, in South Africa) will reintensify the anti-white feelings of the Africans, and make them more susceptible to radical solutions at home and to closer identification with the Communist world abroad. The hope is that with patience the conditions that the Chinese now wish to create will arise from the logic of the developing situation, without excessive risk or cost and without setbacks from premature initiatives (such as the Kirkuk rising in 1958 or the abortive Communist rising in Indonesia).

Indeed, there is at present little likelihood that any of the new African states will espouse Communism or even associate itself fully with the Communist bloc. The desire to be independent and non-aligned is so strong, so intense, and so widely shared that any move in that direction, either through local initiative or under Communist pressure, is likely to result in a strong counterreaction. This is as true in the left-wing government in Guinea and the essentially fascistic regime in Ghana as it is in the more democratic administration of Nigeria. It does not mean, of course, that on many international issues the African states may not occasionally side with Communist states, or that they will either reject Communist aid or be immune to the so-called Communist model of development. But the fundamental sense of values held in the African states will keep them, at least for the near future, partially immune to the proselytizing zeal of the Communists.

As for the more distant future, the picture is less clear, and perhaps the prospects are somewhat darker. Two possibilities, above all, should restrain our optimism. First, there is the real danger, on which the Communists count, that in their domestic development the new states may not succeed in combining rapid modernization with nontotalitarian forms of government, and that the combined pressure of rising expectations from below and growing frustration among the increasingly numerous pseudo-intelligentsia will polarize political forces into radically antagonistic positions. Second, this process could come to a head at a time when African attention is focused on the liquidation of the remaining areas of white supremacy—Southern

Rhodesia, South Africa, and the Portuguese colonies. It is certain that the Communist countries will try to espouse leadership of such a struggle, which would be sure to generate much African enthusiasm.* The coming together of these two crises could provide an opportunity for a large-scale Communist entrance into Africa, an opportunity hitherto denied by the genuine African rejection of Communist dogmatism and the African fear of becoming involved in international power politics.

Much will depend, of course, on the attitudes and the actions of the West. The Communist efforts, as we have seen, are sustained, multifaceted, and geared to a long-range perspective that emphasizes systematic Communist political action to influence the political consciousness of the African elites. The West has tended to lay primary stress on economic relations, although often on an inadequate scale, and to neglect political activity; besides clarifying—for itself as well as for Africans—its sense of historical direction, the West should occasionally be willing to make its own interests clear to Africans, and even to explain the advantages of not alienating the West. A clearer political perspective, including a sharper definition of what is vital to the West and what is not, could help in avoiding those circumstances in which Africans seem to apply a double standard in their foreign policy—one for the West and one for the East—knowing that it is safer to offend the West.

In this connection, the West should also be more careful not to overdo the cultivation, especially at the expense of the more democratic African states, of the one-party, anti-Western dictatorships established in some parts of Africa. This is not merely a matter of money but also of attitudes, official and unofficial (including those of scholars). Offering excessive justifications for the activities of such states simply strengthens the appeal, and the apparent advantage, of anti-Westernism. This plays into the hands of those African leaders whose purpose is to revolutionize the African continent in a generally anti-Western direction. At the same time, however, it is

---

* Communism is already viewed more sympathetically by some of the East Africans who are locked in conflict with the white settlers (e.g., the Oginga Odinga faction of the KANU party in Kenya). For this reason East Africa is also the chief African theater for Communist efforts at political subversion.

essential that the Western democracies, and particularly the United States, prove sensitive to the vital interest of Africans in liquidating the remaining vestiges of colonialism on the African continent. American neutralism on this subject cannot help but produce something less than African neutralism in the East-West conflict.

To a much larger extent, however, Africa's future depends on the sophistication, maturity, and sense of independence of the African elites, as well as on their ability to adapt some of the Marxist-Leninist conceptions they have already absorbed to the realities of the African scene. If these elites, in spite of their higher sensitivity to the threat of "neocolonialism," avoid gradually molding their domestic political institutions to fit a clearly Communist pattern; and if they avoid accepting Communist foreign policy objectives so consistently that the West becomes completely alienated, thereby giving the African anti-Western attitude the character of a self-fulfilling prophecy, then protracted Communist cultivation of these states could gradually destroy the Communist image of the world as two hostile camps. It would deny Communism its self-nourishing sense of historical uniqueness and would help to introduce into it elements of relativity and even far-reaching diversity. This is the historical opportunity and responsibility which so far not all African leaders have perceived.

In a curious way, the Communist world is still politically and ideologically underdeveloped. Even the Soviet Union's growing technological and economic sophistication has not yet destroyed the dogmatic rigidity of the outmoded basic assumptions that shape the world outlook of its political leaders. Nevertheless in Africa and Asia the more advanced parts of the Communist world have been gradually drawn into constructive action (especially in terms of economic and technical aid) in areas not subject to Communist control and not yet even in a revolutionary condition (although the Soviets can always reassure themselves that they are preparing the ground for the revolution, thus meeting the obligations of their own myths). This type of involvement is a radical break with past Communist practices, which were usually designed to destroy in order to prevail, according to the old theory "the worse, the better." To be sure, Lenin had hoped that a Communist Europe might help the underdeveloped world move into socialism, but this presupposed the Communization of the most economically advanced parts of the world. Instead, the task has now fallen on the shoulders of Communist states that are themselves trying to catch up with West. Inherent in this strategy is a subtle evolutionary change in the Communist world perspective, and the Chinese may be quite right in insisting that the real revolutionary is one who engages in revolutions.

Furthermore, there is also the tendency for means to become ends in themselves. Once economic aid is given to achieve a distant political objective, it is difficult to stop giving it, even if the objective remains distant. Cutting off the aid becomes a radical, counterproductive step. The United States has repeatedly faced this dilemma in its relations with Poland and Yugoslavia. The Soviet Union is now facing it in Egypt, and it may face it in Africa, too. Thus the most advanced part of the Communist world may gradually be sucked into constructive international undertakings, irrespective of its proclaimed goals, thereby also widening the gap between itself and the more militant sections of the Communist world. Alternatively, it may at some point suddenly shift back to a more militant posture, having decided that its present strategy was counterproductive. But that decision would be an admission of failure (especially pleasing to those militants who had rejected it) and it would also be likely to provoke a reaction among Africans not unlike Nasser's reaction to the United States' change of policy in 1956. Soviet foreign policy makers are thus facing a "scissors crisis."

The African nations may perhaps draw some benefit from the Communist experience in centralized planning and in rapidly modernizing the economies of notably underdeveloped societies. But in a historical perspective it might be more important, and certainly more ironic, if the Communist world perspective were influenced by Africa. Within a decade or two, it is quite conceivable that the Communist leaders might claim a victory for Communism in Africa on the grounds that the socialist-nationalist African way to modernity is in fact Communism. But if the African states succeed in retaining their external political and ideological independence of the Communist world and do not commit themselves to totalitarian dictatorships at home, Communism will be "subjectively" claiming victory for an "objective" defeat. No one should then begrudge them that small consolation.

NOTES

NOTES

Introduction

1. Editorial, "The Draft Program of the CPSU and Some Problems of the National Liberation Movement of the Nations of Asia and Africa," *Narody Aziia i Afriki*, No. 5, 1961. For a detailed outline of what ought to be studied see E. M. Zhukov, "The Process of Liquidation of the Colonial System and the Tasks of Studying It," *Vestnik Akademii Nauk SSSR*, No. 2, 1961.

2. "The World Twenty Years From Now," *Kommunist*, No. 13, September 1961.

Chapter 1

1. Otto Kuusinen *et al.*, *Fundamentals of Marxism-Leninism* (Moscow, 1960), pp. 425–26.

2. For summaries of some of the Communist discussions of this point in the twenties, see Allen Whiting, *Soviet Policy in China, 1917–1924* (New York, 1954); Demetrio Boersner, *The Bolsheviks and the National and Colonial Question* (Geneva, 1957), chapter 1; and Wladyslaw Kulski, *Peaceful Coexistence* (Chicago, 1959), chapters 9 and 10.

3. The search of Soviet analysts for an "objective" basis to explain changing behavior of national leaders has often been futile, confused, or frankly political in inspiration. Moreover, the concept has failed to distinguish between subgroups which, especially in the new nations, have meaningfully different interests and roles. (See, e.g., H. G. Seton-Watson, "The Communist Powers and Afro-Asian Nationalism," in Kurt London, ed., *Unity and Contradiction* [New York, 1962], pp. 190–94.) Only rarely has a Soviet commentator sought to escape the old dichotomy of good and evil. Anticipating some of the reasoning behind the concept of a national democracy, one Soviet specialist argued that "the leaders of African liberation movements are often not bourgeois and not feudal . . . but rather, as it were, 'Negro democrats.'" (K. Ivanov, "Present-Day Colonialism: Its Socio-Economic Aspects," *International Affairs* [Moscow], 1960, No. 10, p. 20.) However, the issue is at last being discussed squarely. See, for instance, G. Mirsky, "Tvorcheskii marksizm i problemy natsional'no-osvoboditel'nykh revoliutsii," *Mirovaia ekonomika i mezhdunarodnye otnosheniia*, 1963, No. 2, p. 65.

4. See, for instance, Fritz Schatten, *Afrika schwarz oder rot?* (Munich, 1961); David T. Cattell, "Communism and the African Negro," *Problems of Communism* (Washington, D.C.), September–October 1959; and Sergius Yakobson, "Russia and Africa," in Ivo Lederer, ed., *Russian Foreign Policy* (New Haven, 1962).

5. I. I. Potekhin and D. D. Ol'derogge (eds.), *Narody Afriki* (Moscow, 1954). This work, in process since 1948, remains a landmark in Soviet Africanology. A revised German edition appeared in 1961.

6. The Declaration of the twelve "ruling" Communist Parties, in November 1957, described the liberation movement as an ally in the struggle against imperialism, regardless of the subjective attitude of its leaders toward Communism. Substantially the same approach obtained in Kuusinen's textbook, *Fundamentals of Marxism-Leninism*, in the Statement of 81 Parties adopted in Moscow in November-December 1960, and in the 1961 Program of the CPSU—the major documents whose formulations were thereafter borrowed by other Communist writers as authoritative and "safe."

7. N. Inozemtsev, "Razvitie mirovogo sotsializma i novyi etap mezhdunarodnykh otnoshenii," *Kommunist*, 1961, No. 9, p. 101. See also V. P. Nikhamin, "Some Features of the Foreign Policy of Eastern Non-Socialist Countries," *International Affairs*, March 1959, p. 85; and I. Kuzminov, "The New Stage in the General Crisis of Capitalism," *International Affairs* (Moscow), 1961, No. 2, p. 18.

8. G. Mirsky and V. Tiagutenko, "Tendentsii i perspektivy natsional'-no-osvoboditel'nykh revoliutsii," *Mirovaia ekonomika i mezhdunarodnye otnosheniia*, 1961, No. 11, p. 24. On the Soviet concept of neutralism, see also Alexander Dallin, *The Soviet Union at the United Nations* (New York, 1962), pp. 184–85.

9. Akademiia nauk SSSR, Institut Afriki, *Afrika, 1956–1961* (Moscow, 1961), p. 30. Soviet writers maintain (without any attempt at "Marxist-Leninist" explanation) that the West still has economic control but is no longer able to intervene politically and militarily—a fact that makes the achievement of independence easier. (V. P. Nikhamin, *Mezhdunarodnye problemy sovremennoi Afriki*, Moscow, 1960, p. 19.)

10. It is hardly necessary to go into the sustained Soviet attacks on Western "neo-colonialism," "collective colonialism," and such "Trojan horses" as the U. S. Peace Corps; or the corresponding "exposés" of attempts by the EEC to bring the Common Market to Africa under the guise of "Eurafrican" schemes. Most obviously, the grant of military bases to NATO and military agreements with NATO powers have been assailed as betrayals of independence, transforming the governments into tools of imperialism.

11. Editorial in *Narody Azii i Afriki*, 1961, No. 5, p. 4. See also Sivolobov, *Natsional'no-osvoboditel'noe dvizhenie v Afrike* (Moscow, 1961), p. 12ff.

12. Y. Bochkaryov, "New Paths for New States," *New Times*, 1961, No. 41, p. 15.

13. Ye. Zhukov, "Znamenatel'nyi faktor nashego vremeni," *Pravda*, August 26, 1960.

14. B. Ponomarev, "O gosudarstve natsional'noi demokratii," *Kommunist*, 1961, No. 8, pp. 42, 45. The leading British Communist writer on Africa, echoing the Soviet "line," warned against the error of believing "that the morrow of political independence is the signal for an immediate clash between the workers and the new rulers." (Jack Woddis, *Africa: The Lion Awakes* [London, 1961], pp. 288–91.)

15. *Ibid.*, p. 42. Ponomarev also says that the development of "state capi-

talism" can crowd out private capital and "give the progressive forces an opportunity to occupy ever more important positions in production and to increase their political influence." Potekhin's Institute likewise suggests that "the creation of the state sector in industry has a tremendous importance as a matter of principle for determining the further path of development in Africa." (*Afrika, 1956–1961*, p. 126.) Others, however, stress the conclusion that the mobilization of resources under state capitalism takes place "at the expense of the toiling masses, whose standard of living has in most countries hardly risen since the attainment of independence"; hence the fundamental need to alter the maldistribution of the national income and shift political control from "class-alien" to friendly hands. (See, for example, Mirsky and Tiagutenko, "Tendentsii i perspektivy," p. 28.) On state capitalism, see also S. I. Tiul'panov, in *Vestnik Leningradskogo Universiteta (ekonomika, filosofiia, pravo)*, 1961, Nos. 1 and 2; and "Soviet Views on the 'State Sector' in Under-Developed Countries," *The Mizan Newsletter* (London), January 1962, pp. 7–13.

16. Bochkaryov, "New Paths," p. 15.

17. I. I. Potekhin, *Afrika smotrit v budushchee* (Moscow, 1960), p. 20. Italics mine.

18. For some key commentaries on the problem of "by-passing capitalism," see S. N. Rostovsky, "Lininskoe uchenie o nekapitalisticheskom puti razvitiia," *Problemy vostokovedeniia* (Moscow), 1960, No. 2; G. Kim, "Leninizm i sud'by ugnetennykh narodov vostoka," *Aziia i Afrika segodnia*, 1961, No. 4; M. S. Dzhunusov, *Ob opyte stroitel'stva sotsializma v ranee otstalykh stranakh* (Moscow, 1958), and his *O nekapitalisticheskom puti razvitiia* (Moscow, 1963). In his speech to the Eighth Congress of the Chinese Communist Party (September 17, 1956), Anastas Mikoyan had already declared that the growth of state capitalism might provide a "new transitional form and path to avoid the torments of capitalism."

19. Mirsky and Tiagutenko, "Tendentsii i perspektivy," pp. 31–33. The simplest, and most cynical, explanation, was that offered by Hermann Matern, a leading East German Communist, who described the slogan of national democracy as "a tactful formulation . . . which could help the [fraternal] parties in the anti-imperialist countries freed from the colonial yoke, to carry out the democratic and socialist revolution." (*Neues Deutschland*, December 23, 1960.) For a sophisticated analysis, see Richard Lowenthal, "On 'National Democracy': Its Function in Communist Policy," *Survey* (London), No. 47 (April 1963). See also William T. Shinn, Jr., "The 'National Democratic State': A Communist Program for Less-Developed Areas," *World Politics*, April 1963. Some of the conflicting views on national democracy expressed in Soviet media are illustrated by a comparison of G. Kim's analysis (*Aziia i Afrika segodnia*, October 1962) with A. Sobolev's "National Democracy—The Way to Social Progress," *World Marxist Review*, February 1963.

20. Because of lack of space, reference to more thorough studies of this problem must suffice. Fortunately, there are excellent surveys of Soviet academic and other writings on Africa, among them the following: Central Asian Research Centre, London, *Russia Looks at Africa* (London, 1960); Mary Holdsworth, "African Studies in the U.S.S.R.," *St. Antony's Papers*,

No. 10 (London, 1961) ; *The Mizan Newsletter* (since July 1960) ; G. A. von Stackelberg, "The Political Line in Soviet African Studies," *Bulletin* (Munich), August 1958; Christopher Bird, "Scholarship and Propaganda," *Problems of Communism*, March–April 1962; Fritz Schatten, *Afrika schwarz oder rot?* (Munich, 1961), pp. 197–216; and *Soviet Periodical Abstracts: Asia, Africa, and Latin America* (New York, 1961–). The most comprehensive listing of Soviet writings on Africa, with critical annotations, is Mary Holdsworth, *Soviet African Studies, 1918–1959: An Annotated Bibliography* (London, 1961).

21. In 1961 he stated that the tasks before Soviet Africanists are many, such as producing serious studies on the ethnic origins of individual African nationalities; on the great migrations in Africa; on medieval African civilization; and the history of the slave trade. But "it is understood that the basic attention must continue to be concentrated on the history of the collapse of the colonial system," for this is the core around which the "ideological struggle" between progress and reaction is taking place. (I. Potekhin, "Osnovnye problemy istorii narodov Afriki," *Kommunist*, 1961, No. 12, p. 108.)

22. For accounts by disgruntled African students returning from the U.S.S.R., see Stanley Okullo's story in *U.S. News and World Report*, August 1, 1960; Andrew Richard Amar, *A Student in Moscow* (London, 1961); Michel Ayih, *Ein Afrikaner in Moskau* (Cologne, 1961); *Secolo d'Italia* (Rome), November 15, 1960; and the (hardly reliable) series by Anthony G. Okotcha, "Moscow Trained me for Revolution in Africa," *Daily Nation* (Nairobi), August 10–12, 1961. See also Schatten, *Afrika schwarz*, pp. 351–59; Rolf Italiaander, *Schwarze Haut im roten Griff* (Düsseldorf, 1962), pp. 116–27; and Aderogba Ajao, *On the Tiger's Back* (London, 1962). On the Peoples' Friendship University, see Priscilla Johnson, "Apartheid U," *Harper's Magazine*, December 1960; David Burg, "The Peoples' Friendship University," *Problems of Communism*, November-December 1961; and Seymour M. Rosen, *Soviet Training Programs for Africa* (U.S. Office of Education, *Bulletin*, 1963, No. 9).

23. An unusual activity was Soviet distribution of forged documents "implicating" the U.S. or Great Britain. Thus, in Ghana and elsewhere a "photograph" appeared in mid-1960 called "Annexe to Cabinet Paper on Policy in Africa . . . Secret, U.K. Eyes Only," and dated December 21, 1959. This forgery was evidently designed to show how Western "neo-colonialism" operated, stressing particularly U.S. attempts to "steal" Africa from Britain, but also the attempts of both to use Western labor leaders as intelligence agents in Africa. The same document was used, in good faith, by various African organs in the summer of 1960 (and, incidentally, was exposed by Arnold Beichman in the *Christian Science Monitor* of July 30, 1960). Before the end of the year it was published as a booklet, *The Great Conspiracy Against Africa*, with appropriate comment by Leftist labor writers, and was distributed to the ILO conference in Lagos in December 1960. Only then did Moscow take overt cognizance of it, with Soviet newspapers publishing articles on it (*Trud*, January 14, and *Pravda*, February 8, 1961). A formal British protest to Moscow, on February 17, was rejected within two weeks. There are strong suggestions that the forgery was of Soviet origin.

24. For general surveys of Communist parties in Africa, see the annual report of the Department of State, *World Strength of the Communist Party Organizations* (Washington, D.C.); *Ost-Probleme* (Bonn), 1960, No. 4, and 1962, No. 16; Walter Z. Laqueur, "Communism and Nationalism in Tropical Africa," *Foreign Affairs*, July 1961. On the RDA, see also Franz Ansprenger, *Politik im schwarzen Afrika* (Cologne, 1961).

25. As A. B. Rosenthal reported from Accra to *The New York Times* (October 18, 1960), "the indicated aim of the Soviet Union here is not to create a new Communist party, but to indoctrinate and influence enough leaders of Mr. Nkrumah's Convention People's Party so that a take-over of the existing authoritarian political machinery becomes relatively easy."

26. French, Belgian, and Portuguese sources have unfortunately been inclined to suspect virtually every African student, labor, or national organization of Communist ties, financing, or influence. (Pieter Lessing's *Africa's Red Harvest*, London, 1962, is thoroughly unreliable on this account.) Such instances do of course exist, though the extent of commitment to Communism is open to considerable doubt even among the more vehemently "Marxist" figures in Guinea and Ghana. Moreover, it has often been convenient for certain African governments to charge political opponents with having "plotted to overthrow the government and set up a Communist regime with the aid of Moscow." On the other hand, the presence of Communist aides and advisers around Patrice Lumumba, in the fall of 1960, is not in doubt. For Serge Michel's own version, see his *Uhuru Lumumba* (Paris, 1962). Another document of highly improbable authenticity is the memorandum on "conspiratorial centralism," allegedly issued in 1957 by the "Central Committee of the Communist Party of West Africa." (The document has been used in connection with charges of Communist ties of Dr. Nkrumah and appears as an appendix to Dr. Kofi Busia's testimony before the U.S. Senate Subcommittee on Internal Security, December 3, 1962.)

27. The *Parti Africain de l'Indépendance* (PAI), founded in Dakar in 1957, has increasingly limited its ambitions to Senegal. Its Secretary-General, Majhemout Diop, a veteran of "front" organizations, evidently received support from the French Communist Party, visited Eastern Europe, and wrote a volume, *Contribution à l'étude des problèmes politiques en Afrique noire* (Paris, 1958), which received high praise from Moscow. The CPSU does list the PAI among fraternal parties (*e.g.*, among those who sent greetings to the Twenty-second CPSU Congress). The Moroccan Communist weekly, *Al Mukafih* (Casablanca, July 14, 1961), wrote: "The PAI is the first party to raise the torch of national independence and socialism, aiming at the creation of a united democratic front and a great African democratic republic moving forward to socialism." See also Majhemout Diop, "Trebovaniia naroda i politicheskie partii," *Sovremennyi vostok*, 1959, No. 3, pp. 22–24.

28. A recent Soviet survey of Communist parties in Africa declares: "If twenty years ago there were a mere 5,000 Communists in Africa, now there are over 50,000." (L. N. Chernov, "Kommunisty stran Azii i Afriki—v avangarde bor'by za svobodu i natsional'nuiu nezavisimost'," *Narody Azii i Afriki*, 1961, No. 5, p. 30.) This statement is obviously untrue. Even if one includes the U.A.R., the figure hardly exceeds 20,000. Of these, more than half are in

the Arab north, perhaps another thousand in South Africa, and 2,000 in the illegal Sudanese CP.

29. N. Numadé, "Marxism and African Liberation," *The African Communist*, No. 2 (April 1960), p. 39; and N. Numadé, "The Choice Before New Africa," *ibid.*, No. 5 (May 1961), p. 16. Numadé's pieces have been widely reprinted in other Communist organs.

30. *The African Communist*, No. 1 (October 1959), pp. 9, 25, 28.

31. On the South African party, see Madeleine Green Kalb, "The Soviet View of the Union of South Africa," Russian Institute Certificate Essay, Columbia University, 1959; and "The Communist Party in South Africa," *Africa Report*, March 1961.

32. *The African Communist* was repeatedly more outspoken than Soviet commentators. Whether this was due to lack of sophistication on the part of its contributors (unlikely), or a calculated policy of less circumlocution (possibly), or indeed a more militant line due to the situation in South Africa, or some sympathy for the "Chinese" position, cannot be ascertained. It is striking, however, how many references to the Chinese experience the journal carried, stressing the example of China for Africa, the relevance of China's experience, regretting the substitution of negotiations for "militant struggle for freedom" in Tanganyika, Kenya, Uganda, and Zanzibar, and publishing an advertisement for the "famous" volume IV of the English-language edition of Mao Tse-tung's Works, published by the Chinese Foreign Language Press. Being published without Soviet responsibility for its contents, the magazine could afford to be franker than Soviet writings but also chose to be more doctrinaire. In 1961–63 it followed the Soviet "line" on the Albanian and Cuban crises, but came close to endorsing the Chinese position against India. (See, for instance, Vol. II, No. 2 [January-March 1963], pp. 3–6.)

33. As Diallo Seydou told the Fourth World Congress of the WFTU in Leipzig, in 1957, African labor had the choice between "syndical multiplicity" and a united trade-union movement, organized in one great "monolithic trade-union center": the latter was, of course, the wiser course. He made clear that the withdrawals of African unions from the WFTU (in order to join a united labor organization of Black Africa) meant no hostility to the WFTU but were merely a means of uniting African labor in its foremost task —anti-imperialism. (Diallo Seydou, "Profsoiuznoe edinstvo vo frantsuzskoi Afrike," *Vsemirnoe profsoiuznoe dvizhenie*, November 1957, pp. 36–37.) See also Franz Ansprenger, *Politik im Schwarzen Afrika* (Cologne, 1961), pp. 219–26.

34. "In the conditions prevailing in Africa south of the Sahara, where in no territory does the working class possess its own separate political party, neither of the British Labour Party type nor on the basis of Marxist ideology, the trade unions play a particularly important role. They not only mobilize the workers to take part in the general national movement but act as a medium for the workers' political expression on all major questions concerning the struggle for national independence." (Jack Woddis, *Africa: The Lion Awakes*, p. 64.)

35. See *The New York Times*, May 28 and June 6, 1961; Iu. Popov, "Trudovaia Afrika ob'ediniaetsia," *Aziia i Afrika segodnia*, 1961, No. 5; and S.

Valiev, "Sozdana Vseafrikanskaia Federatsiia Profsoiuzov," *Aziia i Afrika segodnia*, 1961, No. 7.

36. See, for instance, Iu. Popov, "O nekotorykh chertakh rabochego dvizheniia v Afrike (iuzhnee Sakhary)," *Narody Azii i Afriki*, 1961, No. 5, pp. 49–56.

37. A leading British Communist writer also discusses the awkward problem of "Black" unions barring "White" members and concludes (in rather "un-Marxian" fashion) that "though both African and European trade unionists are workers, there are very big differences between them": they cannot fight together because the Africans fight against European predominance, while the white workers defend it. Hence African trade unions are likely to continue as separate "Black" organizations at least until the reality and atmosphere of discrimination disappear. (Jack Woddis, *Africa: The Lion Awakes*, pp. 150–52.)

38. *Trud*, January 16, 1962. Unlike AATUF, the new ATUC allowed the unions dual affiliation. The Casablanca powers, Ethiopia, and the Sudan barred participation of their unions in the ATUC.

39. Ali Yata, "New Weapons for Embattled Africa," *World Marxist Review*, December 1961, p. 21.

40. *Moskovskii propagandist*, 1957, No. 11, cited in Robert H. Bass, "Communist Fronts: Their History and Function," *Problems of Communism*, September-October 1960, p. 14.

41. Space permits no detailed discussion of these efforts. See, in addition to Bass, "Communist Fronts," the special issue of *Ost-Probleme*, 1961, No. 18/19, and Schatten, *Afrika schwarz*, pp. 286–344.

42. The official record of the Casablanca Conference (January 1961) does indeed reveal a militant, factious, intolerantly anti-Western spirit and not a word of criticism of the Soviet bloc or of Communism. For typical Soviet comment on it, see *Sovremennyi vostok*, 1961, No. 2, pp. 57–58. For some details on the African alignments, see J. Kirk Sale, "Power Struggle in Africa," *The New Leader*, June 19, 1961; Hans Jaeger, "Gespaltenes Afrika," *Deutsche Rundschau*, November 1961; and the "realistic" appraisal by Potekhin, "The African People Forge Unity," *International Affairs*, 1961, No. 6. I. Plyshevsky, a Soviet foreign office official, in his article, "Some Problems of the Independence Struggle in Africa," *World Marxist Review*, July 1961, goes further than had earlier comments in condemning the pro-French African leaders. By contrast, the previous year, during Soviet efforts at a rapprochement with France, African students at Moscow University had been prevented from publicly protesting French nuclear tests in the Sahara, so as not to antagonize the de Gaulle government. See Richard Amar, *A Student in Moscow*, and Michel Ayih, *Ein Afrikaner in Moskau*, pp. 146–65.

Moscow was manifestly eager not to burn any bridges and continued to deal with and appeal to Libya, Ethiopia, Somalia, and other African members of the Lagos grouping. On the other hand, Soviet journals in 1961–63 carried attacks on the leaders of Tanganyika, Sierra Leone, and Nigeria for excessive friendliness toward the British.

43. For example, Dmitry Volsky, "The 'Gradual Withdrawal' Tactic," *New Times*, 1961, No. 46, p. 13. Perhaps with the Sudan in mind, Plyshevsky

("Some Problems," p. 39) wrote: "There are also the so-called 'neutralists' who, on the pretext of preoccupation with internal affairs and adherence to the principle of non-interference, actually aid the collaborationists." The game, Moscow realized, could be played both ways. Another unexpectedly critical note on neutralism was sounded in a major review article on the prospects of the national liberation movement late in 1961 (Mirsky and Tiagutenko, "Tendentsii i perspektivy," p. 28) : "The neutralism of the bourgeoisie is caused first of all by its desire to stay out of the conflict between the two camps, to reduce to a minimum its risk of being involved in a possible world war." While it may reflect "anti-colonialism," neutralism is also used by the bourgeoisie purely in the interests of business, since "it enables it to trade and cooperate with the West and with the East."

44. See, for example, V. P. Nikhamin, *Mezhdunarodnye problemy sovremennoi Afriki* (Moscow, 1960), pp. 45–47.

45. After giving prompt diplomatic recognition to the Congo, Moscow on August 2, 1960, announced the appointment of Mikhail Yakovlev as ambasdor; he arrived in Leopoldville on August 8. During the following weeks, he presented the Congo government an Il-14 airplane as a gift and other shipments (Moscow had on July 21 announced that it would "consider favorably" any Congolese requests for economic assistance). On August 26 some 100 Soviet trucks were delivered to the government. During the following days, a leading Soviet official, Georgi Zhukov, visited Leopoldville, ostensibly to conclude a cultural exchange agreement with the Congo. After the break between Lumumba and Kasavubu in early September 1960, Colonel Mobutu announced on September 15 that he had asked for the recall of the Soviet and other East European diplomatic missions. On the Soviet reaction, see also Arthur Wauters, ed., *Le Monde Communiste et la Crise du Congo Belge* (Brussels, 1961).

46. In July 1961 the Soviet Union opened a diplomatic mission in Stanleyville without giving Gizenga formal recognition. Its dispatch was not formally announced in Moscow. On August 31, after Gizenga had joined the Leopoldville government, Khrushchev informed Adoula of Soviet recognition (while Peking remained silent). But at the same time the Soviet press hailed the formation of Gizenga's new (and abortive) National Lumumbist Party. During the final three months of 1961, the Soviet press was strikingly reluctant to comment on Congo politics (e.g., whether the Adoula government would remain in control, and whether Gizenga was in it or against it), while the Chinese Communist press roundly attacked Adoula as a puppet of imperialism.

47. On the Soviet-Ghanaian relationship, see Schatten, *Afrika schwarz*, pp. 66–69. On Soviet action in the United Nations, see Alexander Dallin, *The Soviet Union at the United Nations* (New York, 1962), chapter 10.

48. *Le Soir* (Paris), October 26, 1961. See also Drew Pearson's column of October 3, 1961.

49. Philip Decraene, in *The Reporter*, February 1, 1962.

50. Interview with François Mitterand, in *L'Express* (Paris), January 25, 1962; and Colin Legum, "Moskaus Rückschläge in Afrika," *Die Zeit* (Hamburg), March 30, 1962.

51. Moscow Radio in French to Africa, February 21, 1962.

52. Moscow Radio in Hausa to Africa, February 22, 1962. On Mikoyan's trip, see *The Mizan Newsletter*, February 1962.

53. *International Affairs*, 1959, No. 2, p. 88. See also Laqueur, "Communism and Nationalism," p. 617.

54. Potekhin, *Afrika smotrit*, pp. 56–61.

55. *World Marxist Review*, November 1961, p. 45. See also Potekhin's comments in *International Affairs*, 1961, No. 6, pp. 83–84; and Observer, "African Unity," *New Times*, 1963, No. 22, p. 5.

56. Potekhin, *Afrika smotrit*, pp. 8–10, 17; Mirsky and Tiagutenko, "Tendentsii i perspektivy," pp. 29–30; *The Mizan Newsletter*, April 1962, p. 16. In his speech greeting President Keita of Mali, Khrushchev on May 30, 1962, added: "It would be wrong to believe that it is enough to proclaim the slogan, 'We are for socialism,' and that then one can lie down in the cool shadow of a tree and wait for everything to sort itself out." In the case of the U.A.R. and Yugoslavia, the Soviet efforts to denounce "non-Marxist" socialism may also stem from a fear of attempts to unite parts of Africa under the leadership of rival powers. See also *World Marxist Review*, March 1963, p. 64; I. Potekhin, "On 'African Socialism' (A Reply to My Opponents)," *International Affairs*, 1963, No. 1, pp. 71–79.

57. Moscow has identified tribal, national, and religious friction as among the principal impediments to united progressive action in Africa (*Afrika, 1956–1961*, p. 31). See also Lazar Pistrak, "Soviet Views on Africa," *Problems of Communism*, March-April 1962, p. 28.

58. I. Potekhin, "Africa Shakes Off Colonial Slavery," *International Affairs*, 1959, No. 2, p. 88. Others, stressing the intertwining of class conflict with tribal and religious elements (e.g., in the revolts against the dominant Moslem Hausa and Fulba tribesmen in Northern Nigeria by the poorer "pagan" tribes), find a "progressive" content in the tribal struggles. (See L. Kim, "Pervyi god nezavisimosti Nigerii," *Mirovaia ekonomika i mezhdunarodnye otnosheniia*, 1961, No. 8, p. 99.)

59. L. Volodin and O. Orestov, *Trudnye dni Kongo* (Moscow, 1961), pp. 32–33.

60. Potekhin has given the most authoritative exposition of this matter in his *Afrika smotrit*, p. 50ff., and in *World Marxist Review*, November 1961.

61. Stalin's definitions were still accepted: a "tribe" is the product of primitive society; a "nationality" (or "people"), of feudalism; a "nation," of capitalist society. Since before colonization African society was pre-bourgeois, no "nations" could have been formed south of the Sahara. According to Stalin, common territory, economy, language, and culture were the four indispensable conditions of nationhood. In reiterating these terms, Potekhin (*Afrika smotrit*, p. 53) went out of his way to emphasize that the denial of nationhood to the African peoples was in no sense insulting to them.

62. See the 1961 Program of the CPSU on the dual view on nationalism as "containing a democratic element" when directed against imperialist oppression, but being a distinct impediment to "Communist construction," against which "a relentless struggle" must be waged in the U.S.S.R. On the Soviet view of self-determination, see also Elliott Goodman, *The Soviet Design for a World State* (New York, 1961).

63. Sivolobov, *Natsional'no-osvoboditel'noe*, pp. 38–39.

64. A. Arzumanian, "Velikaia Oktiabr'skaia Revoliutsiia," *Kommunist* (Moscow), 1960, No. 16, p. 26. For Potekhin's attacks on African non-violence, see his "Africa Shakes Off," pp. 87–89, and his "Istoricheskii povorot," *Sovremennyi vostok*, 1959, No. 3, pp. 9–10. See also Y. Dolgopolov, "National Liberation Wars in the Present Epoch," *International Affairs*, 1962, No. 2, p. 17.

65. U.S. Department of State, *World Strength* (1962), p. 47. Information on the UPC is based, in addition to personal interviews, on Schatten, *Afrika schwarz*, pp. 87–105, 249–54; Ansprenger, *Politik*, pp. 192–208, 394–404; *Sovremennyi vostok*, 1960, No. 1, p. 19; *Aziia i Afrika segodnia*, 1961, No. 6, pp. 38–41, and No. 7, pp. 49–51. See also V. Larin, "The Cameroons Fight for Unity and Independence," *International Affairs*, 1955 No. 10, pp. 90–98; A. Vetlugin, "Kamerun prodolzhaet bor'bu za nezavisimost'," *Sovremennyi vostok*, 1959, No. 6, pp. 6–8; *The Observer*, March 11, 1962; Italiaander, *Schwarze Haut*, pp. 256–61; *The Times* (London), January 7, 1960. At the Afro-Asian Solidarity Council meeting in April 1960, the Chinese Communists were the only ones to support the UPC against the Cameroun government. Meanwhile, a rival faction of the UPC, under Theodore Mayi Matip, has become a "legal" party and has repeatedly appealed to the remaining guerillas to lay down their arms.

66. While previously the goals of the national-liberation movement were clear, now "a difficult task confronts the people: they must learn to . . . distinguish friend and foe." There is also the possibility of the movement's "mutation of its general democratic content into a reactionary one." Moreover, "the split within the African national-liberation movement undoubtedly weakens the role of the new states in international affairs." (S. Viskov, "The Collapse of Colonialism and New Trends in International Relations," *International Affairs*, 1961, No. 9, pp. 11, 13.)

67. *Narody Azii i Afriki*, 1962, No. 1. See "Tasks for Soviet Africanists," *The Mizan Newsletter*, April 1962.

68. Y. Dolgopolov, "National-Liberation Wars in the Present Epoch," *International Affairs*, 1962, No. 2, pp. 17–20. See also the "tougher" attitude in V. Pavlov, "Soiuz rabochego klassa i krest'ianstva i sotsial'nye preobrazovania na vostoke," *Aziia i Afrika segodnia*, 1961, No. 9, pp. 8–10; and A. Iu. Shpirt, "Inostrannyi gosudarstvennomonopolisticheskii kapital v Afrike," *Narody Azii i Afriki*, 1961, No. 6, pp. 20–31.

69. *Jeune Afrique* (Tunis), February 6–12, 1962.

70. The formation of the Basuto party was formally reported by *Pravda* (November, 6, 1961) as well as the *World Marxist Review*—a highly unusual procedure, unique in African politics. It is likely that South African Communists, some of whom have taken refuge in Basutoland, play an important part there. *Est et Ouest* (No. 271) quoted the Cape Town *Contact* (November 16, 1961) as reporting that John Motloheloa, the Basuto Party's secretary-general, launched the party after a three-months stay in Moscow. Its first congress was held in May 1962. See John Motloheloa, "Lesotho's Road to Independence," *The African Communist*, No. 10 (July-August 1962); and *World Marxist Review*, September 1962, pp. 66–67.

71. *World Marxist Review*, July 1962, p. 50, which states that the CP of

Northern Rhodesia was established "towards the end of 1961"; and TASS, July 18, 1962, cited in *Ost-Probleme* (Bonn), 1962, No. 16, p. 498.

72. A variety of news dispatches in 1962 spoke of a stepping up of Communist activity in Kenya, Uganda, Northern Rhodesia, and Zanzibar. In Angola, a small Communist party, formed in 1955, soon merged with the MPLA, which has been increasingly Soviet-oriented. See *Pravda o portugal'skikh koloniiakh* (Moscow, 1961); *New Times*, 1960, No. 50; L. Korneev, "Narodnaia voina v Angole," *Aziia i Afrika segodnia*, 1961, Nos. 7–9; Russell Howe, "Reds Seek Rebel Split in Angola," *Washington Post*, March 15, 1962. According to a Somalian student who escaped from Prague, the Soviet Union gave money to Somalian Communist students but refused them arms. (*Daily Nation*, Nairobi, February 22, 1962.)

73. *The African Communist*, No. 8 (January 1962), pp. 44–46. See also Jalang Kwena, "National Independence and Socialism," *ibid.*, No. 10, pp. 37–38.

74. *L'Unità* (Rome), November 12, 1961.

75. Raymond Guyot, "Solidarity with the Peoples of Africa," *World Marxist Review*, November 1960, pp. 74–75.

76. *L'Humanité* (Paris), August 16 and 20, and December 7, 1962.

77. *The African Communist*, Vol. II, No. 1, pp. 81–83.

78. *World Marxist Review*, March 1963, p. 82; and TASS, April 17, 1963.

79. *Die Zeit*, March 30, 1962.

80. *The New York Times*, March 25, 1962. The same line was reaffirmed in Khrushchev's speech greeting Premier Mamadou Dia of Senegal on June 14, 1962.

81. K. Ivanov, "The National and Colonial Question Today," *International Affairs*, 1963, No. 5, pp. 3–10.

82. V. Kudryavtsev, "Problems of Afro-Asian Solidarity," *International Affairs*, 1963, No. 5, p. 52. The open letter of the CPSU Central Committee of July 14, 1963 included among its charges against the Chinese Communists the following: "They came out against the participation of representatives of the Afro-Asian Solidarity Committees of the European Socialist Countries in the Third Solidarity Conference [at Moshi]. . . . The leader of the Chinese delegation told the Soviet representatives that 'whites have nothing to do here.'"

83. "End of a Honeymoon," *The Observer* (London), May 26, 1963.

84. *The New York Times*, June 12, 1963.

85. *Pravda*, July 25, 1963.

86. Michel Ayih, Introduction to Branko Lazitch, *L'Afrique et les leçons de l'expérience communiste* (Paris, 1961), pp. 5–6. See also his *Ein Afrikaner in Moskau* (Cologne, 1961).

87. H. Jourdain, "Ideological Moves of Latter-Day Colonialists," *World Marxist Review*, September 1959, p. 67. See also Khrushchev's speech of May 30, 1962.

88. Foreword to George Padmore, *Pan-Africanism or Communism?* (London, 1956), p. 12.

89. See Thomas Hodgkin, "A Note on the Language of African Nationalism," *St. Antony's Papers*, No. 10 (London, 1961), pp. 35–38.

90. See, for instance, *The New York Times,* May 26, 1958; and Edouard Mendiaux, *Moscou, Accra et le Congo* (Brussels, 1960), p. 63.

91. *Afrika, 1956–1961,* p. 32.

92. Woddis, *Africa: The Lion Awakes,* p. 292.

CHAPTER 2

1. "Imperializm kak vysshaia stadiia kapitalizma," *Sochineniia,* XXII, p. 286.

2. *Ibid.,* p. 261.

3. *Ibid.,* p. 229.

4. *Ibid.,* p. 231. It is tempting to read a qualification to this argument into an earlier paragraph which states that "opportunities for export of capital arise because a number of backward countries have already been absorbed into the nexus of world capitalism, the main lines of railroads are either in existence or under construction, the elementary prerequisites of industrial development have been created, etc." Yet there is nothing here to suggest that the "nexus of world capitalism" would not eventually absorb *all* backward countries nor that the creation of the "elementary prerequisites" everywhere would be anything more than a matter of time. This attitude was in complete accord with the letter and spirit of classical Marxism. (See, for example, "The Future Results of British Rule in India," in Karl Marx and Frederick Engels, *Selected Works,* Moscow, 1955, Vol. I, esp. pp. 353, 355, 356.)

5. E. Varga, *Kapitalizm dvadtsatogo veka* (Moscow, 1961), p. 96. It is worth noting that effective criticism of a more sophisticated version of the same position has come from Poland. In a remarkable article ("Nie zgadzam sie z Prof. Langem," *Zycie Gospodarcze,* No. 33, 1957) Zofia Dobrska pointed out that the unwillingness of monopolists to develop industries in backward countries could be properly explained by their anxiety to protect capital already invested from competition only if they had been generally attempting to freeze the size of this capital once and for all; yet this is quite obviously not the case, and the theory under consideration cannot tell us why monopolists would harm themselves more by investing in underdeveloped countries than by investing at home. Furthermore, it is not at all clear why this fear of spoiling the market is inoperative with regard to extractive industries, which have powerfully attracted foreign investment (and which are, one might add, most certainly no less monopolistic or oligopolistic than, say, machine-building).

6. *Kommunist,* No. 16, 1961, p. 34.

7. I. I. Potekhin, *Afrika smotrit v budushchee* (Moscow, 1960), pp. 40–41; the substance of Potekhin's remarks is echoed in R. Avakov and G. Mirskii, "O klassovoi strukture v slaborazvitykh stranakh," *Mirovaia ekonomika i mezhdunarodnye otnosheniia,* No. 3, 1962 (March), p. 93.

8. Report to the Commission on the National and Colonial Question at the Second Congress of the Communist International, July 26, 1920, *Sochineniia,* XXXI, p. 219.

9. Potekhin, *Afrika smotrit,* p. 43.

10. "The Foreign Policy of Mali," *International Affairs,* Vol. XXXVII, No. 4 (October 1961), p. 437.

11. Potekhin, *Afrika smotrit*, p. 24.

12. "State Planning and Forced Industrialization," *Problems of Communism*, Vol. VIII, No. 6 (November-December 1959), pp. 39–40.

13. Kwame Nkrumah, *I Speak of Freedom* (New York, 1961), pp. 53, 137.

14. V. Kollontai, "Burzhuaznaia politekonomiia o problemakh ekonomicheskogo razvitiia slaborazvitykh stran," *Voprosy ekonomiki*, No. 3, 1956 (March), p. 127.

15. A. Aziian, "Raspad kolonial'noi sistemy imperializma i novye otnosheniia mezhdu stranami," *Voprosy ekonomiki*, No. 10, 1956 (October), p. 19.

16. I. I. Potekhin, ed., *Afrika iuzhnee Sakhary* (Moscow, 1958), p. 8.

17. Potekhin, *Afrika smotrit*, p. 42.

18. "Tovarishcham-Kommunistam Azerbaidzhana, Gruzii, Armenii, Dagestana, Gorskoi Respubliki," *Sochineniia*, XXXII, p. 296; quoted by M. Dzunusov, "O zakonomernostiakh nekapitalisticheskogo puti razvitiia otstalykh stran k sotsializmu," *Voprosy filosofii*, No. 2, 1962 (February), p. 18.

19. The chief sources for the statistical material presented in this section are the official Soviet foreign trade statistics; scattered references to aid agreements and projects are contained in *Vneshniaia torgovlia*, the official Soviet foreign trade journal, and in other Soviet publications. The trade statistics now cover the period 1955–61 in detail (as well as the period 1918–40); they list quantity and value of specific commodities of export and import by country, making price calculations possible. (In this connection, it should be noted that Soviet statisticians have recently recalculated their previous yearly figures into new rubles, with 1 ruble to equal $1.11, and published them in a handbook covering 1955–59; the 1960 and 1961 Supplements to *Vneshniaia torgovlia* also use new rubles. While such recalculation due to a currency revaluation seems odd, it must be remembered that Soviet foreign trade ruble prices are based on world market prices valued in a convertible currency and then recalculated into rubles at the official exchange rates, and they bear no relation to domestic prices. The recalculated figures are therefore useful for comparative purposes).

Certain limitations in the trade data must be kept in mind. There are internal inconsistencies in the data, although they seem to be of tolerable dimensions. (See A. Nove and D. Matko, "The Pattern of Soviet Foreign Trade," *The Three Banks Review*, No. 53, March 1962, pp. 18–21. For a contrary assessment, see Robert Loring Allen, "A Note on Soviet Foreign Trade Statistics," *Soviet Studies*, Vol. X, No. 5, April 1959, p. 366.) Further, there are significant discrepancies between the Soviet data and those of the U.S.S.R.'s trading partners. For instance, the Ghanaian figures for tons of cocoa exported to the Soviet Union between 1955 and 1960 vary from the Soviet import figures in a range of +9 per cent to −162 per cent. Such inconsistencies may be due to bad reporting on either end and are present to some degree in all trade statistics.

Using data on Soviet aid is fraught with several dangers, especially if it is done for comparative purposes. In the first place, credits granted do not represent credits actually used. From scattered bits of information on the status of various credit agreements, it is now evident that the use of credits varies so tremendously from country to country that no uniform basis for estimation can be usefully employed. Moreover, projects may easily be counted twice, owing to the publicity attendant upon each stage of the aid-giving process; the exact value of the Soviet contribution to each project is not given; some credit figures are unknown; and finally, the exact terms of each credit agreement are not published. (Only in the 1959 pact with Guinea were the terms made public, although it is generally assumed in Western sources that the other countries received substantially the same terms as Guinea.)

Where possible we have used the African country trade statistics and United Nations and Western periodical and press sources to corroborate the Soviet material. Of the ten countries in sub-Saharan Africa trading with the U.S.S.R. between 1955 and 1961, four (Ethiopia, Ghana, Nigeria, and the Sudan) have statistics available here.

20. U.S.S.R., Ministry of Foreign Trade, *Vneshniaia torgovlia SSSR za 1918–1940 gody* (Moscow, 1960), pp. 1117–19. Figures converted into new rubles.

21. *The New York Times*, Dec. 22, 1952.

22. *Economist*, June 25, 1960, p. 1367. See also A. Nove and D. Matko, "The Pattern of Soviet Foreign Trade," *The Three Banks Review*, No. 53 (March 1962), p. 30.

23. The Ethiopian credit was reported in *Vneshniaia torgovlia*, No. 2, 1961 (February), p. 56. It has also been reported that no drawings on this credit have been made; in fact the Ethiopians are said to have obtained $2 million in dollars through their interpretation of the treaty and to have invested it promptly, at over 3 per cent interest, in United States government bonds. (John D. Montgomery, *Aid to Africa: New Test for U.S. Policy*, New York, 1961, p. 27.) The credit to Guinea was reported in *Vneshniaia torgovlia*, No. 2, 1960 (February), p. 56.

24. Economist Intelligence Unit, *Three-Monthly Economic Review of Ghana, Nigeria, Sierra Leone, Gambia*, No. 40 (December 1962), p. 9.

25. Ghana, Office of the Government Statistician, *Annual Report on External Trade of Ghana and Report of Shipping and Aircraft Movements and Cargo Loaded and Unloaded* (Accra); Federation of Nigeria, Department of Statistics, *Trade Report* (Lagos); *Ethiopian Economic Review*, Vols. I, III, IV (Addis Ababa); Republic of Sudan, Department of Statistics, *Annual Foreign Trade Report* (Khartoum).

26. Economist Intelligence Unit, *Three-Monthly Economic Review of French African Community. French Somaliland, Cameroun, Togo, Guinea, Liberia*, No. 5 (May 1961), p. 13.

27. Raymond F. Mikesell and Jack N. Behrman, *Financing Free World Trade with the Sino-Soviet Bloc* (Princeton, N.J.: Princeton Studies in International Finance, Number 8, 1958), p. 27.

28. See, for example, Kollontai, "Burzhuaznaia politekonomiia," pp. 137, 139.

29. V. Rymalov, "Soviet Assistance to Less Developed Countries," *International Affairs* (Moscow), No. 9, 1959 (September), p. 34.

30. The average percentage of United States International Cooperation Administration project obligations in Africa as a whole going to the "heavy"

field of activity (transport, industry, and mining) from Fiscal Year 1957 to Fiscal Year 1961 was 16.3 per cent. (United States International Cooperation Administration *Operations Report,* 1957–61.)

31. *The New York Times,* Oct. 31, 1960.

32. *Vneshniaia torgovlia,* No. 3, 1962 (March), p. 43.

33. *Ibid.,* No. 8, 1962 (August), p. 12.

34. United States Senate, Committee on Foreign Relations, *Hearings on Foreign Assistance Act of 1962,* 87th Congress, 2nd Session, Testimony of Frank M. Coffin, Apr. 12, 1962, pp. 268–69.

35. Robert B. Stauffer and Mulford J. Colebrook, "Economic Assistance and Ethiopia's Foreign Policy," *Orbis,* Vol. V, No. 3 (Fall 1961), pp. 320–41.

36. *The New York Times,* Nov. 17, 1961.

37. Economist Intelligence Unit, *Three-Monthly Economic Review of Ghana, Nigeria, Sierra Leone, Gambia,* No. 27 (August 1959), pp. 4–5.

38. *Vneshniaia torgovlia,* No. 3, 1962 (March), p. 43.

39. Economist Intelligence Unit, *Three-Monthly Economic Review of French African Community,* p. 13.

40. *The New York Times,* Dec. 5, 1959.

41. *Vneshniaia torgovlia,* No. 10, 1960 (October), pp. 46–47.

42. *Neues Afrika,* Vol. IV, No. 2 (February 1962), p. 47.

43. Economist Intelligence Unit, *Three-Monthly Economic Review of French African Community,* No. 8 (March 1962), p. 16.

44. *The New York Times,* Aug. 20, 1960.

45. *Vneshniaia torgovlia,* No. 5, 1961 (May), pp. 55–57.

46. *Ibid.,* No. 4, 1961 (April), p. 22.

47. *The New York Times,* Oct. 9, 1961.

48. *Vneshniaia torgovlia,* No. 6, 1961 (July), p. 24.

49. *The New York Times,* June 15, 1962.

50. *Ibid.,* June 18, 1961.

51. United States Department of State, *The Sino-Soviet Economic Offensive in the Less Developed Countries,* Department of State Publication No. 6632 (Washington, 1958), pp. 50–52.

52. *Vneshniaia torgovlia,* No. 8, 1961 (August), p. 7.

53. See Mikesell and Behrman, *Financing Free World Trade,* pp. 80–81 and Table 12, p. 84.

54. Joseph S. Berliner, *Soviet Foreign Aid: The New Aid and Trade Policy in Underdeveloped Countries* (New York, 1958), pp. 120–27.

55. See Franklyn L. Holzman, "Soviet Foreign Trade Pricing and the Question of Discrimination," *Review of Economics and Statistics,* Vol. XLIV, No. 2 (May 1962), pp. 134–47. Holzman points out that the prices charged by bloc countries to each other are often higher than prices charged by them to Western countries for the same products. He attributes this phenomenon to the fact that these countries are forced to conduct the maximum of trade within the bloc and must thereby forego many more profitable trading opportunities outside of it.

56. "A highly forced tempo of the development of industry in conjunction with insufficient development of agriculture gave rise to disproportions in the national economy. . . . In some countries planned targets that were too high

were set for development of some lines of heavy industry. Occasionally there were tendencies toward producing all kinds of industrial output without taking into consideration the economic conditions and endowment with natural resources. The adopted rate of growth exceeded the real possibilities of these countries and was not necessary in view of the friendly cooperation of the socialist countries and the broad division of labor between them." (*Ekonomia polityczna,* Polish ed., Warsaw, 1960, p. 527.)

57. See, for example, P. N. Pospelov, "O zadachakh nauchno-issledovatel'-skoi raboty po istorii partii v svete reshenii XXII s"ezda KPSS," *Voprosy istorii KPSS,* No. 2, 1962 (February), pp. 19–20, in which the dire consequences of the early collectivization policy are quite openly discussed and the blame put squarely on Stalin.

58. Paul A. Baran, "A Few Thoughts on the Great Debate," *Monthly Review,* No. 1 (May 1962), pp. 34–45.

CHAPTER 3

1. It is interesting to compare an early warning such as that given in Max Yergan, "The Communist Threat in Africa," in C. Grove Haines (ed.), *Africa Today* (Baltimore, 1955), pp. 267 ff., with more recent and better informed comments such as: Walter Kolarz, "The Impact of Communism on West Africa," *International Affairs* (London), Vol. 38, No. 2 (April 1962), pp. 156–69; David T. Cattell, "Communism and the African Negro," *Problems of Communism* (Washington, D.C.), Vol. VIII, No. 5 (September-October 1959), pp. 35–41; David L. Morison and Walter Kolarz, "Communism in Africa," *ibid.,* Vol. X, No. 6 (November-December 1961), pp. 8–23.

2. Dr. I. I. Potekhin, the leading Soviet Africanist, has said: ". . . great masses of the population in Africa either cannot imagine at all what socialism is or have only a vague notion of it. . . . In Africa socialism is much talked about; the ideas of socialism are widely diffused, but discussion is mostly concerned with ideas that are not in accordance with scientific socialism." ("Afrika: Itogi i perspektivy anti-imperialisticheskoi revolyutsii," *Asiya i Afrika Segodnya,* Moscow, No. 10, 1961.)

3. Fritz Schatten, "Africa: Nationalism and Communism," *Survey* (London), No. 42, June 1962, pp. 148–59.

4. "The Soviet Bloc's Penetration of Africa and Asia," *News from Behind the Iron Curtain* (New York), Vol. V, No. 9 (September 1956), pp. 3 ff. Other useful reviews of the early phases of Soviet and bloc aid to developing countries include: A. Nove, "Soviet Trade and Aid," *Lloyds Bank Review,* No. 51 (January 1959), pp. 1–19; W. A. Nielsen and Z. S. Hodjera, "Sino-Soviet Bloc Technical Assistance: Another Bilateral Approach," *The Annals,* Vol. 323 (May 1959), pp. 40–49; Robert L. Allen, *Middle Eastern Economic Relations with the Soviet Union, Eastern Europe, and Mainland China* (Charlottesville, Va., 1958); Robert L. Allen, *Soviet Economic Warfare* (Public Affairs Press, Washington, D.C., 1960); H. G. Aubrey, "Sino-Soviet Economic Activities in Less Developed Countries," *Comparisons of the United States and Soviet Economies* (Joint Economic Committee, 86th Congress, 1st Session, Washington, D.C., 1959, Part II), pp. 445–66.

5. *Statisticky Obzor* (Prague), No. 10, 1955; Radio Warsaw, December 25, 1955; and *Czechoslovak Economic Bulletin* (Prague), April 1956.

6. *Lidova Democracie* (Prague), Jan. 27, 1956; *Zahranicni Obchod* (Prague), No. 2, 1957; and *Rude Právo* (Prague), Mar. 9, 1957, reporting on the visit to Egypt of the Czechoslovak Minister of Foreign Trade.

7. *Trybuna Ludu* (Warsaw), Dec. 24, 1955.

8. *Czechoslovak Economic Bulletin* (Prague), February 1956.

9. "Communist Traders Look Abroad," *East Europe* (New York), Vol. VIII, No. 12 (December 1959), p. 19; and United Nations, *Direction of International Trade* (New York), Annual Summary issues, Vols. IX and X.

10. Stefan C. Stolte, "The Soviet Union, Communist China, and the Underdeveloped Countries," *Bulletin of the Institute for the Study of the USSR* (Munich), Vol. VII, No. 8, August 1960, pp. 29–36; Gordon Brook-Shepherd, "Red Rivalry in the Black Continent," *The Reporter*, Jan. 18, 1962, pp. 23–25.

11. *Pravda* (Moscow), November 22, 1957.

12. *Current Digest of the Soviet Press*, Vol. XII, No. 49, p. 3.

13. Endre Sik, "Africa's Future," *Nepszabadsag* (Budapest), Dec. 27, 1961.

14. I. Plyshevski, "Some Problems of the Independence Struggle in Africa," *World Marxist Review* (Prague), Vol. IV, No. 7 (July 1961).

15. D. Degtyar and A. Kutsenkow, "Cooperation of the Socialist States with the Economically Underdeveloped Countries," *World Marxist Review*, Vol. IV, No. 6 (June 1961); William Grey, "Imperialist 'Aid'—An Instrument of Enslavement," *ibid.*, Vol. IV, No. 2 (February 1961).

16. Laurice Galico, "The Catholic Church and Africa," *World Marxist Review*, Vol. IV, No. 4 (April 1961). For a very interesting discussion of Communist views regarding economic development see also V. A. Sergeev, "Statement at the First Session of the United Nations Committee for Industrial Development," *U.S.S.R. Mission to the United Nations*, Document No. 15, 1961.

17. *Pravda* (Moscow), Dec. 6, 1960); *Current Digest of the Soviet Press*, Vol. XIII, No. 49.

18. See, for example, D. Matejka on the "national democratic state" in *Pravda* (Bratislava), Jan. 14, 1962.

19. Only Poland, Bulgaria, and the U.S.S.R. are known to have published trade statistics sufficiently detailed to show trade with all African countries. Most of the magnitudes cited here and below are therefore based entirely on data supplied by their trading partners, as published in the United Nations *Direction of International Trade*. This appears to be the most complete set of comparable data available, but there are nonetheless omissions in coverage, stemming from the considerable time lag in reporting and publication and the failure of some of the reporters to distinguish between the two Germanies. A rough allowance has been made for this in the statements here, but the magnitudes are inevitably approximations. For references to the trade of Eastern Europe with underdeveloped countries in general, the basis is the United Nations Economic Commission for Europe, *Economic Bulletin for Europe* (Geneva), Vol. 13, No. 1, pp. 22–28.

20. Radio Warsaw, Nov. 23, 1961; and United Nations, Economic Commission for Europe, *Economic Bulletin for Europe*, Vol. 13, No. 1, p. 25.

21. The U.S.S.R., for example, established "direct" trade with Ghana in 1959 by starting to buy cocoa beans through Ghana's Cocoa Marketing Board's London agent, instead of through British firms, as formerly. (*Vneshnyaya Torgovlya*, Moscow, No. 5, 1961, p. 30.) This kind of shift can affect foreign trade figures without there being any real change in trade.

22. Radio Warsaw, June 1, 1961.

23. Bulgarian Telegraph Agency (BTA), Dec. 7, 1961; East German News Agency (ADN), Apr. 13, 1961; Mogadishu Radio, Feb. 14, 1961; *West Africa* (London), July 8, 1961; Czechoslovak Press Service (CTK), Oct. 16, 1961; *L'Essor* (Bamako), June 6, 1961; Rumanian Press Agency (Agerpress), Feb. 18, 1961.

24. A probably incomplete tally for Poland in the summer and fall of 1961 scores nine African countries visited by at least one Polish delegation to negotiate some sort of trade, and perhaps scholarships and technical assistance as well, and visits to Poland by at least four African delegations on commercial business. Two of the latter were from Ghana, where Poland has had a permanent trade representative since 1959. Meanwhile, Bulgarians, Hungarians, and East Germans were also visiting and being visited by a number of the same African states. (Radio Warsaw, June 1, 1961; PAP, Sept. 23, Oct. 25, Dec. 7 and 11, 1961; Hungarian Press Agency (MTI), Apr. 13, 1961; East Berlin Radio, Oct. 20, 1961; BAT, Oct. 5, 1961; Sofia Radio, June 13, 1961; *Daily Graphic*, Accra, Apr. 17, 1961.)

25. Trade pacts at the government level are quite general in nature. Specific transactions are effected by individual foreign trade organizations that deal in a limited range of goods. The major East European trading countries—Czechoslovakia, Poland, and East Germany—each have 20 to 30 such firms, while Bulgaria and Rumania have about 15 each. (Klaus Billerbeck, *Soviet Bloc Foreign Aid to the Underdeveloped Countries*, Hamburg Archives of World Economy, Hamburg, 1960, p. 28.)

26. *Vneshnyaya Torgovlya* (Moscow), No. 9, 1959, and No. 2, 1961.

27. *Zycie Warszawy* (Warsaw), July 26, 1961.

28. *Vneshnyaya Torgovlya* (Moscow), No. 5, 1960, p. 25; Polish Press Agency (PAP), Aug. 22, 1962.

29. All figures theoretically include both grants and long-term credits for economic and military purposes. All, however, must be regarded as approximate. They refer only to agreements whose values have been made public or may reasonably be estimated to date. More agreements undoubtedly exist. For example, Ghana's President Nkrumah, in a speech broadcast by Accra Radio December 22, 1961, mentioned credits from Bulgaria and Rumania, on which no information appears to be available, and cited a total sum from the bloc which was roughly double the total of identifiable credit commitments. On the other hand, the possibilities of double counting in this field are legion, in view of the repetitious publicity given each phase of procedure, and many sources are vague on the distinction between short-term or revolving trade credits and the longer loans that may properly be considered aid.

Figures here are based on the U.S. State Department's tallies (which are somewhat more generous than those available in United Nations publications or the rare partial totals given by official Communist sources, though less so than President's Nkrumah's), supplemented by United Nations and press and radio sources: U.S. Department of State, *The Sino-Soviet Economic Offensive in the Less Developed Countries* (Washington, 1958) ; *Communist Economic Policy in the Less Developed Areas* (Washington, 1960) ; *The Threat of Soviet Economic Policy* (Washington, 1961) ; *The Sino-Soviet Economic Offensive through 1960,* Intelligence Report No. 8426 (mimeographed), March 1961; *Mutual Security Presentation: Credits and Grants Extended by the Sino-Soviet Bloc to Less Developed Countries of the Free World,* Background Paper B-8, March 1961 (mimeographed) ; United Nations, Economic Commission for Europe, *Ecoonmic Survey of Europe in 1960* (Geneva, 1961), Appendix A; United Nations, Department of Economic and Social Affairs, *International Flow of Long-Term Capital and Official Donations, 1951–1959* (New York, 1961) ; *Vneshnyaya Torgovlya* (Moscow), No. 3, 1961, pp. 42–44, and No. 6, 1961, pp. 29–30; *Ekonomicheskaya Gazeta* (Moscow), June 3, 1961; *Daily Graphic* (Accra), Apr. 21, 1961, May 24, 1961, and Dec. 18, 1961; *L'Essor* (Bamako), June 23, 1961, and Nov. 3 and 4, 1961; *The Times* (London), May 29, 1961; MTI, Oct. 13, 1961; Mogadishu Radio, June 27, 1961.

30. *The Economist* (London), Aug. 26, 1961, pp. 788–90. This is not, of course, a strictly valid comparison, since the data on bloc aid refer to amounts committed, not to amounts disbursed, on which information is all but non-existent. Deliveries under bloc agreements from 1954 to the end of 1960 have been estimated at about one-third of the total commitments to all underdeveloped countries, with rather lower rates under economic agreements than under military. Ratios in sub-Saharan Africa should be even lower, since credits there were more recently contracted.

31. *Figyeloe* (Budapest), Mar. 1, 1961.

32. Radio Accra, Jan. 13, 1962; *Africa Diary* (New Delhi), Vol. II, No. 8 (Feb. 17–23, 1962) ; Economic Commission for Europe, *Economic Bulletin for Europe* (Geneva) Vol. 14, No. 1, p. 49.

33. PAP, Mar. 3, 1962; *Daily Graphic* (Accra), Apr. 21, 1961.

34. Radio Accra, Mar. 6, 1962.

35. *Voprosy Ekonomiki* (Moscow), No. 4, 1958, p. 92; U.N. *Economic Survey of Europe in 1960,* Appendix A.

36. Michel Lubrano-Lavadera, *l'Ours dans la Bergerie* (Paris, 1960), p. 103; *Christian Science Monitor* (Boston), Aug. 29, 1961.

37. *Daily Graphic* (Accra), Apr. 21, 1961; PAP, Apr. 22, 1961.

38. Radio Budapest, June 23, 1961.

39. International Monetary Fund, *International Financial News Survey,* Vol. XIII, No. 47, Dec. 1, 1961, p. 377.

40. U. S. Department of State, *Mutual Security Presentation,* p. 16.

41. PAP, Apr. 22, 1961; Radio Accra, Dec. 18, 1961.

42. Radio Accra, Dec. 18, 1961.

43. *Daily Graphic* (Accra), May 24, 1961; *Ghanaian Times* (Accra), June 8 and 9, 1961.

44. Radio Warsaw, Dec. 28, 1960; PAP, Jan. 11 and Oct. 25, 1961.

45. CTK, June 30, 1961; Radio Sofia, Feb. 20, 1961.

46. Radio Warsaw, Mar. 3, 1961.

47. PAP, Sept. 20 and Nov. 8, 1961; *Présence Congolaise* (Leopoldville), July 28, 1962; *West Africa*, July 21, 1962.

48. *Horoya* (Conakry), Aug. 22, 1961; *Lidova Democracie* (Prague), Feb. 23, 1961.

49. *Narody Asii i Afriki* (Moscow), No. 2, 1961.

50. *Ghanaian Times* (Accra), Aug. 28 and Sept. 11, 1961; CTK, Jan. 14, 1961.

51. United Nations, Department of Economic and Social Affairs, *International Economic Assistance to the Less Developed Countries* (New York, 1961), pp. 22 and 52.

52. *Afrique Action* (Tunis), May 29, 1961.

53. AFP, Nov. 21, 1961.

54. *Tribüne* (Berlin), July 19, 1961; MTI, July 15, 1961.

55. *Polish News and Views* (Warsaw), September-October 1961, p. 53; *Pravda* (Bratislava), Feb. 14, 1961.

56. ADN, Jan. 9, 1961.

57. *Tribüne* (Berlin), May 15, 1961.

58. Ethiopian Herald (Addis Ababa), May 26, 1961.

59. Brook-Shepherd, "Red Rivalry in the Black Continent," *The Reporter*, *loc. cit.*

60. The background to the Soviet Ambassador's recall from Guinea in December 1961 was reported by *Forum Service* (London), Nos. FS 450 (Dec. 23, 1961) and FS 454 (Jan. 1961). Invitations from foreign diplomatic missions to Guinean citizens to visit their respective countries must now be submitted through the Guinean Foreign Ministry (*Afrique Nouvelle*, Dakar, Dec. 27, 1961). The recall of the Guinean students from Czechoslovakia was cited from a Radio Conakry broadcast by Jerusalem Radio, Jan. 23, 1961.

61. *New York Times*, Mar. 25, 1961, reporting a statement published in *Rude Právo*, official organ of the Czechoslovak Communist Party.

62. *Manchester Guardian*, Mar. 3, 1961.

63. Radio Moscow, Feb. 19, 1961; Radio Warsaw, Feb. 23, 1961.

64. L. Holubek in *Vysoka Skola* (Prague), Jan. 1959, cited in *East Europe* (New York), April 1959, pp. 33–34.

65. *Lidova Democracie* (Prague), Sept. 17, 1961.

66. Radio Bratislava, Jan. 8, 1961; Radio Prague, June 29, 1961; CTK, Oct. 18, 1961.

67. For a recent comment on Friendship University, based on first-hand observation, see David Burg, "The People's Friendship University," *Problems of Communism*, Vol. X, No. 6, November-December 1961; pp. 50–54; an earlier and shorter note is "The University of Friendship of Peoples," *Youth and Communism*, Vol. III, No. 1–2, pp. 36–37; historical background is given in "Friendship University—The Early Versions," *Survey*, No. 39, July-September 1961, pp. 18–23.

68. The sources of information on this training in the sciences are: *L'Essor* (Bamako), Nov. 4, 1961; Radio Warsaw, Mar. 9, 1961; *Ghanaian Times* (Accra), Nov. 1, 1961; ADN, Sept. 14, 1961; Radio Warsaw, Apr. 22,

1961, and CTK, Oct. 18, 1961; *Africa Diary* (New Delhi), Vol. II, No. 6, Feb. 3–9, 1962, and Radio Bucharest, Dec. 3, 1960.

69. A useful short review of the WFDY and the IUS is available in N. M. Apeland, *World Youth and the Communists* (London, 1958). See also R. H. Bass, "Communist Fronts: Their History and Function," *Problems of Communism*, Vol. IX, No. 5, September-October 1960, pp. 8–16.

70. *Daily Graphic* (Accra), Feb. 17, 1961; ADN, May 26, 1961.

71. Any information on actual affiliation is difficult to obtain. A number of recent visitors to Africa have supplied the authors with the names of several organizations assumed to have IUS and/or WFDY affiliation, but no claim regarding accuracy or completeness can be made. The groups mentioned are the West African Students Union, General Union of West African Students, National Union of Cameroun Students, Cameroun Democratic Youth, Youth Union of Dahomey.

72. Christopher Bird, *Soviet Views on Africa* (a lecture delivered at the World Institute of the University of Southern California, October, 1961. Mimeographed) ; Billerbeck, *op. cit.*, p. 155.

73. *World Trade Union Movement* (London), November-December 1961.

74. For a discussion of some organizational problems encountered by non-Communist trade unions in Africa, see "Outline for Action in Africa," *Free Labor World* (Brussels), No. 127, January 1961.

75. *World Trade Union Movement* (London), November-December 1961.

76. *Christian Science Monitor* (Boston), Mar. 21, 1961.

77. ADN, Jan. 2, 1961.

78. "WFTU Congress Shows East Bloc Strains," *Forum Service* (London), No. 452, Jan. 6, 1962; "The Fifth Congress of the WFTU," *East Europe*, Vol. XI, No. 2 (February 1962).

79. TASS, Dec. 5–12, 1961.

80. Radio Accra, Feb. 5, 1962.

81. Radio Accra, Feb. 10, 1962.

82. Radio Prague, July 17, 1959; *Polish News and Views* (Warsaw), September-October 1961; Radio Warsaw, July 25, 1961; MTI, July 28, 1961; Radio Prague, July 31, 1961; East German Radio, Aug. 1, 1961.

83. *East Europe*, Vol. X, No. (January 1961), pp. 17 ff.

84. *Ibid.*, No. 2 (February 1961), pp. 27 ff.

85. *Ibid.*, No. 3 (March 1961), p. 29. Bulgaria, Czechoslovakia, Hungary, Poland, and Rumania also had observers at the 3rd session of the UN Economic Commission for Africa which met in Addis Ababa in February 1961, while East Germany attended as a "guest." (*Narody Asii i Afriki*, Moscow, No. 2, 1961.)

86. Brook-Shepherd, *op. cit.; West Africa*, April 20, 1963.

87. Radio Prague, July 16, 1960.

88. *Trybuna Ludu* (Warsaw), July 21, 1960.

89. Radio Budapest, Feb. 17, 1961.

90. PAP, February 22, 1961. Poland has also begun to publish a periodical in English and French for distribution in Africa and Asia. Also Radio Warsaw, Aug. 31, 1961.

91. Czech and East German aid to Guinean broadcasting was reported in *Lidova Democracie* (Prague), Feb. 23, 1961; the receipt of East German printing equipment in *Horoya* (Conakry), Aug. 22, 1961; and Czech agreements to provide news services on Radio Prague, Feb. 14 and Mar. 26, 1961, and in CTK, Mar. 30, 1961.

92. Radio Prague, Feb. 21, 1961; *The Democratic Journalist* (Prague), No. 5 (May 1961), pp. 100–101.

93. *The Democratic Journalist* (Prague), Nos. 6–7 (July 1961), pp. 127–29; *Neue Zeit* (Berlin), Feb. 16, 1961. This meeting was an outgrowth of an initiative taken by the IOJ at one of its periodic conferences in Baden, Austria, during October 1960, when a "provisional committee" to encourage cooperation among African journalists was formed. (See C. S. Stolte, "Africa between Two Power Blocs." Bulletin of the Institute for the Study of the USSR, Munich, Vol. VIII, No. 5, May 1961, pp. 37–81.) This source quotes *Die Feder* (Frankfurt, A.M., No. 2, 1960, p. 204) to the effect that the press department of the Soviet government made $250,000 available to launch the work of this committee.

94. *East African Standard* (Nairobi), May 10, 1961.

95. ADN, Dec. 30 and Jan. 6, 1961.

96. *Neues Deutschland* (Berlin), Jan. 31, 1962.

97. *Geschichte und Geschichtsbild Afrikas* (Studien zur Kolonialgeschichte, Vol. II), Berlin, 1960, esp. pp. 164 ff., and 189 ff.; W. Markow and P. Freidlaender, "Le néo-colonialisme et la politique africaine ouest-allemande," *Afrique Noire*, No. 22, 1961; "Afrikanische Gegenwartsfragen," *Deutsche Aussenpolitik* (Berlin), Special Issue, No. 1, 1960; U. Ruhmland, "Sowjetzonale Aktivitaet in den Staaten Afrikas," *Aussenpolitik* (Stuttgart), Vol. XI, No. 3 (March 1960).

98. *IWE—Informations und Archidienst* (West Berlin), No. 101, Apr. 17, 1961.

99. *Ibid.*

100. *The Times* (London), July 23, 31, and Aug. 1, 1961, reported that Nigerian officials had complained of "disruptive forces" at work in their country, and that British officials in Cameroon had reported clandestine traffic in Czechoslovak weapons. *The Guardian* (London), Sept. 29, 1961, said that an official Liberian statement alleged the existence of a Communist plot to subvert the republic. Czechoslovak arms were reported in the hands of Angolan rebel forces as early as the spring of 1961. (See *The Observer*, London, May 21, 1961, and *The Daily Telegraph*, London, May 18, 1961.)

CHAPTER 4

1. For general post-1945 Yugoslav developments, see George W. Hoffman and Fred Warner Neal, *Yugoslavia and the New Communism* (New York, 1962); Fred Warner Neal, *Titoism in Action* (Berkeley, 1958); Charles McVicker, *Titoism* (New York, 1957); and Ernst Halperin, *The Trimphant Heretic* (London, 1958).

2. Viktor Meier, *Das neue jugoslawische Wirtschaftssystem* (Zurich und St. Gallen, 1956); Benjamin Ward, "Workers' Management in Yugoslavia,"

Journal of Political Economy, LXV, 5 (October 1957), pp. 373–86; and Hoffman and Neal, *Yugoslavia*, pp. 239–381.

3. Stephen Clissold, *The Whirlwind* (New York, 1949); and Fitzroy H. Maclean, *The Heretic* (New York, 1957).

4. See Edward R. F. Sheehan, "The Birth Pangs of Arab Socialism," *Harper's Magazine*, February 1962, pp. 85–91; Georg von Huebbenet, "Der östliche Einfluss auf Kairo," *Aussenpolitik*, XII, 5 (May 1961), pp. 348–53; "Socialism on the Nile," *The Economist*, May 5, 1962, pp. 457–58; and Walz from Cairo in *The New York Times*, May 21, 1962.

5. Stojan Petrović, "The Belgrade Conference and Economic Integration," *Review of International Affairs*, XII, 281 (Dec. 20, 1961), p. 4. See also R. Kozarać, "African Dilemmas," *Rad*, Feb. 10, 1962.

6. For information on the Belgrade Conference, see the proceedings in *Borba* and in *The Conference of Heads of State or Government of Non-Aligned Countries* (Belgrade, 1961); a convenient collection of excerpts in *Review of International Affairs*, XII, 274–75 (Sept. 5–20, 1961); and a brief summary and an interview concerning it with *L'Unità* and *Avanti!* in *Yugoslav Life*, VI, 60 (September 1961), p. 2.

For the arrangements made during Tito's African tour, see the issue of *Borba* for the dates given in parentheses: speech by Tito to Ghanaian parliament and speeches by Tito and Nkrumah (Mar. 3, 1961); Yugoslav-Ghanaian joint communiqué (Mar. 5, 1961); speeches by Tito and Sylvanus Olympio (Mar. 7, 1961); Yugoslav-Togo joint communiqué (Mar. 8, 1961); Tito's and Tubman's speeches (Mar. 14, 1961); Tito's speech to the Liberian parliament (Mar. 15, 1961); speeches of Tito and Sekou Touré at Conakry (Mar. 21, 1961); and of Tito and Modibo Keita at Bamako (Mar. 27, 1961).

7. See "Yugoslav Attitude to Events in Congo," *Yugoslav Survey*, I, 3 (October-December 1960), pp. 411–16; "How Yugoslavia Views the Worsening Situation in the Congo," *ibid.*, II, 4 (January-March 1961), pp. 559–67; "Yugoslavia's Attitude Regarding Events in the Congo," *ibid.*, II, 5 (June 1961), pp. 747–50; and Djordje Jerković, "New Complications in the Congo," *Review of International Affairs*, XIII, 284 (Feb. 5, 1962), pp. 4–6.

8. Janez Stanovnik, "The Struggle of Two Opposite Tendencies in the Economy of Underdeveloped Countries," *Naša Stvarnost*, No. 3 (March 1961). See also his "Historical Roots of the Problem of Economic Underdevelopment," *ibid.*, No. 5 (May 1960), pp. 569–87; "Yugoslav View on Assistance to Economically Underdeveloped Countries," *Yugoslav Survey*, I, 2 (September 1960), pp. 265–73; "International Assistance for the Economic Development of Underdeveloped Countries in the Light of the Evolution of the World Economy," *Medjunarodna Politika*, No. 4, 1957; "The Uncommitted Countries in the World Economy," *Borba*, June 23, 26, 28, 1961; and, for a more extended treatment, *Socijalisticki Elementi u Ekonomskom Razvoju Nerazvijenih Zemalja* (Belgrade, 1960). Stanovnik's articles on the July 1962 Cairo Conference, "The Cairo Conference and International Economic Relations," *Borba*, Aug. 19, 21, 23, 25, 26, 1962, do not add significantly to his general analysis. Stanovnik's influence on African leaders can be seen from the fact that in a recent article in *Foreign Affairs* Sekou Touré quoted extensively from an article of his about the Cairo Conference; see Sekou Touré, "Africa's Fu-

ture and the World," *Foreign Affairs*, XLI, 1 (October 1962), pp. 141–51, p. 148.

9. Aleš Bebler, "Africa Rediscovered," *Review of International Affairs* (Belgrade), Feb. 16, 1960, p. 6; see also his "Problems of Social and Political Change of Black Africa," *Socijalizam*, No. 6, 1959, pp. 82 ff.

10. See, for example, the speeches of the trade union leader Svetozar Vukmanović-Tempo at the Moscow WFTU Congress in December 1961, in *Borba*, Dec. 12, 1961, at the Feb. 12, 1962, plenum of the Central Committee of the Yugoslav Trade Union Federation, *ibid.*, Feb. 13, 1962; and Anon., "International Activities of the Yugoslav Trade Unions in 1960," *Jugoslovenski Preglad*, No. 1 (January 1961), pp. 2–6.

11. See, for example, "A New African Initiative," *Komunist*, Oct. 19, 1961.

12. The most extensive account of this aspect of Yugoslav-African relations is "Jugoslawiens Aktivität in Afrika," *Wissenschaftlicher Dienst Südosteuropa*, X, 3 (March 1961), pp. 25–28; see also [Fritz Schatten], "Tito in Afrika," *Neues Afrika*, April 1961, pp. 126–28; Paul Yankovitch, "Belgrade intensifie ses efforts de pénétration sur le continent africain," *Le Monde*, July 22, 1960; and "Africa—Our Youngest Foreign Trade Partner," *Borba*, Mar. 12, 1961.

13. "President Tito's Interview with Yugoslav Journalists in Conakry," *Borba*, March 31, 1961.

14. Kardelj at Oslo, Oct. 28, 1954; text given in *Borba*, Jan. 1, 1955.

15. "Tito in Africa—Understanding and Equality," *Komunist*, April 6, 1961.

16. "The Process of Decolonialization in Ghana, Guinea, and Mali Is Closely Connected with the Development of Socialist Social Relations, States Svetozar Vukmanović," *Komunist*, April 26, 1962.

17. For example, SAWPY-PDG conversations in Conakry, broadcast in English to Europe, April 9, 1962.

18. See Jože Smole, "Preparations for 'The World Without the Bomb' Conference," *Review of International Affairs*, XIII, 287 (Mar. 20, 1962), pp. 8–10.

19. See an interview with Vukmanović-Tempo in *Avanti!*, Mar. 18, 1962; M. Milenković, "Difficulties About the Unity of African Trade Union Organs," *Borba*, Jan. 8, 1962; Mika Spiljak, "The First Pan-African Trade Union Conference," *ibid.*, June 11, 1961, M. Marinović, "Pan-Africa in Casablanca," *Rad*, June 3, 1961. For joint declarations between the Yugoslav and national African trade unions, see, for Liberia, *Borba*, Mar. 29, 1961; for Kenya, *Vjestnik* (Zagreb), Feb. 9, 1962; for Mali and Aden, *Borba*, Dec. 1, 1961.

20. For the Yugoslav view, see "Yugoslavia and the European Common Market," *Commercial News of Yugoslavia*, VII, 16 (Aug. 15, 1961), p. 1, and "Yugoslavia and the European Free Trade Area," *ibid.*, VII, 18 (Sept. 15, 1961), p. 1; "Two Theories of Economic Stabilization to Further the Development and the Role of Underdeveloped Countries of Africa and Other Regions," *Vestnik Jugoslovenske investicone banke*, No. 54–55, June-July 1961, pp. 27–28; an interview with Tito in *The Observer* (London), April 1, 1962; for analysis, see C. K. [Christian Kind] (from Belgrade), "Jugoslawien und die EWG," *Neue Zürcher Zeitung*, Apr. 29, 1962.

21. Quoted from *Review of International Affairs*, XII, 274–75 (Sept. 5–20,

1961), pp. 28–29. See Stojan Petrović, "The Belgrade Conference and Economic Integration," *ibid.*, XII, 281 (Dec. 20, 1961), pp. 1–3.

22. Bogdan Crnobrnja, "Cooperation on a Wider Basis," *Kommunist*, Jan. 11, 1962; see Underwood from Belgrade in *The New York Times*, Jan. 30, 1962.

23. See the excellent analysis by the Vienna correspondent of *The Times* (London), Feb. 13, 1962; also the Belgrade dispatch in *Süddeutsche Zeitung*, Mar. 8, 1962. The Tito-Nasser communiqué is in *Borba*, Feb. 22, 1962. For a Yugoslav report of anti-EEC sentiment in Ghana, see F. Drenovać, "Africa and the Common Market," *Borba*, July 13, 1961.

24. Popović in *Al Goumhouria*, Jan. 31, 1962, quoted from a Cairo dispatch by Walz in *The New York Times*, Feb. 12, 1962.

25. Dj. Jerković, "Legitimate Defence of the Threatened," *Review of International Affairs*, XIII, 389 (Apr. 20, 1962), p. 2.

26. See C. K. [Christian Kind], "Titos Idee einer Dritten Kraft," *Neue Zürcher Zeitung*, Apr. 13, 1962, and "Jugoslawien und die EWG," *ibid.*, Apr. 29, 1962, and Eric Bourne from Belgrade, "Yugoslavia and the Blocs," *Christian Science Monitor*, May 18, 1962.

27. Nataša Djurić, *Jugoslovenska Preduzeća na Inostranim Gradilištima* (Belgrade: Kultura, 1960), pp. 5–30. Most of this activity had hitherto been carried out in the Middle East; no separate statistical breakdown for Africa is available. Statistics converted at the official rate: $1.00 = 300$ dinars.

28. John C. Campbell, "Jugoslavia: Crisis and Choice," *Foreign Affairs*, XLI, 2 (January 1963), p. 386; also *Commercial News of Yugoslavia*, IX, 3 (Feb. 1, 1963).

29. See William E. Griffith, "The Sino-Soviet Schism" (to be published in late 1963 by *The China Quarterly* and the M.I.T. Press.

30. For the December 1961 WPC meeting, see Griffith, *Albania and the Sino-Soviet Rift* (Cambridge, Mass., 1963), pp. 124–29. For Moshi, see especially the resolution and speech by Liu Ning-yi, in English from the New China News Agency in Moshi, Feb. 4 and 5 (SCMP 2915, Feb. 8, 1963, and 2916, Feb. 11, 1963); the final resolution (in English from the New China News Agency in Peking, broadcast to Europe and Asia, Feb. 11, 1963, 1519 GMT); and "Solidarity My Way," *The Economist*, Feb. 16, 1963.

31. Griffith, *Albania*, pp. 122–25.

32. Two recent activities have been the African Students' Conference at Belgrade in August-September 1962 (*Borba*, Aug. 30, 1962 *et seq.*) and the establishment of a Center for the Study of Africa at the University of Zagreb (*Sveucilisni Vjesnik—Aktuelne Vijesti*, A Suppl. 135–37, May 1, 1962).

CHAPTER 5

1. "The Chinese Revolution and the Chinese Communist Party," in *Selected Works of Mao Tse-tung*, Vol. III (London 1954), pp. 72–101.

2. *Ibid.*, p. 97.

3. *Ibid.*, p. 96.

4. *World Trade Union Movement*, No. 8, December 1949; cited hereafter as *WTUM*.

5. *Ibid.*

6. *For a Lasting Peace, For a People's Democracy,* Dec. 30, 1949; *Pravda* Jan. 4, 1950.

7. "Mighty Advance of the National Liberation Movement in Colonial and Dependent Countries," *For a Lasting Peace,* Jan. 27, 1950. For this whole development, compare John Kautsky, "Moscow and the Communist Party of India" (New York, 1956).

8. *World Marxist Review,* December 1960.

9. "The Victory of Marxism-Leninism in China," *World Marxist Review,* October 1959.

10. W. Kolarz, "Communism in Africa: The West African Scene," *Problems of Communism,* June 1961.

11. A Sudanese, I. A. Zakharia, was appointed WFTU secretary for Africa at the Warsaw meeting of the Executive Council in April 1959 (*WTUM,* May 1959); but in practice he seems to have handled only relations with Arab trade unions, including those in Algeria. Both at the official founding conference of UGTAN (Conakry, Jan. 1959) and at that of the All-African Trade Union Federation (Casablanca, May 1961), however, the official spokesman for the WFTU was the Frenchman Marcel Bras; the Chinese trade unions sent their own fraternal delegates as well, but so did the French CGT and the Italian CGIL (*WTUM,* March 1959, August 1961). Again, the WFTU school for African trade unionists was opened in Budapest in the late summer of 1959 under the direction of the Frenchman Jean Marillier (*WTUM,* November 1959).

12. In 1956 Chinese cultural missions visited, besides Egypt, the newly independent states of Sudan, Morocco, and Tunisia, as well as Ethiopia, and began to stimulate cultural exchanges of various kinds. Following the major cotton purchases from Egypt, Peking concluded its first commercial contracts with other African countries in 1956, beginning with the Sudan and Morocco; China also made a big impression at the 1957 Casablanca fair.

13. See Robert H. Bass, "Communist Fronts: Their History and Function," in *Problems of Communism,* May 1960; *Ostprobleme* (Bonn) No. 18/19, 1961; Kurt Mueller, "Der Ostblock und die Entwicklungsländer," in *Das Parlament* (Bonn) July 12, 1961. The Soviet account of the origin of the new organization is in *International Affairs* (Moscow), February 1958.

14. On the strength of Chinese delegations, see Donald Zagoria, "Sino-Soviet Friction in Under-Developed Areas," in *Problems of Communism,* February 1961; the Chinese pledge was announced in *Rose al Yusuf* (Cairo), Nov. 17, 1958.

15. Texts of the reports are in *Conférence des Peuples Afro-Asiatiques, 26 Décembre 1957–1er Janvier 1958, Principaux Rapports* (Cairo, 1958).

16. The Chinese delegate reported on it at the Executive meeting of the International Union of Students held at Leipzig in January 1958.

17. For estimated figures, see Gordon Brook-Shepherd, "Red Rivalry in the Black Continent," in *The Reporter,* Jan. 10, 1962.

18. *New China News Agency* (NCNA), Apr. 13, 1961.

19. See the report of Abdulcadir Scek Mohammed, a Somali student returning from Peking early in 1962.

20. On Feb. 6, 1961, immediately after the MPLA's attempted coup in Luanda, *Pravda* published an article by MPLA President Mario de Andrade,

who described his organization as having originated from the merger of a "small Marxist underground group" with a broader African organization that had a near-Marxist program. In 1962, an official Soviet handbook disclosed that the "small Marxist group" in question was the Communist Party of Angola, created in 1955. ("Afrika Segodniya," Moscow, 1962, p. 119.)

21. See Philippe Schneyder, "Pekin à l'assaut du Tiers Monde," in *Revue Militaire d'Information* (Paris) April 1960. The amount of the Chinese "loan" was given as 12 million dollars by Premier Kassem when opening the Chinese economic exhibition in Baghdad in November 1960.

22. See the report of the Fourth Congress of the WFTU, held at Leipzig in October 1957, and the article by I. A. Zakharia in *WTUM*, November 1959.

23. See the *Revue Militaire* article quoted in note 21 above.

24. For a concise and documented account of this development, see David Dallin's *Soviet Foreign Policy after Stalin* (Philadelphia, 1961), pp. 476–79.

25. *Neue Zürcher Zeitung*, July 17, 1960.

26. Fritz Schatten, *Afrika Schwarz oder Rot?* (Munich, 1961). The general picture presented in this chapter owes much to this pioneering study.

27. *Neue Zürcher Zeitung*, July 17, 1960; Ho Wei-Yang, "Peking in Afrika auf eignen Wegen," in *Aussenpolitik* (Stuttgart) March 1961.

28. *Ostprobleme*, No. 4, 1960.

29. This was admitted by Diallo Seydou, UGTAN general secretary in charge of organization, press, and education; see *WTUM*, October 1960.

30. Schatten, *Afrika Schwarz*, p. 250.

31. *Ibid.*, p. 224.

32. See, for example, *People's Daily*, editorial "Victory Belongs to the Congolese People," in *Survey of the China Mainland Press* (SCMP), Hong Kong, No. 1944, Jan. 25, 1959, and statement by Liao Cheng-shih, *ibid.*, No. 1946, Jan. 26, 1959.

33. Representatives of these two parties were received by Foreign Minister Chen Yi in Peking on the day independence was declared (*SCMP*, No. 2292, June 30, 1960). No representative of the Mouvement National Congolais (MNC) seems to have been in Peking at the time. See, however, Schatten, *Afrika Schwarz*, p. 255, for a report alleging that Chinese contact with the MNC was established and a decision to support it taken during the Second All-African People's Conference in Tunis in January 1960.

34. Cairo Conference, *Rapports Principaux*; see note 15 above.

35. On Sept. 18 and again on Oct. 1, according to later account by Larbi Bouhali, Secretary-General of the Communist Party of Algeria, in *Aus der internationalen Arbeiterbewegung*, East Berlin, October 1960.

36. *SCMP*, No. 2106, Sept. 25, 1959; No. 2108, Sept. 27, 1959.

37. In his address to the Supreme Soviet, Moscow Radio, Oct. 31, 1959.

38. *NCNA*, Oct. 17, 1959.

39. Radio Peking in Indonesian, Nov. 12, 1959; quoted by Zagoria, "Sino-Soviet Friction"; *NCNA*, Nov. 30, 1959.

40. Schatten, *Afrika Schwarz*, p. 246.

41. *Peking Review*, May 24, 1960.

42. For example, see E. Arab-Ogly, "1960—Africa's Year" in *WMR*, May 1960.

43. *Peking Review*, July 5, 1960.

44. Akoa Azambo in an article in the (Communist) *France Nouvelle*, reprinted in *Aus der internationalen Arbeiterbewegung*, June 1960.

45. Schatten, *Afrika Schwarz*, p. 252.

46. Quoted in the article by E. Arab-Ogly cited in note 42 above; see Azambo's article cited in note 44 above.

47. Schatten, *Afrika Schwarz*, pp. 252–54.

48. Message of the Permanent Secretariat of the Afro-Asian People's Solidarity Organization to the All-African People's Conference.

49. Rawle Knox, "Afro-Asian Snub for Peking," *Observer Foreign News Service*, London, Feb. 15, 1960; Schatten, *Afrika Schwarz*, p. 260.

50. According to a statement by the Indian delegate Harsh D. Malaviya to the Press Trust of India, May 5, 1960, quoted by Zagoria, "Sino-Soviet Friction."

51. Arab-Ogly, cited in note 42 above; also the report in *Sovremennyi Vostok*, February 1960.

52. For an unusually full account of the Conakry conference, see G. Zinke in *Aus der internationalen Arbeiterbewegung*, October 1960.

53. Mikoyan's press conference, Moscow Radio, Apr. 18, 1960.

54. Zinke, cited in note 52 above.

55. Kurt Mueller, cited in note 13; Zinke, cited in note 52 above.

56. A full account of the Fund is in *Der Ostblock und die Entwicklungsländer: Vierteljahresbericht der Friedrich-Ebert-Stiftung*, Hannover, No. 4/5. The statute was first published in *Aziia i Afrika segodnia*, May 1961.

57. Schatten, *Afrika Schwarz*, p. 224.

58. *Pravda*, July 13, 1960.

59. Khrushchev's reply of July 15 to an appeal by Kasavubu and Lumumba, *Pravda*, July 16, 1960.

60. Chinese government statement of July 19, *Peking Review*, July 26, 1960.

61. Speech of July 23, *ibid.*

62. *Ibid.*

63. *People's Daily*, Aug. 22, 1960; translation in *Peking Review*, Aug. 30, 1960.

64. The texts of Gizenga's messages to Peking of September 8 and to Moscow, September 10, 1960, are in "Congo 1960—Annexes et Biographies," published by the Centre de Recherche et d'Information Socio-Politiques, Brussels.

65. *People's Daily*, Nov. 25, 1960; *Peking Review*, Nov. 29, 1960.

66. The Chinese Chargé d'Affaires arrived on July 31, according to *NCNA*, Aug. 1, 1961. Elisabethville Radio reported on July 17 that the Soviet mission had reached Stanleyville "about July 6."

67. For example: Moscow Radio for Africa, Aug. 21, on the Adoula government; *Pravda*, Sept. 15, supporting the Congo parliament against Katanga; Moscow Radio, Sept. 22 and 26, cirticizing the U.N. for yielding to Tshombe. The new Soviet Chargé d'Affaires, Leonid Podgornov, arrived in Leopoldville on September 19, before the formalities for an *agrément* had been fulfilled. (Leopoldville Radio, Sept. 22, 1961.)

68. *NCNA*, Sept. 18, 1961.

69. Radio Peking in Swahili, Sept. 15, 1961.

70. *Peking Review*, Aug. 25, 1961, for the text of the treaty, the official communiqué, and the authoritative Chinese comment.

71. All the documents on this are in *Peking Review*, Sept. 14, 1960.

72. All of Prof. Potekhin's *original* contributions to the class analysis of African society fall into the period mentioned in the text; see his paper in *Problemy Vostokovedenye* (January 1960), his 1960 pamphlet *Africa Looks at the Future*, and his article in *Aziia i Afrika segodnia* (October 1961). Further Soviet publications on Africa stressing the class aspect in that period are quoted by David L. Morison, "Moscow's First Steps in Africa," in *Problems of Communism*, July 1961. "National Democracy" is first defined in the declaration of the Moscow conference of 81 Communist parties, *WMR*, December 1960. For a fuller analysis of the origin and development of the concept, see R. Lowenthal, " 'National Democracy' and the Post-Colonial Revolution," *Survey*, No. 47.

73. For example, by the British Communist Idris Cox, in *Mezhdunarodnaya Zhizn*, December 1959, and by the French Communist and Research Director of the government of Guinea, J. Suret-Canale, in *Cahiers du Communisme*, November 1960.

74. *WTUM*, November 1959.

75. For example, articles appear repeatedly in *Aus der internationalen Arbeiterbewegung* (East Berlin).

76. For the general line, see N. Numadé, "Marxism and African Liberation," *The African Communist*, April 1960; this has become the first article to be translated into an African language, as announced in issue No. 8 (January 1962). Criticism of the PDG appears in "Guinea as an Example," quoted from No. 2 by W. Z. Laqueur, "Communism and Nationalism in Africa," *Foreign Affairs*, July 1961. For criticism of Dr. Nkrumah, see issue No. 8, January 1962.

77. I. Kumalo, "Nigeria's Struggle for Independence," *ibid.*, No. 3, September 1960.

78. *Ibid.*, No. 8, January 1962.

79. See M. Yassin, "Problems of the National Struggle in Somalia—Letter from a Communist," *WMR*, November 1960; Andrade's statement is cited in note 20 above.

80. Radio Conakry, Nov. 20, 23, 26, 1961; *Le Monde*, Dec. 13, 1961; *Afrique Nouvelle*, Dakar, Jan. 3, 1962.

81. *WTUM*, July 1960.

82. *Ibid.*

82. Li Wei-han, "The Chinese People's Democratic United Front: Its Special Features." Reprinted from *Red Flag*, No. 12, 1961, in *Peking Review*, Aug. 18 and 25, and Sept. 1, 1961.

84. Feng's article appeared in the *Peking Review*, July 5, 1960.

85. See *Al Cha'ab*, Algiers, Feb. 16, 1963, on Chinese-Algerian discussions on military cooperation; *NCNA*, Mar. 14, and *Alger Républicain*, Apr. 3, on Chinese gifts; Algiers Radio, Apr. 23, on invitation of an "official" delegation of Algerian journalists to China.

86. Details were quoted from the diaries of the arrested men in the *Sunday Telegraph*, London, July 23, 1961.

87. See the joint communiqué of the UPC and the French CP, endorsing the decisions of the Moscow Peace Congress in *Humanité*, Aug. 20, 1962, and the joint declaration of the UPC, the Senegalese PAI, and the Sawaba party of Niger in *Humanité*, Dec. 7, 1962; also the analysis of the split in *Est et Ouest*, Paris, Nos. 285 and 287.

88. See for instance the speech by Liu Ning-yi at the Moshi Afro-Asian conference, *NCNA*, Feb. 6, 1963.

89. A "Zimbabwe Day" rally was held in Peking and the ZANU leader, Joshua Nkomo, was interviewed by *NCNA* on Mar. 17, 1963.

90. According to the Albanian Telegraph Agency, Feb. 16, 1963, the first secretary of the Madagascar CP had sent a message of "Marxist-Leninist solidarity" to the Albanian CP for the New Year.

91. Robert Counts, "Chinese Footprints in Somalia," *The Reporter*, Feb. 2, 1961. Regarding Soviet caution on the issue, see I. Plyshevski, "Some Results of the Struggle for Independence in Africa," *WMR*, July 1961.

92. For the Chinese orientation of Abulrahman Moahmud Babu, the general secretary of the ZNP, see *Die Welt*, Hamburg, Dec. 28, 1961. He has since served a sentence for sedition but lately returned to active propaganda; some of the ZNP's publications are smuggled in from Cuba (*Tanganyika Standard*, Jan. 26, 1963). For the Chinese dependence of the ZFPTU, see *Daily Telegraph*, Feb. 26, 1963. For the possibility of a change in the Moscow line toward the East African federation, see A. Zanzolo in *The African Communist*, No. 5, May 1961.

93. Liao's speech in *Peking Review*, Dec. 22; Liu's speech, *ibid.*, Dec. 29, 1961.

94. *Unità*, Dec. 23, 1961, where the voting figures cited below are also given.

95. *NCNA*, Dec. 19/20, 1961.

96. *Reuters* dispatch from Cairo, Feb. 16, and Colin Legum in *The Observer*, London, Mar. 12, 1962.

97. *TASS*, Dec. 20, 1961.

98. See the article by Nicolas Lang on the Moshi conference in *Est et Ouest*, Paris, No. 297; also the letter of the French CP to the Chinese CP of Jan. 24, 1962, published in *Problèmes du Mouvement Communiste International*, Paris, January 1963.

99. *Bulletin of the WPC*, October 1962.

100. *TASS*, Aug. 28, 1962.

101. *WFDY News*, February 1963.

102. See the first-hand report by Fritz Schatten in *Ostprobleme*, May 31, 1963.

103. Only the Chinese and Mali members of the WPC were mentioned as having addressed the conference Radio Dar es Salaam, Feb. 4, 1963). That the others were not admitted because they were "whites" was disclosed in V. Kudryavtsev's article "Thoughts at the Foot of Mt. Kilimanjaro," in *International Affairs*, Moscow, May 1963, and confirmed in the open letter of the Central Committee of the CPSU of July 14, 1963 (*Pravda*, same date).

104. The above and some further details are taken from an unpublished British report.

105. *Pravda*, Feb. 4, 1963.

106. *Pravda*, Feb. 6.

109. *NCNA*, Feb. 6.

108. He is the only speaker quoted on that point in *Pravda*'s editorial summing up the conference, Feb. 13, 1963.

Chaman Lall's walkout occurred on Feb. 7. See the summing up of the Peking *People's Daily* in *NCNA*, Feb. 13.

110. *Pravda*, Feb. 11 and 12.

111. *NCNA*, Feb. 13.

112. *Pravda*, March 23, 1963.

113. In the Indian Communist weekly *New Age*, Mar. 24, 1963.

114. *La Dépêche d'Algérie*, Apr. 28 and 30, 1963; Radio Algiers, Apr. 23–28.

115. *NCNA*, Apr. 24 to May 1, 1963.

116. V. Kudryavtsev, "Thoughts at the Foot of Mt. Kilimanjaro," *International Affairs*, Moscow, May 1963.

117. "More on the Differences between Comrade Togliatti and Us," English translation of editorial in *Red Flag* (Peking), No. 3–4, March 4, 1963.

118. *NCNA*, June 14, 1963.

119. In the open letter of the Central Committee of the CPSU to all party members, in *Pravda*, July 14, 1963.

CHAPTER 6

1. In the words of Harold Lasswell, "the specific process by which the universal was parochialized was that of partial adaptation and countersymbolization." (*World Politics and Personal Insecurity*, Glencoe, Ill., 1950, p. 121.)

2. See, for example, the speeches in *V'toraia Konferentsiia Solidarnosti Narodov Azii i Afriki* (Moscow, 1961).

3. Ye. Zhukov, "Significant Factor of Our Times—On Some Questions of the Present-Day National Liberation Movement," *Pravda*, August 26, 1960.

4. For a discussion, see A. Nove, "The Soviet Model and Underdeveloped Countries," *International Affairs*, No. 1, January 1961.

5. However, the Czech Communists explicitly assert it. See, for example, Jan Kozek, *How Parliament Can Play a Revolutionary Part in the Transition to Socialism and the Role of the Popular Masses* (English translation, London, 1961).

6. M. Syrucek, "Peaceful Coexistence and the Struggle Against Colonialism," *Mlada Fronta*, February 22, 1962.

7. For contrasting views, see Mamadou Dia, *Nations Africaines et solidarité mondiale* (Paris, 1960); and *Obshche Zakonomernosti Perekhoda K Sotsializmu i Osobennosti Ikh Proiavlenia v Raznikh Str.nakh* (Moscow, 1960).

8. See, for example, T. Lychowski, *Stosunki Ekonomiczne Miedzy Krajami o Roznych Ustrojach* (Warsaw, 1957), especially pp. 590–605.

9. *Jen Min Jih Pao*, December 10, 1961.

10. A later reference to "strict international control" made it clear that

its meaning was defined in the Soviet draft proposal submitted to the Geneva meeting in 1962.

11. For a discussion of varieties of strategy, see D. Zarin, "Some aspects of the National Liberation Movement of the Colonial Nations," in *Voprosy Filosofii,* January 1961.

12. *World Marxist Review,* No. 7, 1962 (Russian edition).

13. TASS, May 19, 1962.

14. K. N. Brutens, *Protiv Ideologii Sovremennovo Kolonializma* (Moscow, 1961), p. 183 ff.

15. For a comprehensive Soviet statement, see Brutens, *Protiv Ideologii.*

16. L. Senghor in *West Africa,* No. 4, 1961, p. 12; quoted by Rupert Emerson, "Pan-Africanism," *International Organization,* No. 2, 1962.

17. Radio Moscow, June 5, 1962.

18. *The New York Times,* July 15, 1962.

19. E. Paloncy, "Build-up of the Anti-Imperialist Front," *Rude Právo,* March 21, 1962. (Italics mine.) For a critique of Nasser's claims to be building socialism, see V. Mayevsky in *Pravda,* July 19, 1962; Mayevsky objects particularly to the religious basis for Arab socialism (explicitly postulated by Nasser) and to the Egyptian denial of open class conflict; he complains that some Arab commentators see in Nasser's Arab socialism an alternative to the dictatorship of the proletariat.

20. Similar criticisms have been voiced by I. I. Potekhin in his pamphlet *Afrika smotrit v budushchee.* See also L. Labedz's introduction to the special *Survey* issue (August 1962) on *Nationalism, Communism and the Uncommitted Nations,* in which he shows the contrast between domestic Soviet criticisms of "African socialism" and Soviet flattery of the new African leaders.

INDEX

INDEX